F. SCOTT FITZGERALD

A Study of the Short Fiction

Twayne's Studies in Short Fiction

Gordon Weaver, General Editor
Oklahoma State University

Photograph courtesy of the Yale Collection of American Literature, Beinecke Rare Book and Manuscript Library, Yale University; reprinted by permission of the Estate of Carl Van Vechten, Joseph Solomon, executor.

F. SCOTT FITZGERALD

A Study of the Short Fiction

John Kuehl
New York University

TWAYNE PUBLISHERS • BOSTON
A Division of G. K. Hall & Co.

Twayne's Studies in Short Fiction Series No. 22

Copyright 1991 by G. K. Hall & Co.
All rights reserved.
Published by Twayne Publishers
A division of G. K. Hall & Co.
70 Lincoln Street
Boston, Massachusetts 02111

Copyediting supervised by Barbara Sutton.
Book design and production by Janet Z. Reynolds.
Typeset by Compset, Inc., Beverly, Massachusetts.

First published 1991.
10 9 8 7 6 5 4 3 2 1

The paper used in this publication meets the minimum requirements
of American National Standard for Information Sciences—Permanence
of Paper for Printed Library Materials, ANSI Z39.48-1984. ∞™

Printed and bound in the United States of America.

Library of Congress Cataloging-in-Publication Data

Kuehl, John Richard, 1928–
      F. Scott Fitzgerald : a study of the short fiction / John Kuehl.
         p.   cm.—(Twayne's studies in short fiction ; no. 22)
      Includes bibliographical references and index.
      ISBN 0-8057-8332-6 (alk. paper)
      1. Fitzgerald, F. Scott (Francis Scott), 1896–1940—Criticism and
   interpretation.   2. Short story.   I. Title.   II. Series.
   PS3511.I9Z6735   1991
   813'.52—dc20   90-48727
                                                                                       CIP

For Alexander P. Clark
and, in Memoriam,
Sheilah Graham

Contents

Preface

During his brief twenty-year career as a professional writer, F. Scott Fitzgerald "developed" less than most literary figures of comparable stature. Thus, half his major stories had already been published before his masterpiece, *The Great Gatsby*, appeared in 1925 when he was twenty-eight. It is for another reason, then, that this book proceeds chronologically: doing so enabled me to treat the four story collections as individual achievements, whose contents and titles were chosen by their maker.

After the Introduction, which focuses on characteristic Fitzgerald dichotomies—novelist versus short story writer; artist versus businessman; "putter-inner" versus "leaver-outer"—I consider a large body of work termed "Apprenticeship" that, owing to various interconnections, encompasses the prep-school and college fiction (1909–17), *Flappers and Philosophers* (1920), and *Tales of the Jazz Age* (1922). In these first stories, Fitzgerald introduced the settings, the narrative voices, the structural strategies, the characters (especially the femme fatale and *homme manqué*), and the themes he would subsequently explore. These elements recur in *All the Sad Young Men* (1926), in which the marriage motif dominates his popular pieces, and unrequited love his artistic ones. If *All the Sad Young Men* is notable for the stories clustered around *The Great Gatsby* (1925), *Taps at Reveille* (1935) is notable for those clustered around *Tender Is the Night* (1934), as well as the eight Basil and Josephine selections. The latter, a transitional collection, shifts from the theme of lost youth/illusion to that of "emotional bankruptcy," which surfaces again in the posthumous collections. The chapter on those collections discusses several superior efforts excluded by the four Scribner compilations. It also compares Fitzgerald's expansive and elliptical styles, concluding with his Pat Hobby yarns.

This panoramic view of the formal and conceptual patterns that emerge throughout the short fiction, however, represents only one critical preoccupation. My second, even more important task, concerns what I take to be the eight major Fitzgerald stories. Three ("The Ice Palace," "May Day," and "The Diamond as Big as the Ritz") receive extended treatment in the chapter titled "Early Triumphs"; three ("Absolution," "Winter Dreams," and "The Rich Boy") in *"All the Sad Young Men"*; and two ("Babylon Revisited" and "Crazy Sunday") in *"Taps at Reveille."* Because these stories make a permanent contribution to American letters and are thus urged upon the reader, their quoted passages are cited parenthetically, the pagination coming from the available and affordable Macmillan Scribner Classic edition *Babylon Revisited and Other Stories*. References also appear for some additional primary and for all secondary material, but not for the lesser stories, which may be found in various editions. Such additional Scribner Classics as *Afternoon of an Author, Flappers and Philosophers, The Pat Hobby Stories, Six Tales of the Jazz Age and Other Stories*, and *The Stories of F. Scott Fitzgerald* contain many. Out-of-print paperback collections like *The Apprentice Fiction of F. Scott Fitzgerald, Bits of Paradise*, and *The Price Was High* contain more. Along with *Taps at Reveille*—still a hardcover book—these nine volumes constitute virtually the entire Fitzgerald story output.

The Conclusion to Part 1 synthesizes the diverse ingredients manifested by the eight major tales, whose themes and techniques define Fitzgerald's art and place him among the few modern American masters of the form.

Acknowledgments

I am grateful for permission to reprint the following material:

Excerpts from "TO: *The Editor*," in the *Correspondence of F. Scott Fitzgerald*, ed. Matthew J. Bruccoli and Margaret M. Duggan (New York: Random House, 1980). © 1980 by Frances Scott Fitzgerald Smith.

"F. Scott Fitzgerald's Critical Opinions," revised and expanded from my essay published in *Modern Fiction Studies* (Spring 1961). © 1961 by Purdue Research Foundation, West Lafayette, Indiana.

Excerpts from three essays published in *Studies in Short Fiction:* "The Tension of Opposites in Fitzgerald's 'May Day'" by Anthony J. Mazzella (Fall 1977), "Four Voices in 'Winter Dreams'" by Gerald Pike (Summer 1986), and "'Babylon Revisited': A Story of the Exile's Return" by Roy R. Male (Spring 1965).

Excerpts from "Scott Fitzgerald and the Collapse of the American Dream," in *The Eccentric Design: Form in the Classic American Novel* by Marius Bewley (New York: Columbia University Press, 1963). © 1959, 1963 by Columbia University Press.

Excerpts from "Toward *The Great Gatsby:* The Apprenticeship Period," in *The Achieving of "The Great Gatsby": F. Scott Fitzgerald, 1920–1925* by Robert Emmet Long (Lewisburg, Pa.: Bucknell University Press, 1979). © 1979 by Bucknell University Press. Reprinted by permission of Associated University Presses.

Excerpts from "F. Scott Fitzgerald's Revision of 'The Rich Boy'" by James L. W. West III and J. Barclay Inge, *Proof* 5 (1975).

Excerpts from "The Sane Method of 'Crazy Sunday'" by Sheldon Grebstein, in *The Short Stories of F. Scott Fitzgerald: New Approaches in Criticism*, ed. Jackson R. Bryer (Madison: University of Wisconsin Press, 1982). © 1982 by the Board of Regents of the University of Wisconsin System.

"The Perfect Life" by William Troy, *Nation*, 17 April 1935. © 1935 by *The Nation Magazine*/The Nation Co., Inc.

I also want to thank Gordon Weaver of Oklahoma State University and Liz Fowler of Twayne Publishers for expert editorial advice and steady personal support.

Part 1

THE SHORT FICTION

Introduction

Although the tradition of the short story in the United States had boasted Washington Irving, Edgar Allan Poe, Herman Melville, Nathaniel Hawthorne, Henry James, Stephen Crane, and other luminaries, F. Scott Fitzgerald, like most early twentieth-century writers, editors, and critics, considered short fiction inferior to long fiction. No doubt this negative attitude was influenced by O. Henry (William Sydney Porter), whose formulaic works became notorious for their trick endings. Moreover, mass circulation magazines such as the *Saturday Evening Post* published innumerable stories at high prices, which, since they were "commercial," often induced serious craftsmen—Fitzgerald included—to compromise themselves. During the 1920s, the brief form was further denigrated by the publishers' practice of bringing out story collections immediately following novels as a way of keeping their authors before the public between full-length narratives. Thus, in Fitzgerald's case, *Flappers and Philosophers* (September 1920) followed *This Side of Paradise* (March 1920); *Tales of the Jazz Age* (September 1922) followed *The Beautiful and Damned* (March 1922); *All the Sad Young Men* (February 1926) followed *The Great Gatsby* (April 1925); and *Taps at Reveille* (March 1935) followed *Tender Is the Night* (April 1934).

Fitzgerald began publishing stories in 1909, eleven years before the appearance of his first novel; at the end of his career, in the month he died (December 1940), *Esquire* printed "A Patriotic Short" while Fitzgerald was working on *The Last Tycoon*. The author commented on these interdependent and parallel careers to interviewer Charles C. Baldwin:

> I became an advertising man at ninety dollars a month, writing slogans that while [*sic*] away the weary hours in rural trolley cars. After hours I wrote stories—from March to June. There were nineteen all together; the quickest written in an hour and a half, the slowest in three days. No one bought them, no one sent personal letters. I had one-hundred-and-twenty-one rejection slips pinned in a frieze about my room. I wrote movies. I wrote song sketches. I wrote jokes. Near

the end of June I sold one story for thirty dollars ["Babes in the Woods," *The Smart Set*, 1919]. . . . On September 15 *This Side of Paradise* was accepted by special delivery.

In the next two months I wrote eight stories and sold nine. The ninth story was accepted by the same magazine that had rejected it four months before. In November I sold my first story to the *Saturday Evening Post* ["Head and Shoulders"]. By February I had sold them half a dozen. Then my novel came out.[1]

Though Fitzgerald combined professions as both novelist and story writer, he identified exclusively with the former role, proclaiming over and over, "I hate writing short stories . . . and only do my six a year to have the leisure to write my novels."[2] The difference between the two fictional modes is summarized by his statement, "So in my new novel [*The Great Gatsby*] I'm thrown directly on purely creative work—not trashy imaginings as in my stories but the sustained imagination of a sincere and yet radiant world."[3] If the story represented a "poor old debauched form," the novel represented "the strongest and supplest medium for conveying thought and emotion from one human being to another."[4] The first could "be written on a bottle," while the second required "mental speed"; the first was impermanent, the second, permanent. Therefore, Fitzgerald felt no compunction about going through the stories, extracting the best phrases and passages, having his secretary enter these in his notebooks, and then designating the affected texts as "stripped" and never to be republished. Later, the pirated material would grace a long prose work.

Ironically, it was the "poor old debauched form" and not "the strongest and supplest medium" that sustained Fitzgerald financially. Appendix A of Anthony Bryant Mangum's unpublished 1974 University of South Carolina dissertation, "The Short Stories of F. Scott Fitzgerald: A Study in Literary Economics" draws on Fitzgerald's Ledger and Matthew J. Bruccoli's *As Ever, Scott Fitz——* to chart authorial income between 1919 and 1940. Various categories were used, including "Writing for Movies," but only "From Stories" and "From Novels" appear here.

Year	From Stories	From Novels
1919	$ 770.00	——
1920	13,025.00	$ 6,200.00
1921	4,280.00	14,749.87
1922	6,286.00	15,583.00
1923	8,928.21	15,111.00
1924	16,253.40	1,177.00
1925	13,924.52	3,952.39
1926	5,123.99	20,098.34
1927	15,766.69	8,971.56
1928	22,178.50	2,217.63
1929	27,075.42	913.84
1930	25,529.85	3,732.57
1931	31,687.00	79.35
1932	14,280.67	480.00
1933	7,766.84	6,450.00
1934	12,692.76	6,840.33
1935	14,989.86	359.92
1936	10,099.79	81.18
1937	2,550.00	——
1938	31.54	——
1939	1,150.00	225.00
1940	5,340.00	——

Most of this story income came from the *Saturday Evening Post*, whose fee rose from $400 in 1919 to $4,000 in 1929. The sixty-five *Post* stories published during a period of seventeen years brought Fitzgerald nearly $200,000.

The conflict between the hackwork/money/success homology and the artwork/penury/failure homology extended beyond considerations of genre (story versus novel) to embrace the larger question of commercial versus serious fiction. Five of eight major short stories were published in magazines that paid very little, prefiguring Fitzgerald's subsequent situation at *Esquire*, where he was paid an average of $250 per story. For "May Day" and "The Diamond as Big as the Ritz," he received $200 and $300 respectively from *The Smart Set*; for "Absolution" and "Crazy Sunday," $118 and $200 respectively from *The Amer-*

ican Mercury; and for "Winter Dreams," $900 from *Metropolitan*. The author, a professional, understandably wanted to locate his superior creations more lucratively, yet often the big journals rejected his best work. The fate of "Crazy Sunday" is typical: "Fitzgerald promised to write an article on 'Hollywood Revisited' for *Scribner's Magazine* but in January 1932 wrote instead the story 'Crazy Sunday.' . . . The story was declined by the *Post* as too sexually frank, and it was not accepted by any of the other mass-circulation magazines. Fitzgerald later wrote his agent, Harold Ober: 'Do you remember how the Hearst publicity men killed my story "Crazy Sunday" for *Cosmopolitan*. That was in case someone would get hurt.'"[5] During an earlier letter to Ober, he had lamented: "I am rather discouraged that a cheap story like *The Popular Girl* written in one week while the baby was being born brings $1500.00 + a genuinely imaginative thing into which I put three weeks real enthuesiasm [*sic*] like *The Diamond in the Sky* [i.e., "The Diamond as Big as the Ritz"] brings not a thing."[6]

Since the three remaining major stories were published by *Red Book* ("The Rich Boy") and *Saturday Evening Post* ("The Ice Palace" and "Babylon Revisited"), clearly the big journals sometimes accepted outstanding work. Indeed, other quality Fitzgerald fiction appeared in the *Post*, including "Jacob's Ladder," "The Last of the Belles," "The Rough Crossing," "The Swimmers," "One Trip Abroad," and thirteen Basil and Josephine stories. He could thus honestly praise George Horace Lorimer, the great *Post* editor between 1899 and 1936, informing Zelda on 18 May 1940: "As you should know from your own attempts, high-priced commercial writing for the magazines is a very definite trick. The rather special things that I brought to it, the intelligence and the good writing and even the radicalism all appealed to old Lorimer who had been a writer himself and liked style" (*Letters*, 117–18). True, Lorimer had composed *Letters from a Self-Made Merchant to His Son* (1902) and *Old Gorgon Graham* (1904), but his pro-Hoover/anti-Roosevelt stance was hardly radical. Yet Lorimer seemed superior to the "man who runs the magazine now [Wesley W. Stout]," "an up-and-coming young Republican who gives not a damn about literature and who publishes almost nothing except escape stories about the brave frontiersmen, etc., or fishing, or football captains—nothing that would even faintly shock or disturb the reactionary bourgeois" (*Letters*, 118). In this 1940 communication, Fitzgerald connected his recent difficulties with the *Post* to Lorimer's retirement: "I wrote them three stories that year and sent them about three others which they didn't like" (*Letters*, 117). Though these difficulties had begun earlier, it is interesting to note that his final contribution to the *Post*, a story aptly titled "Trouble," came out in March 1937, a few months before Lorimer died and many years after Fitzgerald had vowed, "[B]y God + Lorimer, I'm going to make a fortune yet" (*As Ever*, 36).

He commenced auspiciously enough, publishing six stories there during 1920 alone: "Head and Shoulders," "Myra Meets His Family," "The Camel's Back," "Bernice Bobs Her Hair," "The Ice Palace," and "The Offshore Pirate." Comic except for "The Ice Palace," they all contained strong, unconventional females. Of the first, which Lorimer had renamed, Henry Dan Piper says: "The college setting, the unexpected twist in the plot at the end, and the characters—a shy young hero and an attractive, aggressive working-girl heroine (from a vaudeville show)—were to become familiar staples in his subsequent commercial fiction."[7] Later, his output increased: seven *Post* stories in 1928, eight in 1929, seven in 1930, eight in 1931, and six in 1932; then it slackened to four in 1933, three in 1934, one in 1935, two in 1936, one in 1937, and none thereafter.

Fitzgerald became more and more discouraged about his efforts to write commercially acceptable short fiction. In a letter of 1925, he complains to H. L. Mencken:

> My trash for the *Post* grows worse and worse as there is less and less heart in it. Strange to say, my whole heart was in my first trash. I thought that "The Offshore Pirate" was quite as good as "Benediction." I never really "wrote down" until after the failure of *The Vegetable* [1923] and that was to make this book [*The Great Gatsby*] possible [financially]. I would have written down long ago if it had been profitable—I tried it unsuccessfully for the movies. People don't seem to realize that for an intelligent man writing down is about the hardest thing in the world. (*Letters*, 481)

By 1929 he had grown artistically dissolute, or so he told another friend, Ernest Hemingway: "The *Post* now pays the old whore $4000 a screw. But now it's because she's mastered the 40 positions—in her youth one was enough" (*Letters*, 307).

Although "The Jelly-Bean" was turned down at the *Post* and elsewhere in 1920, thanks to the unhappy ending, from 1927 on, while America approached and then entered the Great Depression, such endings seemed more commonplace and admissible, as the publication of

"One Trip Abroad" and "Babylon Revisited" illustrates. By the end of the Depression, in 1940, however, Fitzgerald remarked to Zelda: "Their new attitude is that you no longer have a chance of selling a story with an unhappy ending." Since his pen froze and his talent vanished if he was "writing according to cheap specification," he did not blame the *Post* for its rejections through "the past three or four years" (*Letters*, 118). Mrs. Fitzgerald, who would soon leave Highland Hospital after several mental breakdowns, must have understood why her impecunious, unwell, neglected, and alcoholic husband could never again tack happy conclusions on sad tales. Earlier he had told fellow writer Julian Street: "It was easier when I was young and believed in things and hoped that life might be a happy matter for some people. But . . . you learn that happiness is a prerogative of the perennial children of this world, and not too many of them" (*Letters*, 526).

Fitzgerald was unlikely to "write a great many more stories about young love," as *Colliers* editor Kenneth Littauer discovered in 1939:

> I was tagged with that by my first writings up to 1925. Since then I have written stories about young love. They have been done with increasing difficulty and increasing insincerity. I would either be a miracle man or a hack if I could go on turning out an identical product for three decades.
>
> I know that is what's expected of me, but in that direction the well is pretty dry and I think I am much wiser in not trying to strain for it but rather to open up a new well, a new vein. You see, I not only announced the birth of my young illusions in *This Side of Paradise* but pretty much the death of them in some of my last *Post* stories like "Babylon Revisited." Lorimer seemed to understand this in a way. Nevertheless, an overwhelming number of editors continue to associate me with an absorbing interest in young girls—an interest that at my age would probably land me behind the bars. (*Letters*, 588)

Young love and happy endings were only two aspects of the popular romance nurtured by George Lorimer, whose *Saturday Evening Post* generally typified the taste of the big journals. It was a family publication with a wide middle-class audience and therefore printed no liquor advertisements and permitted no sexual innuendoes. Conservative formally as well as politically, this patriotic weekly opposed brief, shapeless fiction, not to mention fiction that lacked verisimilitude. What little satire appeared there had to be sugar-coated. Some idea of the restrictions imposed on contributors may be gained from a deposition Fitzgerald's agent prepared for "the Collector of Internal Revenue" in 1932:

> During 1929 and 1930 Mr. Fitzgerald wrote a total of fifteen stories at the request of the editors of The Saturday Evening Post, all of which were copy-righted by that publication and published therein. The arrangement, pursuant to which these stories were written for The Saturday Evening Post, specified the length of each, subject matter, avoidance of certain topics and at an agreed price for each. . . . The Post's requirements in this connection are for stories from 5,000 to 8,000 words. The stories would not have been acceptable to certain publications known as women's magazines, which have a large circulation, since they are written from the male angle. (*As Ever*, 192–93)

It has been argued that the popular romance, with its conventional form and content, was ill-suited to the Fitzgerald talent, but, as we shall see, his prep-school and college stories contradict this. Long before he sold "Head and Shoulders" to the *Post*, he had regularly employed both Lorimer- and O. Henry–like fictional strategies. Initially, Fitzgerald shared Lorimer's idealism, summarized thus: "I found he made a sharp distinction between a sordid tragedy and a heroic tragedy—hating the former but accepting the latter as an essential and interesting part of life" (*Letters*, 565). Later, while the disillusioned author treated broken marriages rather than young lovers, he admitted that "the commercial short story . . . requires a certain ebullience about inessential and specious matters which I no longer possess."[8] His work—now darkly, not lightly comic—substituted ironic for happy endings, yet its form remained more or less traditional.

Fitzgerald told Marxist author V. F. Calverton, "To a great extent I have used the accepted technique of my time, feeling that what observations I have made need all the help that I can give the reader" (*Correspondence*, 460). This "accepted technique," which he found in native writers like Henry James, Edith Wharton, and Willa Cather, characterizes "most traditionalist literature: a deliberate and unhurried narrative; a consecutive chronology; and a solid recognizable social world."[9] Consequently, his stories tend to be full, heavily plotted constructs involving several mechanical divisions. Fitzgerald, usually employing a third-person perspective, can become almost as intrusive as an eighteenth-century novelist. When first-person narration is employed, the storyteller plays observer rather than hero, though he or she may be the actual protagonist. These figures sometimes seem unreliable (cf. James's "publishing scoundrel" of "The Aspern Papers" and Faulkner's Jason Compson of *The Sound and the Fury*), but creating a deliberately unreliable central intelligence was probably too innovative for a fictionist indebted to O. Henry's "clever twists and turns, and abrupt climaxes and surprise endings."[10]

The modern realists, convinced that life lacked Aristotelian symmetry and predictability, revolted against plot, or the artificial ordering of events. Instead, Anton Chekhov, whose first story collection was published during 1884, offered the episode focused on a static situation, and James Joyce, whose *Dubliners* was completed around 1905, offered the epiphany derived from a sudden revelation. Though Fitzgerald had probably read Chekhov's *Letters on the Short Story, the Drama, and Other Literary Topics*, he made no memorable recorded statements about him. Joyce is another matter, since Fitzgerald ranked *Dubliners* among the "great English classics." His notebooks contain the admonition, "Must listen for conversation style a la Joyce," but the Joycean influence remained largely thematic.

Two other contemporary American authors profited most from the formal revolution inspired by Chekhov and Joyce. Nobody opposed "The Poison Plot" more than Sherwood Anderson: "What was wanted I thought was form, not plot, an altogether more elusive and difficult thing to come at. . . . [A]s for the plot short stories of the magazines—those bastard children of De Maupassant, Poe and O. Henry—it was certain there were no plot short stories ever lived in any life I had known anything about."[11]

Anderson substituted the word *tale* for the word *story*, implying a strict distinction between two modes often considered interchangeable, the tale defining a simpler prose or verse narrative without plot complications. When he published twenty-one such pieces as *Winesburg, Ohio* (1919), modern short autochthonous fiction was launched. Each tale combined Chekhov's episode and Joyce's epiphany to dramatize a single bizarre moment of small-town life. This art has been succinctly summarized: "In Anderson, the representational mode, the tripartite structure, the assumption of verifiable patterns of behavior and the moral concomitant disappear. In their place is a form at once more allusive and epigrammatic, more mystical and poetic, and more psychologically suggestive than anything that had gone before it in

American fiction" (Kimbel, 62). Innovative too was the *Winesburg* structure, for, reminiscent of Edgar Lee Masters's *Spoon River Anthology* (1915), it revealed novelistic properties, paving the way for Ernest Hemingway's *In Our Time* (1925), whose "oblique" sketches, which "reverberate, in the Chekhovian manner, with aftereffects," were "trying to extend the possibilities of the short story cycle" (Gullason, 90).

By contrast, Fitzgerald's two extended sequences, the *in*clusive Basil Duke Lee stories (*Post*, 1928–29) and the *ex*clusive Pat Hobby stories (*Esquire*, 1940–41) are certainly not "experimental." Yet he greatly admired *In Our Time*, which he reviewed for *The Bookman* in May 1926.[12] After describing Anderson as "the possessor of a brilliant and almost inimitable prose style, and of scarcely any ideas at all," he turns from this "difficult simplicity" to the main subject, Hemingway:

> "In Our Time" consists of fourteen stories, short and long, with fifteen vivid miniatures interpolated between them. When I try to think of any contemporary American short stories as good as "Big Two-Hearted River," the last one in the book, only Gertrude Stein's "Melanctha," Anderson's "The Egg," and Lardner's "Golden Honeymoon" come to mind. It is the account of a boy on a fishing trip— he hikes, pitches his tent, cooks dinner, sleeps, and next morning casts for trout. Nothing more—but I read it with the most breathless unwilling interest I have experienced since Conrad first bent my reluctant eyes upon the sea.

Fitzgerald asserts that the stories make the reader "aware of something temperamentally new," citing Hemingway's ability to give people an emotion "without the aid of a comment or a pointing finger." The reader understands the meaning sans authorial exposition; the dialogue says it all: "a picture—sharp, nostalgic, tense—develops before your eyes. When the picture is complete a light seems to snap out, the story is over. There is no tail, no sudden change of pace at the end to throw into relief what has gone before." Hemingway, who "turns a corner" with *In Our Time*, cultivates words that spare "not a bit," and so he implicitly shares the Fitzgerald view that "material, however closely observed, is as elusive as the moment in which it has its existence unless it is purified by an incorruptible style and by the catharsis of a passionate emotion."

The first reference Fitzgerald made to Hemingway appears in a letter to Scribner editor Maxwell Perkins: "This is to tell you about a young man named Ernest Hemmingway [*sic*], who lives in Paris . . . writes for the transatlantic Review & has a brilliant future. . . . He's the real thing" (*Dear Scott*, 78). Fitzgerald's admiration for Hemingway persisted throughout his career. In 1939 he called *A Farewell to Arms* one of the "great English classics"; in 1940 he declared *For Whom the Bell Tolls* "a fine novel, better than anybody else writing could do"; and, in the same letter, said of *To Have and Have Not:* "There is observation and writing in that that the boys will be imitating with a vengeance—paragraphs and pages that are right up with Dostoyevsky in their undeflected intensity" (*Letters*, 312). Meanwhile, Fitzgerald had recognized how dangerous such esteem might become:

> I think it is obvious that my respect for your artistic life is absolutely unqualified, that save for a few of the dead or dying old men you are the only man writing fiction in America that I look up to very much. There are pieces and paragraphs of your work that I read over and over—in fact, I stopped myself doing it for a year and a half because I was afraid that your particular rhythms were going to creep in on mine by process of infiltration. Perhaps you will recognize some of your remarks in *Tender,* but I did every damn thing I could to avoid that. (*Letters*, 309)

He also told Hemingway the latter had reinforced Conrad's concept of "lingering after-effects": "you felt that the true line of a work of fiction was to take a reader up to a high emotional pitch but then let him down or ease him off. You gave no aesthetic reason for this—nevertheless, you convinced me" (*Letters*, 309–10). Not only did Hemingway extend his technical knowledge of writing, but he symbolized the artistic ideal Fitzgerald found in Keats and Conrad, as the notebook entry "value of Ernest's feeling about the pure heart when writing—in other words the comparatively pure heart, the 'house in order'" indicates.[13]

This same admiration for writers with a "pure heart" lies behind Lionel Trilling's comment in *The Liberal Imagination*, "It is hard to overestimate the benefit which came to Fitzgerald from his having consciously placed himself in the line of the great."[14] That Fitzgerald thought about fictional craft is evidenced by his many comments on reading and writing described in "Critical Opinions" (see part 2), where, among other things, he advocates "shaping" and "pruning," concepts manifested as early as *The Great Gatsby* (1925) and its cluster stories. Referring to *The Last Tycoon* fifteen years later, Fitzgerald wrote Zelda, "I am deep in the novel, living in it, and it makes me happy. It is a *constructed* novel like *Gatsby*, with passages of poetic prose when it fits the action, but no ruminations or side-shows like *Tender*. Everything must contribute to the dramatic movement" (*Letters*, 128).

Clearly, then, the general assumption regarding Fitzgerald's so-called "late style"—that it emerged during the mid-1930s when *Esquire*, which paid $250 per submission, but would accept two thousand words or less, displaced the *Post*, which paid $2,000–$4,000 per submission, but expected five thousand words or more—is misleading. His economical prose was not necessarily a late development, nor did this displace his rhetorical prose altogether. The two styles were antithetical, the first marked by brevity, objectivity, indirection, simplicity, and dialogue; the second by the reverse of these. Yet they sometimes coincided, the one-part "Outside the Cabinet-Maker's" appearing in the *Post* period (1928) and the seven-part "Trouble" appearing in the *Esquire* period (1937), for example. Fitzgerald the "leaver-outer" owed a debt to the school of selection, while Fitzgerald the "putter-inner" owed a debt to the school of saturation. Though he associated selection with artistry and saturation with commercialism, he wrote more major *in*clusive stories than *ex*clusive ones. And even when Fitzgerald's work bore traces of the experimental, pared-down stories of Chekhov, Joyce, Anderson, and Hemingway, it remained fundamentally conservative. Thus even his fantastic "second manner," which flourished through the publication of *The Great Gatsby*—especially in *Tales of the Jazz Age* and *The Vegetable*—depends for the most part on established conventions.

Fitzgerald's traditionalism, his orientation and negative valuation on brief fiction during its modern renaissance, helps to explain why his stories have suffered "the critical neglect" charted by Jackson R. Bryer, whose *The Short Stories of F. Scott Fitzgerald: New Approaches in Criticism* is ameliorative:

> The disparate critical attention which Hemingway's and Fitzgerald's short stories have received is astonishing. . . . Through 1979, there were 287 articles or book chapters devoted to Hemingway's short stories: 46 Hemingway stories—nearly half he wrote—were the subjects of at least 1 full essay or chapter. For the same period, Fitzgerald's stories were the subjects of 75 articles or chapters; and only

22 stories—just about one-eighth of his total output—were dealt with in full essays or chapters. . . . The number of serious critical essays on the stories is probably no greater than 20. . . . Each year, some 50 essays or chapters on Fitzgerald are published; rarely do more than 2 or 3 of these deal in more than a cursory way with the stories. Again by contrast, Hemingway's stories generate an annual figure of 15 or 20 essays.[15]

Such past neglect is difficult to understand in view of John O'Hara's 1949 comment to John Steinbeck, which also cited Hemingway and Faulkner: "Fitzgerald was a better just plain writer than all of us put together."

Apprenticeship

Prep-School and College Fiction

Fitzgerald's "Thoughtbook," which inspired Basil Duke Lee's "The Book of Scandal" nearly two decades later, extends from August 1910 to 24 February 1911 and shows the author to have been a born story-teller even in the keeping of a diary. At age fourteen, he already con-sidered himself so, as self-conscious references like "and that is the story of Violet Stockton" indicate. Having developed the storyteller's temporal sense, juxtaposing past and present, he was able to dramatize factual events and render them in natural, though heightened dia-logue. For example:

> "Jim was so confident the other night that you had a crush on him."
> "Well Jim gets another think"
> "Shall I let him know you dont like him."
> "I'll do that."
> "Now if you had thought that it might be different."
> "Good" said I
> "Good" repeated she and then the convestion lagged.[16]

Further evidence in the "Thoughtbook" of Fitzgerald's storytelling instinct may be gathered from his successful endeavors as an amateur psychologist/sociologist. He recorded his reactions to other people and their reactions to him, with the special attention to group status that would later produce a renowned novelist of manners. Competition with rival boys over girls who prefigure the femme fatale is a central motif of his diary. At eleven, he found Kiddy Williams irresistible:

> I dont remember who was first but I know that Earl was second and as I was already quite over come by her charms I then and there resolved that I would gain first place. . . . It was impossible to count the number of times I kissed Kitty that afternoon. At any rate when we went home I had secured the coveted 1st place. I held this until

dancing school stopped in the spring and then relinquished it to Johnny Gowns a rival.

The childish affair immediately succeeding the one with Kiddy involved Violet Stockton:

> She was very pretty with dark brown hair and eyes big and soft. She spoke with a soft southern accent leaving out the r's. She was a year older than I but together with most of the other boys liked her very much. . . . She had some sort of book called flirting by sighns and Jack and I got it away from Violet and showed it too all the boys. . . . The day she went away was my birthday and she gave me a box of candy. Her latest fancy is Arthur Foley.

The "Thoughtbook" breaks off with Margaret's crush on Reuben and Scott's crush on Alida.

Actually, his apprenticeship had started about four years before the composition of this diary, according to the "Ledger" Fitzgerald began during the summer of 1922. An entry for January 1907 reads: "He began a history of the U.S. and also a detective story about a necklace that was hidden in a trapdoor under the carpet. Wrote celebrated essay on George Washington & St. Ignatius." Another entry for June 1909 commences: "Wrote the Mystery of the Raymond Mortgage. Also 'Elavo' (or was that in Buffalo) and a complicated story of some knights."[17] Of these pieces, only "The Mystery of the Raymond Mortgage" has survived. It was published in the St. Paul Academy *Now and Then*, October 1909. Three other *Now and Then* stories followed: "Reade, Substitute Right Half" (February 1910), "A Debt of Honor" (March 1910), and "The Room with the Green Blinds" (June 1911). They all treat heroism: solving a murder mystery; winning a football game single-handed; an act of physical courage during the Civil War; avenging the murder of a son.

At the Newman School, where Fitzgerald moved to spend most of his fifteenth and sixteenth years, he served on the *News*'s editorial staff and published three more stories. Their subjects are giving away money on Christmas Eve, doing unto a religious fanatic what he has done unto you, and searching futilely for a nobleman. While "Pain and the Scientist" (1913) resembles the other two *News* stories technically, it otherwise stands alone in its focus on Christian Science; "A Luckless

Santa Claus" and "The Trail of the Duke," by contrast, introduce the femme fatale and treat the wealthy class in an urban environment.

Fitzgerald's career at Princeton, where, besides fiction, he wrote fifty-five musical comedy lyrics, several poems, parodies, and book reviews, and where he became secretary of the Triangle Club and an editor of the *Tiger* and *The Nassau Literary Magazine*, may be divided into two phases, the first extending from matriculation (September 1913) to initial departure (December 1915) and the second from readmittance (September 1916) to final departure (November 1917). During the earlier period, Fitzgerald contributed the plot and lyrics to one Triangle Club show, lyrics to another, and composed the one-act play *Shadow Laurels* (printed April 1915), while publishing but a single story, "The Ordeal" (June 1915). During the later phase, however, he published five stories in *The Nassau Literary Magazine*—"The Spire and the Gargoyle" (February 1917), "Tarquin of Cheepside" (April 1917), "Babes in the Woods" (May 1917), "Sentiment—and the Use of Rouge" (June 1917), "The Pierian Springs and the Last Straw" (October 1917)—while contributing lyrics to only one Triangle Club show and composing the one-act play *The Debutante* (printed January 1917).

These musical comedy lyrics and one-act plays extended a life-long commitment to the theater that had already produced the four melodramas Fitzgerald submitted to the St. Paul Elizabethan Dramatic Club between August 1911 and September 1914. During the school years, he participated in various histrionic activities and saw several Broadway shows. Later, *This Side of Paradise* (1920) and *The Beautiful and Damned* (1922) would include passages of formal stage dialogue. Later still, Fitzgerald's theatrical interest would inspire a full-length play, *The Vegetable*, and a screenwriting career that would supply material for the Pat Hobby stories, *The Last Tycoon*, and other works of fiction. Though Fitzgerald never mastered drama as such, the arts of theater and cinema exerted considerable influence on him.

Both prep-school and college stories employ dramatic beginnings, surprise endings, and lively scenes. Like his earlier subjects, the Princeton subjects are sometimes sensational: rediscovering a father; overcoming doubt before joining the Jesuits; the debut of a vain female; regret at having flunked out of college; Shakespeare raping Lucrece's "real-life" model, then writing a poem about it; a boy's attempt to kiss a fickle girl; demoralization and death during World War I; a man finally winning an old flame only to lose his writing ability.

Diversity also marks the settings of Fitzgerald's prep-school and college fiction, with New York appearing four times, Southern locations three times, and Princeton and London twice each.

That New York, the dominant setting of his early stories, supplied more than just a place may be surmised from "Forging Ahead" (1929), where Basil Duke Lee is "attuned to the vast, breathless bustle of New York, to the metropolitan days and nights that were tense as singing wires." There, "nothing needed to be imagined . . . for it was all the very stuff of romance—life was as vivid and satisfactory as in books and dreams." Manhattan had been the opening, though not the central setting, of "The Mystery of the Raymond Mortgage" twenty years before. But except for the first few sentences—"It was about six o'clock and the lights were just going on. All down Thirty-third street was a long line of gayly illuminated buildings"—references to the metropolis are perfunctory. Not so with "A Luckless Santa Claus" and "The Trail of the Duke." The heroine of the first lives "somewhere east of Broadway" and the hero of the second owns a "house on upper Fifth Avenue." Largely because of Harry Talbot's walk down Broadway to Union Square, Cooper Square, and the Bowery, then up Third Avenue, locale takes on greater significance and utility in "A Luckless Santa Claus" than in "The Trail of the Duke," which nonetheless commences with Fitzgerald's most ambitious descriptive passage to date. Its 168 words conclude:

> In the flats that line upper New York, pianos (sweatting [*sic*] ebony perspiration) ground out rag-time tunes of last winter and here and there a wan woman sang the air in a hot soprano. In the tenements, shirt-sleeves gleamed like beacon lights in steady rows along the street in tiers of from four to eight according to the number of stories of the house. In a word, it was a typical, hot New York summer night.

Obviously, his 1912 trips from Hackensack, New Jersey (home of the Newman School), to New York City, where he saw *The Little Millionaire*, with George M. Cohan, *The Quaker Girl*, with Ina Claire, *Over the River*, and *The Private Secretary*, influenced the author's prep-school stories, college librettos, and, later, the Basil Duke Lee sequence.

Experimentation with point of view may help determine whether an apprentice writer is an incipient artist. Like subjects and settings, the voices that tell the early tales are various. Five of the prep-school pieces employ the omniscient narrator and two the first-person observer. Two of the college pieces employ the omniscient narrator, one employs the first-person observer, and three employ the central intelligence. A general shift from the omniscient narrator in the prep-school stories to the central intelligence in the college stories shows Fitzgerald's growing awareness of his characters' psychological reactions.

He had less success with structure, an aspect of fiction that would give him trouble even after he discovered the framework narrative and the quest motif, as the two published versions of *Tender Is the Night* prove. The prep-school pieces extend from about 800 words to about 3,000, their typical length being 2,000 words; the college pieces extend from about 2,000 words to about 5,700, their typical length being 3,500 words. Except in the one-act plays, which preserve the unities, increasingly complex structures accompany the tendency toward greater bulk. While two of the seven prep-school stories have two parts, all six college stories have bi- and tripartite constructions. Only rarely—for instance, in "Pain and the Scientist," whose plot depends upon a reversal—do mechanical divisions furnish organic support. Most often they merely separate body and denouement or introduce a change of setting, both of which Fitzgerald also managed in one-part stories. "The Trail of the Duke" (in one part) treats a situation almost identical to that in "A Luckless Santa Claus" (in two parts), and "The Mystery of the Raymond Mortgage" (in one part) uses more settings than "The Room with the Green Blinds" (in three parts).

Among his early characters who represent roles—detective, athlete, soldier, priest, student, writer—two archetypal figures dominate: *l'homme manqué* (the inadequate man) and *la femme fatale* (the destructive woman). Failure on the part of males in the Princeton fiction had been foreshadowed in the St. Paul fiction, whose heroes, through personal weakness or some external force, became the *homme manqué*, a term the author would use to describe Dick Diver of *Tender Is the Night*, though it applies equally well to many other Fitzgerald protagonists. Besides upper-class boys like Harry Talbot ("A Luckless Santa Claus"), Dodson Garland ("The Trail of the Duke"), John Cannel (*The Debutante*), Kenneth Powers ("Babes in the Woods"), and Clay Syneforth ("Sentiment—and the Use of Rouge"), Fitzgerald's *homme manqué* will include failed aristocrats like Diver or ambitious parvenus like Gatsby. His bourgeois heroes eventually believe that anything is possible and so grow disillusioned in the end. He would not write the tragedy of the rich, nor of the poor; instead, he would write the tragedy of the unstable middle class.

Two Newman stories introduce the femme fatale, Fitzgerald's vampiric antagonist. "A Luckless Santa Claus" (Christmas 1912) begins: "Miss Harmon was responsible for the whole thing. If it had not been for her foolish whim, Talbot would not have made a fool of himself." What is "her foolish whim"? A challenge to wealthy, indolent, "faultlessly dressed" Harry Talbot to give away twenty-five dollars, two dollars at a time, in an hour-and-a-half period one Christmas Eve, a challenge her words explain: "Why you can't even spend money, much less earn it!" And how does her fiancé make a fool of himself? By accosting people who greet his generosity with a mistrust and contempt that reach their climax when he gets badly mauled and must return to Dorothy's house "hatless, coatless, tieless."

"The Trail of the Duke" (1913) closely resembles "A Luckless Santa Claus." We are given another aimless rich boy as victim and another silly girlfriend as victimizer. Compared to Harry Talbot's experience, however, Dodson Garland's seems trivial: it hinges on a simple misunderstanding rather than an ironic, thematically important circumstance. "Crestfallen and broken-hearted," he returns to Mirabel Walmsley after having futilely and erroneously quested after the Duke of Matterlane rather than the "small white poodle" called "Dukey" that she has lost.

The femme fatale also plays a crucial role in three Princeton pieces prior to "The Pierian Springs and the Last Straw," Fitzgerald's last college story. Throughout *The Debutante*, a "huge pier-glass" constantly reminds us of the narcissism of the heroine, a latter-day Helen and typical debutante who will soon metamorphose into flapper or vamp. She despises her maid; toys with her father's advice; tells her mother, "You can't run everything now, the way they did in the early nineties"; and, enacting her acknowledged fickleness, dismisses John Cannel.

Like Helen Halycon, Isabelle of "Babes in the Woods" is based on Fitzgerald's college sweetheart, Ginevra King, and like Helen, Isabelle differs from Dorothy Harmon and Mirabel Walmsley only to the extent that calculation differs from capriciousness. After pitting Peter Carroll against him, Isabelle becomes Kenneth Powers's dinner partner, a circumstance that precedes Kenneth's attempt to kiss her. The closing section depicts the situation thus: "[Kenneth] was aware that he was getting this particular favor now because she had been coached. He knew that he stood for merely the best thing in sight, and that he would have to improve his opportunity before he lost his advantage."

"Sentiment—and the Use of Rouge" introduces a slightly older set. In it, Lieutenant Clay Harrington Syneforth, son of Lord Blachford and "champion of sentiment," comes home from the war to find the girls' heavily painted faces expressing "half enthusiasm and half reck-lessness," a sight more depressing "than any concrete thing." One girl, with a voice "like the grey creed of a new materialistic world," embod-ies the breakdown of traditional sexual standards. We discover that Eleanor's fiancé (Clay's dead brother) and her younger sister have been killed during the war, and we observe Eleanor's successful effort to seduce the moralistic lieutenant. Though not destroyed by this femme fatale, Clay Harrington Syneforth, like John Cannel and Kenneth Pow-ers, is more seriously affected than Harry Talbot and Dodson Garland, who suffer temporary humiliation at the hands of Dorothy Harmon and Mirabel Walmsley. Just as Helen rejects John and Isabelle uses Ken-neth, Eleanor entices Clay into betraying himself and his dead brother.

The femme fatale represents no mere foil. Her development into an independently significant personage became one of the major achieve-ments of Fitzgerald's juvenile writing. Eventually, Judy Jones of "Win-ter Dreams," Jonquil Cary of "The Sensible Thing," and Josephine Perry of the five Josephine stories will surround themselves with de-voted males, whom they seem to delight in torturing with uncertainty. Judy was destined to "bring no end of misery to a great number of men," and Josephine "had driven mature men to a state of disequili-brium." Another girl, Ailie Calhoun of "The Last of the Belles," is proud of the fact that a man committed suicide over her. Clearly, the creator of Daisy Buchanan and Nicole Warren had suffered from *la belle dame sans merci*, whether Ginevra King, his Princeton sweetheart, or Zelda Sayre, his Southern fiancée. Clearly, too, he was "half femi-nine—at least my mind is. . . . Even my feminine characters are fem-inine Scott Fitzgeralds."[18]

"The Pierian Springs and the Last Straw": Adumbrations of *The Great Gatsby*

The school fiction of F. Scott Fitzgerald—stories that he wrote be-tween the ages of thirteen and twenty-one and submitted with un-qualified success to his prep-school and college magazines—contain, as has been demonstrated, many prototypical themes, characters and techniques that would reappear, fully developed, in his mature work. In most cases the points of similarity between early and later fiction are scattered rather than clustered; no one juvenile story shares themes, characters, and techniques with any single corresponding story written in maturity. The only exception to this rule happens to be Fitzgerald's final college piece, "The Pierian Springs and the Last Straw" (1917),[19] which appeared in the October 1917 *Nassau Literary Magazine*. It is also his best juvenile story, despite the curious fact that he never placed it in *The Smart Set*, H. L. Mencken's chic avant-garde monthly, where four other college pieces—none as good as "The Pierian Springs and the Last Straw"—were reprinted. Perhaps the explanation is that Mencken never had a chance to consider the story because Fitzgerald deliberately set it aside, planning to rework it eventually. Whether this is in fact what happened cannot be known, but its plausibility is undeniable, for "The Pierian Springs" and *The Great Gatsby* (1925), while worlds apart in quality, bear so many and such striking similarities that the undergraduate story seems a kind of crude template for the masterwork Fitzgerald was to publish seven and a half years later.

The story contains two parts. The opening section of the long first part elaborates the statement, "My Uncle George assumed, during my childhood, almost legendary proportions": he drank heavily and was a "mesogamist" [*sic*] who "had been engaged seven times" and "had written a series of novels" about bad or not-quite-good women. The closing section takes the narrator—now a twenty-year-old Easterner—to "the prosperous Western city that still supported the roots of our family tree," where, in the Iroquois Club, his uncle explains why his life stopped "at sixteen minutes after ten" one October evening. The woman responsible for this figurative death, Mrs. Fulham, subsequently ridiculed Uncle George, her willing victim, for an entire decade. Then she added "the last straw" of insult when she announced sarcastically in public that she had often talked her dead husband out of horsewhipping George for fawning on her. At this, George flew into a rage, wrenched her wedding ring from her, breaking Myra's finger in the process. With that touch of melodrama, the first part ends and the nephew departs. The second part, consisting of two brief paragraphs, describes the uncle's fate and implies the nephew's relation to it. We learn that the older man and the widow eloped soon after the incident, with the result that he "never drank again, nor did he ever write or in fact do anything except play a middling amount of golf and get comfortably bored with his wife." And we feel that the nephew—whose comments such as, "The story ought to end here," and, "Unfortunately the play continues into an inartistic sixth act," illustrate his self-consciousness—may become the new family author, even though this creative role may entail similar instability.

The resemblance between the nephew of "The Pierian Springs" and Nick Carraway of *The Great Gatsby* is remarkable. Both young men and both self-referential, they share an upper middle-class heritage, their families possessing firmly established roots and sufficient resources to send sons to Eastern schools. The nephew's father practices law; Nick's engages in wholesale hardware. Mr. Carraway advises his son, "Whenever you feel like criticizing any one . . . just remember that all the people in this world haven't had the advantages that you've had";[20] similarly, the nephew's father acts the part of moral touchstone, conservative yet sympathetic too: "Is that damn father of yours still defending me against your mother's tongue?" asks George. Like Nick's, the nephew's hometown is a "prosperous Western city," though the initiatory journey of the story runs from east to west to east rather than from west to east to west. Thus, "The Pierian Springs" employs geographic oppositions in a journey context, introducing Fitzgerald's most successful structural mode.

But even more remarkable than the nephew-Nick parallels are the correspondences between George Rombert and Tom Buchanan, on the one hand, and George Rombert and Jay Gatsby, on the other. Both Buchanan and Rombert drink heavily and act promiscuously, yet these general resemblances seem slight when compared with what may be termed the analogue of the injured finger, for just as George breaks Myra's ring finger, Tom hurts Daisy's little finger. If the second injury is accidental, the first is intentional. Neither victim seems to resent this violence; indeed, it may well have inspired Mrs. Fulham to elope with Uncle George. Physical violence will recur during *The Great Gatsby*, where Tom embodies what Daisy calls him: "a brute of a man" (*GG*, 12).

Both about thirty and both purveyors of disreputable merchandise, Rombert and Gatsby assume mythical stature, the former being pictured by the nephew as Romeo, Byron, Bernard Shaw, Don Juan, Havelock Ellis, "the Thomas Hardy of America," "the Balzac of his century," and the latter being described by Nick as Trimalchio and by acquaintances as a relative of Kaiser Wilhelm or Von Hindenburg, a German spy or a murderer. Uncle George's personality is "a series of perfectly artificial mental tricks . . . gestures," and Jay Gatsby's is "an unbroken series of successful gestures" (*GG*, 2). Uncle George tells his story to the nephew and Jay Gatsby tells his to Nick. Like Gatsby, who "knew women early" and "became contemptuous of them" (99), George evolves into a misogynist. And like Gatsby, who also collected "presentable" trophies, George was inspired by a young lady to do something for her, to get something to show her. Each perishes— Gatsby actually and Rombert figuratively—because, as romantics, they believe they can repeat the past when they fell in love, a past that both story and novel frequently juxtapose with the present.

The similarities between Myra Fulham—the most treacherous femme fatale of the college stories—and Daisy Buchanan are also remarkable. Uncle George applies adjectives to the former that apply equally to the latter: "unprincipled," "selfish," "conceited," "uncontrolled." He claims, "When she wanted a boy there was no preliminary scouting among other girls for information, no sending out of tentative approaches meant to be retailed to him. There was the most direct attack by every faculty and gift that she possessed. She had no divergence of method—she just made you conscious to the highest degree that she was a girl." Just as this sexuality expresses itself in Myra's "eternal mouth," it is present in Daisy's voice full of money. And if Myra betrays George—first with a man "from another college," and then with "a crooked broker—the damn thief that robbed me of everything in this hellish world"—Daisy betrays both Gatsby and Tom.

Not only does "The Pierian Springs and the Last Straw" contain the most impressive early manipulation of the prototypical *homme manqué* and femme fatale, but also the most effective use of the observer-narrator focus, later made famous in *The Great Gatsby* and other superior fictions. This figure had already appeared in the prep-school canon, but there it had not matured beyond its basic function as reporter.[21] Such is not the case, however, with "The Pierian Springs"—the third instance of the observer technique in Fitzgerald's juvenile work—for, while recreating Uncle George, the nameless nephew learns a critical lesson: if he should become an author ("your son here will be George the second"), artistic fulfillment might hinge on personal frustration.

Long before Fitzgerald published his masterpiece, then, he had discovered and even developed one significant storytelling technique and two significant characters central to its achievement. The technique— observer as raconteur—was still rather crude, but the two characters— *homme manqué* and femme fatale—were already quite sophisticated. If Dorothy Harmon of "A Luckless Santa Claus" and Mirabel Walmsley

of "The Trail of the Duke" humiliate their boyfriends by capricious-
ness, Helen Halycon of *The Debutante,* Isabelle of "Babes in the
Woods," and Eleanor Marbrooke of "Sentiment—and the Use of
Rouge" inflict far greater pain by calculation. And if Harry Talbot and
Dodson Garland revenge themselves when deserting Dorothy and
Mirabel, John Cannel, Kenneth Powers, and Clay Syneforth seem
completely helpless. These prototypical characters, as well as the observer-narrator point of view, reach their preprofessional apotheosis in
"The Pierian Springs and the Last Straw," where the relationship be-
tween femme fatale and *homme manqué* reveals considerable psychological complexity.

Flappers and Philosophers and Tales of the Jazz Age

That nearly all of Fitzgerald's college stories were considered publish-
able is attested to by the inclusion of "Babes in the Woods," *The Debutante,* and "The Ordeal" in *The Smart Set,* edited by H. L. Mencken
and George Jean Nathan, while "Jemina" appeared in *Vanity Fair.*
Moreover, Fitzgerald's first novel, *This Side of Paradise* incorporated
versions of "Babes in the Woods" and *The Debutante* as well as material
from "The Spire and the Gargoyle" and "Sentiment—and the Use of
Rouge." One college effort—"The Ordeal" (retitled "Benediction")—
recurred in the first published story collection, *Flappers and Philosophers*
(1920), and two—"Tarquin of Cheapside" and "Jemina," in the second, *Tales of the Jazz Age* (1922). Eight of the thirteen stories Fitzgerald
had already published, including several from the *Saturday Evening
Post,* constituted *Flappers and Philosophers,* rejects of which (such as,
"The Camel's Back" and *Mr. Icky*) helped to flesh out *Tales of the Jazz
Age* two years later. The second volume contains three important
works: "The Jelly-Bean" and "May Day" (both from 1920) would have
been part of *Flappers and Philosophers* were they not awaiting magazine
publication; "The Diamond as Big as the Ritz" (*The Smart Set,* June
1922) was the only one chosen for *Tales of the Jazz Age* among the three
written since the summer of 1920. Because the selections in *The Nassau
Literary Magazine, Flappers and Philosophers,* and *Tales of the Jazz Age*
were all composed during 1915–21 and share obvious connections,
they, like the author's prep-school efforts, may be said to comprise his
apprentice fiction.

The established patterns persist. For example, the wide range of subject matter that characterized earlier stories also characterizes those making up the first two Scribner collections. Thus, *Flappers and Philosophers*, a book focused on its two title-figure types, explores the maritime romance between a clever young man and a rebellious young woman; the broken engagement between a Southern girl and a Northern boy; the marriage between an intellectual and an actress; the catastrophic life and death of an unfaithful wife; the triumph of an inexperienced debutante over her seasoned counterpart; the journey of a sceptical sister to an older brother joining the Jesuits; the peacetime adventures of a disillusioned World War I hero; and, finally, the education through hard knocks of a privileged snob.

Similarly, Fitzgerald, whose already-published *This Side of Paradise* was a potpourri of literary forms reflecting his student work at Princeton, no doubt calculatedly employed diversity in *Tales of the Jazz Age*, since its annotated table of contents lists selections under three separate categories: "My Last Flappers," "Fantasies," and "Unclassified Masterpieces." Insofar as these annotations elucidate the genesis and history of each offering, they are valuable, but, more often than not, they are merely personal and flippant. Fitzgerald is obviously being facetious when he says that wife Zelda—"an expert on technique and terminology"—contributed "the crap-shooting episode" to "The Jelly-Bean"; that "The Camel's Back" was written during one day . . . with the express purpose of buying a platinum and diamond wrist watch"; that he likes the frivolous "Offshore Pirate" (of *Flappers and Philosophers*) better than the serious "Diamond as Big as the Ritz"; that one correspondent called him a "fanatic" after reading "The Curious Case of Benjamin Button"; that "none of the characters in 'O Russet Witch!' need be taken seriously"; that "The Lees of Happiness" won "the quadruple gold laurel leaf"; that "Jemina" is "worth preserving . . . until the ennui of changing fashions suppresses me, my books, and it together." Fitzgerald concludes, "I tender these tales of the Jazz Age into the hands of those who read as they run and run as they read," perhaps acknowledging the thinness of a volume built largely upon old performances and new rejects.

Authorial self-consciousness, which had marked his earlier work as well, burgeons in *Flappers and Philosophers* and *Tales of the Jazz Age*, appearing in about half of the stories. Often Fitzgerald introduces an anonymous "I" (presumably himself) and an anonymous "you" (presumably the reader) at or near the beginning of the narrative. For instance, "The Jelly-Bean" opens, "Much as I desire to make him [Jim Powell] an appealing character, I feel that it would be unscrupulous to deceive you on that point." And he sometimes offers pseudo-philosophical passages such as the one toward the end of "The Offshore Pirate": "Most of us are content to exist and breed and fight for the right to do both, and the dominant idea, the foredoomed attempt to control one's destiny, is reserved for the fortunate or unfortunate few." Coming from the twenty-three-year-old author of commercial comic fictions, such remarks seem pretentious. Fitzgerald is much more effective when comments such as these emerge in dialogue from his flappers and philosophers. We more readily accept similar pronouncements made by the nineteen-year-old protagonist Ardita Farnam, whom we first encounter reading Anatole France's *The Revolt of the Angels*, because she has an unconventional personality.

In keeping with this self-consciousness bordering on self-indulgence, the author's voice tends to intrude upon and dominate the stories, whether narrated in the third person or in the no less omniscient first person. The characters tell neither their own nor other people's tales; with few exceptions, they are objects viewed through authorial eyes instead of filters through whom the action unfolds. The egotistical foregrounding of the author as entertainer/pundit causes Fitzgerald to avoid his two most successful perspectives, first-person observer and central intelligence, and minimizes the mental reactions of individuals. Consequently, the implicit psychologist of the late college fiction becomes the explicit performer-preacher of the first two Scribner collections. This emphasis on telling over showing, on asserting over dramatizing, mars not only Fitzgerald's later mediocre fiction, but even an otherwise superior achievement like "Winter Dreams."

Fitzgerald's intrusiveness occasionally resembles the postmodern antirealism practiced by Gilbert Sorrentino. Few metafictions—that is, imaginative prose pieces that convey "the story of writing" as much as they do "the writing of story"[22]—are more absurdly self-reflexive than "Jemina," which begins, "This don't pretend to be 'Literature.' This is just a tale for red-blooded folks who want a *story* and not just a lot of 'psychological' stuff or 'analysis.' Boy, you'll love it! Read it here, see it in the movies, play it on the phonograph, run it through the sewing machine." Composed at Princeton during October 1916, "Jemina," like the equally ridiculous short play *Mr. Icky,* is trivial when compared to the dreamlike surrealism of "The Diamond as Big as the Ritz," one

27

Ritz," one of the four "Fantasies" in *Tales of the Jazz Age*. These "Fantasies," said Fitzgerald, were "written in what . . . I should call my 'second manner.'"

The structure of the early Scribner selections, if not their narrative foci, follows the school model. We encounter here the same voluble writer, only now his bi- and tripartite pieces have grown to stories of four to eleven sections, with an average of six. Sometimes a section is irrelevant, contributing little or nothing to plot development. For instance, the reception-room (3) and grass (5) scenes in "Benediction" represent mere interludes, while three of the eight scenes in "Dalyrimple Goes Wrong" (4, 6, and 7) are extraneous. Fitzgerald's omnipresent chronological organization affords a structure as predictable (and monotonous) as it is arbitrary. Hours, days, weeks, months, even years march forward, punctuated by considerable exposition but few flashbacks. This tendency to narrate rather than dramatize past events seems contradictory in view of Fitzgerald's theatrical background.

More than ever, recurrent images ("The Ice Palace"), symbols ("The Cut-Glass Bowl"), and actions ("The Four Fists") reinforce the coherence achieved by means of linear time. In "The Cut-Glass Bowl," an angry jilted suitor buys Evylyn the title object, a gift "as hard as you are and as beautiful and as empty and as easy to see through." It causes four accidents, one in each of the four sections, which treat Evylyn at different ages. Finally, the cut-glass bowl crushes its owner after "telling" the unfortunate woman, "You see, I am fate . . . and stronger than your puny plans; and I am how-things-turn-out and I am different from your little dreams, and I am the flight of time and the end of beauty and unfulfilled desire."

Similarly, repetition again fortifies temporal progression in "The Four Fists," this time with a recurrent action instead of a recurrent symbol. Samuel Meredith absorbs four punches that, like the accidents in "The Cut-Glass Bowl," occur successively, as roommate, workman, husband, and rancher chastise him from age fourteen to thirty-five.

Obviously, chronological sequence serves as more in these fictions than a mere device to get the protagonists from one age to the next. Symbolized by the title object, it becomes "fate" in "The Cut-Glass Bowl," and in "The Four Fists," a painful educational vehicle. Other chronological stories treat temporal phenomena thematically. "'O Russet Witch!'", where Fitzgerald records a male-female relationship over many decades, contains this assertion: "The years between thirty-five and sixty-five revolve before the passive mind as one unexplained, confusing merry-go-round. . . . For most men and women these thirty years are taken up with a gradual withdrawal . . . as, by turns frightened and tired, we sit waiting for death." A more memorable, albeit similar, pseudo-philosophical pronouncement appears in "Bernice Bobs Her Hair": "At eighteen our convictions are hills from which we look; at forty-five they are caves in which we hide."

His obsession with time and its disastrous effects inspired Fitzgerald to write "The Curious Case of Benjamin Button," which, the *Jazz Age* table of contents informs us, was based on "a remark of Mark Twain's to the effect that it was a pity that the best part of life came at the beginning and the worst part at the end." This assumption is tested throughout an "astonishing history" composed of eleven divisions carrying the protagonist from seventy back to babyhood. If the chronological inversion of Benjamin's life is ignored, the pattern of events seems normal, for he attends college, finds work, gets married, becomes brigadier general. However, these events are made grotesque, particularly by the fact that his wife Hildegarde grows older while he grows younger: "She went out socially with him, but without enthusiasm, *devoured already by that eternal inertia which comes to live with each of us one day and stays with us to the end.*" Ironically, then, Benjamin Button cannot escape the ravages of time despite his progressive juvenescence, since deterioration and death are impressed upon him by the experience of others.

The school fiction had also used such plot reversals, the most vivid example occurring in "Pain and the Scientist," where the protagonist, who was victimized by Christian Science in the first section, turns the antagonist's religion against him in the second. But they become more commonplace later. Though not as elaborately as "The Curious Case of Benjamin Button," "Head and Shoulders"—a *Flappers and Philosophers* story—employs this technique. It prefigures *The Beautiful and Damned* and *Tender Is the Night* by reversing conjugal roles. When Horace Tarbox meets Marcia Meadow, he is a seventeen-year-old prodigy studying philosophy at Yale and she is a nineteen-year-old stage performer. They marry, have children, and encounter money problems. So Marcia bargains with Horace: "You join a gym and I'll read one of those books." He soon becomes a successful trapeze artist and she a successful writer; prodigy and performer are now switched. An anonymous magazine clipping caps Fitzgerald's irony: "It is said that the young couple have dubbed themselves Head and Shoulders, referring doubtless to the fact that Mrs. Tarbox supplies the literary and mental qualities, while the supple and agile shoulders of her husband contribute their share to the family fortunes."

The related strategy of the O. Henry surprise ending had permeated the school fiction: the title figure in "The Trail of the Duke" turned out to be a dog, and the rapist in "Tarquin of Cheepside," Shakespeare. It permeates the early Scribner pieces too. In "The Offshore Pirate" Carlyle is actually Toby; Evylyn dies in "The Cut-Glass Bowl"; Bernice gets even in "Bernice Bobs Her Hair"; Dalyrimple joins the state senate in "Dalyrimple Goes Wrong." Surprise endings may accompany reversals, as "The Camel's Back," which Fitzgerald liked least among the *Jazz Age* selections, shows. This tale begins when Perry Parkhurst and Betty Medill quarrel after he has offered her "his heart, his license, and his ultimatum." When Perry has won Betty back, she exclaims, "I love you and if you can wake up a minister at this hour and have it done over again I'll go West with you."

Not only Perry Parkhurst but also Toby Moreland of "The Offshore Pirate" are amorously triumphant through schemes that impress their girls, schemes related to the reversal, the surprise ending, or both. These entail disguise, Perry becoming a camel, and Toby a thief. Kenneth Eble, who cites further instances of the clever stratagem, argues, "The device obviously appealed to Fitzgerald's theatrical nature: in an otherwise realistic story, the hero stages an elaborate fantasy complete in all its details and convincing to both the reader and the heroine of the story."[23]

Thanks to their imaginations, Perry and Toby avoid the inadequacy usually associated with the *homme manqué;* indeed, they more or less trick Betty and Ardita into marriage. All four are upper-class characters, yet Toby/Carlyle seduces Ardita by impersonating "a poor kid in a Tennessee town," who "wants to be a rajah, then an aristocrat." His courage, which has included "stealing nearly one million dollars," impresses her, for she also defies Victorian conventions, scorning family and smoking cigarettes.

Though the indolent rich continue to dominate stories like "The Camel's Back" and "The Offshore Pirate," Toby Moreland's "elaborate fantasy" of metamorphosing from rich to poor boy (Carlyle), to rich boy again, indicates that Fitzgerald is now interested in more than inherited wealth. Now earned money (obtained by working in wholesale hardware or dry goods, for instance) runs his world, where, along with the privileged few, we find businessmen, writers, performers, priests, and white collar workers. There upward mobility is becoming prevalent, as lower middle-class Marcia Meadow marries Ivy Leaguer Horace Tarbox; as indigent war hero Bryan Dalyrimple successively occupies the roles of stock clerk, criminal, and state senator; as small-town John T. Unger attends an Eastern prep school and visits wealthy Percy Washington's fabulous Western home; and as bookstore employee Merlin Grainger acquires the business. This "democratic" focus reaches its apotheosis in "May Day," where various socioeconomic classes meet.

Settings like Princeton, New York, London, and the South reappear in *Flappers and Philosophers* and *Tales of the Jazz Age*, but now we are also transported to Florida and Maryland. The pretentious Midwestern city emerges here: in "The Ice Palace," St. Paul, Minnesota, "is a three-generation town," and in "The Camel's Back," Toledo, Ohio, is the home of Mrs. Howard Tate, who "was a Chicago Todd before she became a Toledo Tate, and the family generally affect that conscious simplicity which has begun to be the earmark of American aristocracy." As before, Fitzgerald's locations are essentially urban, though he introduces his most interesting small town, Tarleton, Georgia ("The Jelly-Bean"), and the equally fictitious Marlowe, Illinois ("The Lees of Happiness"), "a comparatively old settlement" that "had only recently acquired a 'society.'"

Tarleton, Georgia, is the home of three very different femmes fatales, one of whom we encounter in "The Ice Palace" (discussed in the next section) and another in "The Jelly-Bean." Later, Ailie Calhoun of "The Last of the Belles" will join Sally Carrol Happer and Nancy Lamar as the most destructive among them. Sally Carrol is more victim than victimizer, but Nancy, the boyish, crap-shooting, liquor-drinking Southern belle notorious for "crazy stunts," hurts a failed aristocrat, the "weak and wobbly" Jim Powell. He gets sick when she suddenly weds another man after leaving "a trail of broken hearts from Atlanta to New Orleans." Jim represents the typical *homme manqué* of the early fiction, where except for ingenious fellows like Perry Parkhurst and Toby Moreland, the male is usually far less assertive than the female. The relationships between Marcia and Horace ("Head and Shoulders"), Edith/Jewell and Gordon/Peter ("May Day"), Caroline and Merlin ("'O Russet Witch!'"), and Roxanne and Jeffrey ("The Lees of Happiness") illustrate this.

Toward the end of "The Pierian Springs and the Last Straw," George Rombert and Myra Fulham elope, anticipating the focus on marriage in the first two Scribner collections. Some characters are married (for example, Marcia and Horace, Evylyn and Harold, Benjamin and Hildegarde, and Roxanne and Jeffrey) and others (Ardita and Toby, Perry and Betty) will marry. Similar to the situation of George Rombert, who stopped writing after his elopement, matrimony affects most of these individuals adversely because of economic, psychological, or other problems. Nor do its victims number only the very young, such as those populating the school canon. In "The Lees of Happiness," writer Jeffrey Curtain and actress Roxanne Milbank wed, yet soon a blood clot destroys his brain and he dies paralyzed. Meanwhile, Harry Cromwell, their best friend, suffers a hopeless marriage, too, since his wife Kitty divorces him and takes an older man. The story concludes, "To these two life had come quickly and gone, leaving not bitterness, but pity; not disillusion, but only pain." The tragic marriage motif that will dominate Fitzgerald's fiction in the 1930s and that will culminate with *Tender Is the Night* has already surfaced, as has so much else, in these apprentice stories.

By the time Scott Fitzgerald published *Flappers and Philosophers* and *Tales of the Jazz Age*, he had gained considerable writing experience with plays, poems, and songs as well as imaginative prose. In the school works (1909–17), which took the author from thirteen to twenty-one, he created his typical short story, with traits the initial Scribner collections developed, collections that borrowed four college pieces. Those stories are almost always long, each containing several sometimes arbitrary divisions. Interrelated reversals, surprise endings, and clever stratagems often characterize the plots, which depend on a linear organization in which sequential time figures not only as a structural device but also as a thematic concern. The various points of view include the successful observer-narrator and the unsuccessful self-conscious author. Diverse characters and classes manifest themselves, yet Fitzgerald's fundamentally bourgeois world features the ubiquitous *homme manqué* and femme fatale, for courtship and marriage comprise the all-important sexual element. "The Pierian Springs and the Last Straw," where these figures and the observer-narrator attain early sophistication, prefigures *The Great Gatsby*, a 1925 masterwork whose stature several antecedent major stories, if not two mediocre novels, help to explain.

Early Triumphs

Fitzgerald was not merely being flippant when he expressed his preference for "The Offshore Pirate" over "The Diamond as Big as the Ritz." There were other times when he betrayed bad taste about his own work: for instance, he overrated "Tarquin of Cheapside" and "Benediction," while underrating "The Jelly-Bean" and "Bernice Bobs Her Hair." Most often, though, Fitzgerald estimated his work accurately. For example, he told Maxwell Perkins, "I've always hated & been ashamed of that damn story *The Four Fists*. Not that it is any cheaper than *The Off Shore Pirate* because it isn't but simply because its a mere plant, a moral tale & utterly lacks vitality" (*Dear Scott*, 44).

Only "The Diamond as Big as the Ritz," "The Rich Boy," "The Curious Case of Benjamin Button," and "May Day" ranked with the best modern short stories, averred Fitzgerald in 1929, an assessment most critics would partially endorse. Except for "Benjamin Button," which he should have excluded, and "The Ice Palace," "Absolution," and "Winter Dreams," which he should have included, these do indeed represent his major stories before 1930; later, "Babylon Revisited" and "Crazy Sunday" would join them.[24]

Among the eight stories in *Flappers and Philosophers*, only "The Ice Palace" transcends entertainment, and among the ten stories constituting *Tales of the Jazz Age*, only "May Day" and "The Diamond as Big as the Ritz" are exceptional, while "The Jelly-Bean" is good. The discrepancy between those artworks and their companion pieces, whose quality varies, would be incomprehensible if Fitzgerald had not been similarly erratic throughout his entire literary career, notably when *The Great Gatsby* succeeded *This Side of Paradise* and *The Beautiful and Damned*. Rarely regarded as innovative in imaginative prose— whether story or novel—the author was, nonetheless, an occasional master. This should be evident from the ensuing examination of three early triumphs: "The Ice Palace," "May Day," and "The Diamond as Big as the Ritz." They, along with "Winter Dreams" and "Absolution" (discussed in the next section), demonstrate Fitzgerald's thematic seriousness and technical range before he created his greatest novel.

"The Ice Palace"

Like Ernest Hemingway, Scott Fitzgerald experienced landscape as a psychic phenomenon. He had emotional ties in six geographical areas that formed three sometimes interrelated dichotomies: North vs. South, East vs. West, America vs. Europe. *The Great Gatsby* and *Tender Is the Night* most eloquently dramatize the second and third, but the first remarkable story written by the author best renders the North-South conflict. "The Ice Palace" (1920) launches the so-called Tarleton trilogy, whose other members are "The Jelly-Bean" (1920) and "The Last of the Belles" (1929). All three superior tales treat the South (Georgia) and Southern women, though neither "The Jelly-Bean" nor "The Last of the Belles" matches "The Ice Palace" for complexity: in that story, South and North become symbolic settings, and protagonist Sally Carrol Happer reveals more ambivalence than her rather one-dimensional femme fatale successors Nancy Lamar and Ailie Calhoun. "The girls come from the same town, they shop at the same drug store together, but there is a world of difference between them,"[25] comments one critic. Linguistically, too, "The Ice Palace," which employs considerable iterative imagery, surpasses the sequel pieces.

That Sally Carrol was based on Zelda Sayre is clear from the genesis of Fitzgerald's story, since twin episodes, one involving a Northern girl and one a Southern girl, figured in its composition.[26] The Southern girl, Montgomery-born Zelda, represented only the most important autobiographical element in his first trenchant exploration of the North-South antithesis.

Having explained, "I want to live where things happen," and having rejected Southern men as "ineffectual," Sally Carrol defends her divided personality: "There's two sides to me. . . . There's the sleepy old side . . . an' there's a sort of energy" (*BR*, 4). Unfortunately, the story, which begins and ends with images of inertia connecting heroine and landscape, lacks a really credible psychological conflict; although "she like[s] all the winter sports," her "sleepy old side" completely dominates. (The recurrent allusion to "home" is a rationalization when applied to the North by Sally Carrol—whose previous excursions terminated in Asheville, North Carolina—but a certitude when applied to the South.)

A six-part narrative, "The Ice Palace" is structured around a quest for identity. Since Sally Carrol's journey produces confirmation of her identity rather than transformation of it, however, the journey is circular, starting and stopping at Tarleton, "in southernmost Georgia" (that is, Montgomery, Alabama). Section 3, after fiancé Harry Bellamy's visit (in section 2) to establish a March wedding date, occurs on the transitional Pullman train, and sections 4 and 5 in the nameless Northern city that stands for St. Paul, Minnesota. The first and sixth sections transpire during the summer and spring respectively, while the framed sections transpire during the fall and winter. Section 6 repeats, sometimes verbatim, the introductory paragraphs of section 1.

If the South and its embodiment, Sally Carrol, are associated with inertia, the North and its embodiment, Harry Bellamy, are associated with energy. Therefore, enthusiastic Harry, who mentions "pep in the air" and claims "Everybody's healthy here," ridicules small-town Southerners. Conversely, he praises the North as "a man's country," which has not only produced "the best athletes in the world" but also John J. Fishburn, the "greatest wheat man in the Northwest, and one of the greatest financiers in the country" (*BR*, 12). The story's real conflict is cultural, then, for the antagonism between Sally Carrol and Harry Bellamy symbolizes a conflict between temperaments geographically determined. She makes this apparent to Roger Patton when she tells him that Southerners are feline and Northerners canine.

Sally Carrol's hostility toward Northern women or "glorified domestics" like her future sister-in-law ("spiritless conventionality") and her future mother-in-law ("ungracious dumpiness of carriage") is unrelieved, whereas there are at least two exceptions among the men—Mr. Bellamy, because "he was born in Kentucky" and forms "a link between the old life and the new" (*BR*, 15) and Professor Patton, an Easterner with "blue eyes that had . . . some quality of appreciation" (*BR*, 12). Perhaps this Dangerous Dan McGrew, "the man she preferred," shares an attribute discussed by Edwin Moses: "In a death-oriented society, the child-like has no place; thus, for instance, Harry's angry tirade on the subject of Southerners, who, according to him, have become lazy and shiftless like the colored people (those archetypes of the child-like nature) whom they live with. The attack on the child-like in Sally Carrol—that is, essentially, on her Southernness—extends even to her typically Southern double name: Harry's mother insists on calling her 'Sally.'"[27]

Geographical antithesis, which poses masculine against feminine and grown-up against childlike, transcends national boundaries. When Patton asks Sally Carrol, "How's Carmen from the South?" he anticipates other allusions involving Latin races. They are supposed to be "tragic," but actually it is the "Ibsenesque" Scandinavians, maintaining "the largest suicide rate in the world," that appear "gloomy," "melancholy," "righteous," "narrow," and "cheerless" (*BR*, 14).[28] Drawn toward a similar fatal climate, "thousands of Swedes" have migrated there, where Patton has taught French for ten years. These contemporary locals exhibit atavism in section 5: "the full-throated resonant chant of the marching clubs . . . grew louder like some paen of a viking tribe traversing an ancient wild." Moments after, Sally Carrol interprets their shout as "the North offering sacrifice on some mighty altar to the gray pagan God of Snow" (*BR*, 21).

The snow god is opposed by the sun god in "The Ice Palace," whose images of heat and cold are even more pervasive than its related images of inertia and energy. Section 1 commences, "The sunlight dripped over the house like golden paint" (*BR*, 1), and section 6, "The wealth of golden sunlight poured . . . heat over the house" (*BR*, 24), while section 2—outside the frame yet still inside Georgia—evinces a "cheerful late sun." An emblem of life, this god has created "tangled growths of bright-green coppice and grass and tall trees" (*BR*, 5).

Up North, however, the "summer child" will walk beneath a sun she will barely recognize, but first she must ride through "white hills and valleys and scattered pines" revealing occasional farmhouses, "ugly and bleak and lone." Each causes Sally Carrol "an instant of chill compassion for the souls shut in there waiting for the spring" (*BR*, 9). The city—winter carnival notwithstanding—proves to be equally "dismal," "as though no one lived here" (*BR*, 19). It seems loveless as well as lifeless, a condition Sally Carrol intuits when she asks Harry Bellamy, "I don't guess this is a very kissable climate, is it?" (*BR*, 11). Their ecstatic kiss of section 2 in the South becomes the dispassionate kisses of section 3 in the North, where "his cold lips kissed the tip of her ear." Thus we are prepared for Harry's symbolic desertion later.

Comments like "sometimes I look out an' see a flurry of snow, an' it's just as if somethin' dead was movin'" (*BR*, 13) and phrases like "tombing heaps of sleet" echo James Joyce's most celebrated story. Though Fitzgerald possessed the 1922 Egoist Press edition of *Dubliners* (originally published in 1914), he may have read "The Dead" before he composed "The Ice Palace," since other early works were influenced by Joyce—*This Side of Paradise* by *A Portrait of the Artist as a Young Man*, "Absolution" by "The Sisters." Besides, Fitzgerald ranked *Dubliners* among the "great English classics" and in his copy he checked three titles, including "The Dead," in the table of contents. There also, snow is associated with extinction.

A real edifice supplied Fitzgerald with the physical model for the ice palace, his ultimate expression of death and frozen water: "When I reached St. Paul I intrigued my family into telling me all they remembered about the ice palace. At the public library I found a rough sketch of it that had appeared in a newspaper of the period" (*Correspondence,* 62).

Hans Christian Andersen's "The Ice Maiden," containing Swedes, a journey, a new home, and a broken engagement, may also have influenced him. The "wondrous palace of crystal" in Switzerland resembles the "hard, glittering crystalline object" John A. Higgins designates "a central symbol" of "The Cut-Glass Bowl" and "The Diamond as Big as the Ritz" as well as "The Ice Palace,"[29] which, incidentally, bears these two lines from "Kubla Khan": "It was a miracle of rare device, / A sunny pleasure-dome with caves of ice!" Being lost and entombed in such a place is prefigured by Andersen, too, for his "young hunters and young girls, men and women who had been lost in the crevasses of the glacier, stood there, lifelike, with open eyes and smiling lips; and far beneath them arose from buried villages the church bells' chimes."[30]

Concerned about character and plot, Fitzgerald emphasized "lost" over "entombed." His palace, Canuck-built and fortresslike in aspect as the Viking invaders are hostlike, harbors many "labyrinths downstairs." After Harry vanishes, Sally Carrol experiences typical confusion: "She reached a turn—was it here?—took the left and came to what should have been the outlet into the long, low room, but it was only another glittering passage with darkness at the end" (*BR*, 22). Her symbolic crisis terminates finally when Roger Patton, heralded by "a pale-yellow sun," arrives. Both psychological and cultural dilemmas resolved, Sally Carrol screams, "Take me home . . . tomorrow."

Still, the concept of entombment is thematically more important than that of bewildered estrangement. One "wide passage" was "like a damp vault connecting empty tombs." Then the protagonist "was alone with this presence that came out of the North. . . . It was an icy breath of death . . . rolling down . . . to clutch at her." She feels "damp souls . . . haunted this place," and reminiscent of "The Ice Maiden," fears "she might . . . freeze to death and lie embedded in the ice like corpses she had read of, kept perfectly preserved until the melting of a glacier" (*BR*, 22–23).

Part 1

These ominous allusions are countered by a vision of dead Margery Lee, "with a young, white brow, and wide, welcoming eyes," and faded Tarleton "tombstones," which precede Sally Carrol's deliverance in section 5 but which derive from "one of her favorite haunts," the cemetery of section 2. This vision comforts partly because of climatic considerations: "Oh, if there should be snow on her grave! . . . Her grave—a grave that should be flower-strewn and washed with sun and rain" (*BR*, 19).

However, it is the tie between the past and the Southern cemetery— a tie Fitzgerald would reforge personally and fictionally—that makes Sally Carrol happy and strong there. Margery Lee died young (1844– 73), yet continues to inspire romantic speculation: "And she was the sort of girl born to stand on a wide, pillared porch and welcome folks in. I think perhaps a lot of men went away to war meanin' to come back to her; but maybe none of 'em ever did." Those men might rest over the hill among the Confederate dead, whose inscriptions show "only a name and a date, sometimes quite indecipherable." Though obscure, they "died for the most beautiful thing in the world—the dead South" (*BR*, 6–7).

The alive North, on the other hand, lacks tradition—a fact Sally Carrol notes when she compares "the battered old library at home, with her father's huge medical books, and the oil-paintings of her three great uncles, and the old couch that had been mended up for forty-five years and was still luxurious to dream in" to the Bellamy library, "neither attractive nor particularly otherwise . . . a room with a lot of fairly expensive things in it that all looked about fifteen years old" (*BR*, 10). Harry claims he inhabits "a three-generation town," where "everybody has a father, and about half . . . grandfathers," but he must admit, "back of that we don't go." Their "social model" is, consequently, the daughter of "the first public ash man" (*BR*, 10–11). And their current ice palace, while impressive—"a hundred and seventy feet tall," "six thousand square yards," "walls twenty to forty inches thick" (*BR*, 20)—will be as temporary as the last one of 1885. Whatever history it connotes seems barbaric, foreign, vague.

According to Sally Carrol, there are people even now who embody the Southern past. That Fitzgerald intended his heroine to be the reincarnation of an archetypal predecessor becomes clear during two separate incidents when Sally Carrol invokes the archetype's ghost. At the cemetery, she says, "Dear Margery Lee. . . . Can't you see her?" and, again, at the ice palace, "Why, it's Margery Lee. . . . I knew you'd come." Reincarnation means the South achieves perpetuity through the empathy between Sally Carrol and her forebears, a sharp contrast to the North's preservation through refrigeration. As concomitant, Southern-life-in-death represented by Sally Carrol, the resurrected antebellum woman, opposes Northern death-in-life represented by Harry Bellamy, the kiss of death. "Energy," which he relates to health, and "inertia," which he relates to degeneracy, are equally ironic states.

The conflict between North and South is not, per se, the most impressive thing about "The Ice Palace," since, after all, Fitzgerald had treated that dichotomy elsewhere, notably in "The Jelly-Bean," a story critical of the Southern style. But neither "The Jelly-Bean" nor "The Last of the Belles" equals "The Ice Palace," his first Tarleton piece and most brilliant formal achievement to date. Here, several interrelated antitheses project the North-South tension—canine vs. feline, masculine vs. feminine, Scandinavian vs. Latin, snow god vs. sun god, energy vs. inertia—through rich recurrent imagery. Fitzgerald fortifies this linguistic coherence by making the realistic/fantastic title symbol more convincingly dominant than its crystalline forerunner, the cut-glass bowl. Other types of coherence appear too: for example, tonal unity arises from Sally Carrol as the central intelligence experiencing, if not reporting, the action; and structural unity from the quest or journey motif, which, thanks to its framework, brings the adventure full circle. These techniques seem perfectly suited to "The Ice Palace," whose heroine confirms her identity in an orderly world.

"May Day"

Probably a discarded prologue to *The Beautiful and Damned*, as "Absolution" would be to *The Great Gatsby*, "May Day" (1920) is Fitzgerald's only major "occasional" story, the occasion being the first of May, when, annually, labor parades and political demonstrations occur. Moreover, for him 1 May 1919 initiated his self-proclaimed "Jazz Age," which "extended from the suppression of the riots on May Day 1919 to the crash of the Stock Market in 1929" (*Dear Scott*, 171).[31] Some critics believe that the title also ironically refers to the spring festival of crowning the May Queen and dancing around the Maypole, or even to the French expression, *m'aidez* ("help me"), yet such ambiguities seem unlikely. Other critics detect the influence Frank Norris and H. L. Mencken exerted on the story, an influence Fitzgerald cited at the time. Indeed, he published "May Day" in Mencken's *The Smart*

Set, receiving two hundred dollars, five times as much as the magazine usually paid, but, then, like "The Diamond as Big as the Ritz" and "The Rich Boy," it could be considered a novella. According to James W. Tuttleton, Mencken provided "the theme of character in decay, and . . . the satiric treatment of socialism as a political ideology" (Bryer, 186). Typically, however, "May Day" reflects the author's life, with the Delmonico material drawn from an actual dance, at which Fitzgerald and Porter Gillespie played Mr. In and Mr. Out.

Between *The Smart Set* publication of "May Day" (1920) and the *Tales of the Jazz Age* version, the work underwent "thorough polishing and refinement," involving hundreds of variants. The most pronounced single change affects the end, where Fitzgerald replaced four paragraphs that treat Gordon Sterrett's death with a single explicit one. He improved the "tone" to eliminate sentimentality, particularly as regards Sterrett, who is now less victimized by liquor than by sex. Much triteness, wordiness, vagueness, abstraction, and implausibility also disappeared. Dialogue became less sloppy, less stiff, while old section 6 became new sections 6 and 7. The characters, bearing new names, are "more mature and imposing" than before.[32] Thus, "May Day," like Fitzgerald's fiction in general, was painstakingly revised. The revisions, often based on sound and mood, attest to his artistic control.

Some critics believe "May Day" was "poorly plotted." Among them, only Henry Dan Piper, who nevertheless regards the piece as the "finest work until *The Great Gatsby*," offers a practical explanation: Fitzgerald "told Max Perkins that he had decided 'to break up the start of my novel and sell it as three little character stories to *Smart Set*.' Nothing else he wrote that spring, or that *Smart Set* published, seems to fit this description except 'May Day,' which is really three independent episodes tied together by an unconvincing plot—probably imposed at the last minute" (Piper, 70). In *Tales of the Jazz Age*, Fitzgerald more or less affirmed Piper's explanation, for in his annotated table of contents he mentions three memorable events from the previous spring. They "were unrelated except by general hysteria," yet he "tried, unsuccessfully I fear, to weave them into a pattern." His uncertainty about the story's action surfaces again at the end of the prologue, where we learn, "so during all this time there were many adventures that happened in the great city, and, of these, several—or perhaps one—are here set down" (*BR*, 26).

Both "one" and "several" adventures, the story is structurally the most innovative fiction Fitzgerald ever wrote, prefiguring books like *Manhattan Transfer* (1925) by John Dos Passos. It eliminates the old dramatic concept of a chief character and distributes the protagonal energy among many characters. This affected the form of the story, since a controlling plot could not be sustained without an individual hero or heroine. Thus "May Day" became "decentralized," and decentralization, which adumbrates fragmentation, became an effective way to render disjointed modern life.

Though decentralized works lack conventional main characters, they usually treat one character as slightly more important than the others: for example, Jimmy Herf in *Manhattan Transfer*, Darl Bundren in Faulkner's *As I Lay Dying*, Lieutenant Hearn in Mailer's *The Naked and the Dead*, Tyrone Slothrop in Pynchon's *Gravity's Rainbow*. Technically, such characters are descendants of Gordon Sterrett, whose circular journey frames "May Day," carrying him from the Biltmore, where he begs Philip Dean for money (section 1), to the "small hotel just off Sixth Avenue" (*BR*, 74), where he commits suicide (11). However, his deterioration as *homme manqué* / failed artist, caused by Jewel Hudson as femme fatale / blackmailer, is intermittent, since he appears during only about half of the remaining sections.

Weaving through the Sterrett plot are plots involving lower-class Carrol Key and Gus Rose and upper-class Peter Himmel and Philip Dean, alias Mr. In and Mr. Out. All three plots contain peripatetic movement, yet another feature of decentralized fiction. In section 3 we follow Carrol and Gus on Sixth Avenue, soon headed toward Fifth, then down to Tenth and up to Forty-fourth; in section 10 Peter and Philip, after abandoning Childs', stop at Delmonico's, the Commodore, and the Biltmore. These perambulations anticipate the lonely meanderings Herf will make around labyrinthine New York City.

If he, the slightly more important character of *Manhattan Transfer*, evolved from Gordon Sterrett, his wife, Ellen Thatcher, evolved from Edith Bradin, for both function as linking characters or those who encounter everybody and so unite their tales. Edith, having dated Gordon at Yale before he went overseas, still loves him, but rejects Peter, her present escort to the Gamma Psi dance. The girl is identified with Delmonico's, which she leaves to visit her radical brother "Henry's office . . . across the street and just around the corner" (*BR*, 54). There "two very drunken soldiers" (*BR*, 61) are among the anticommunist mob; there she watches one, Carrol Key, disappear "helplessly out through the open window" (*BR*, 62). Clearly, then, Edith Bradin (as well as Delmonico's) bridges the three plots of "May Day."

The upper-class party and the lower-class riot embody aimless motion, dramatized by frequently changing partners during the dance, and by the ebb and flow of the clamorous crowd during the riot. About this "shifting world," Colin S. Cass writes, "Fitzgerald was working to *emphasize* the sense of hectic coming and going that at first inspection would seem to be a defect of the novelette. The restlessness and instability of the new-born Jazz Age is a major theme in 'May Day,' one which is epitomized in the next to the last chapter, in the much reiterated symbol of Mr. In and Mr. Out" (Cass, 77).

For Anthony J. Mazzella, Fitzgerald's story, "structured on the careful modulation of opposites, of integration and disintegration," has chaotic content but orderly form.[33] The latter depends partly on his commitment to the unities: incoherent action transpires amid a circular journey; several locations materialize amid a single city. Most detailed, time begins at 9:00 A.M. on 19 May and moves to 4:00 P.M., 5:30 P.M., 9:00 P.M., after 10:00 P.M., 12:00 A.M. on 20 May, 1:00 A.M., 4:00 A.M., and ends at 9:00 A.M., exactly twenty-four hours later. Unity of time (one day) and of place (Manhattan) are fortified by the opening (Biltmore Hotel; "sunshine") and closing (Sixth Avenue hotel; "sunlight") of "May Day." Therefore, Gordon Sterrett's dissolution—a synecdoche for the story's total experience—is, ironically, circumscribed as well as circular.

Additional unity is revealed during section 9, "Childs', Fifty-ninth Street," through what James Joyce termed an "epiphany": "Dawn had come up in Columbus Circle, magical, breathless dawn, silhouetting the great statue of the immortal Christopher, and mingling in a curious and uncanny manner with the fading yellow electric light inside" (*BR*, 67). This historical revelation tacitly extols the American past and condemns the American present. It foreshadows other similar moments: for instance, the one evoking the Dutch sailors' eyes in *The Great Gatsby* and the one evoking Andrew Jackson's shrine in *The Last Tycoon*. If Sterrett's odyssey is symbolic of what is, Columbus's statue is symbolic of what was.

Separated from section 1 by spaces and from the entire text by its Biblical/epical style, the prologue to "May Day" projects the timeless and the universal such moments imply. Here, abstractions dominate; we read about "a war" instead of World War I, a "great city" instead of New York. Prologue and story both treat postwar periods when soldiers were returning (spring); however, the prologue focuses on "peace and prosperity," with the young men "pure and brave," while the text focuses on pandemonium and poverty, whose soldier victims form an angry mob. The doom that lurks just beneath the hedonistic surface of the prologue is actualized by the text, where Manhattan becomes the Nineveh and Babylon later depicted by Dos Passos.

Though Fitzgerald provides fewer typical characters and groups and no interpolated material, "May Day" was probably *Manhattan Transfer*'s model. Its prologue imagery, which "The Diamond as Big as the Ritz" echoes, suggests wealth: "merchants," "splendor," "luscious feasts," "lavish entertainments," "furs," "bags of golden mesh," "varicolored slippers of silk and silver," "rose satin," "cloth of gold." This imagery recurs in section 1, where Philip Dean's "silk pajamas," "silk shirts," "impressive neckties," and "soft woollen socks" are contrasted to Gordon Sterrett's soiled, frayed, and faded garments. These two occupied the same privileged class until Gordon became the lover of lower-class Jewel. Once well-off, though poor now, his confrontations with them are hardly Marxian, no more than are the confrontations between the benighted mob and leftists like the little Jewish orator ("What have you got outa the war? . . . Who got anything out of it except J. P. Morgan an' John D. Rockefeller?" [*BR*, 37]) and idealistic Henry Bradin at the *New York Trumpet*. The first receives a pummeling and the second a broken leg, tokens of the violence epitomized by the parallel deaths of Carrol Key and Gordon Sterrett. As fallen "aristocrat," the latter is merely weak, but as representative proletarians, the former and buddy Gus Rose look "ugly, ill-nourished, devoid of all except the lowest form of intelligence." An unconscious bias for the elite and against the alien manifests itself when Fitzgerald says the name *Key* (compare Francis Scott Key) indicated "blood of some potentiality," "however thinly diluted," while semitic Rose "was swart and bandy-legged, with rat-eyes and a much-broken hooked nose" (*BR*, 35).

James W. Tuttleton, after tracing the author's political affinities from *This Side of Paradise* through *Tender Is the Night*, concludes "that Fitzgerald was an individualist, hustling with the best of the entrepreneurs to make a dollar. . . . And it is unarguable that his views were sketchy and based more on feeling than on dialectical materialism. But his socialist sympathies color his fiction and should not be lightly regarded. . . . In "May Day," however, the treatment of socialism is a rather confused and ambivalent affair" (Bryer, 189–90). Tuttleton attributes the confusion and ambivalence to Mencken's influence, yet he quotes Fitzgerald's self-confessed inability "to reconcile my double allegiance to the class I am part of, and the Great Change I believe in" (Bryer, 189).

Consequently, private (that is, "individualist") and public (that is, "socialist") spheres tend to alternate, with pairs such as Sterrett and Dean, Key and Rose, Sterrett and Edith, Edith and Henry, and Himmel and Dean moving in and out of group scenes focused on the juxtaposition of dance and riot. Endless variety amid terrible sameness is the impression communicated by the eleven-part story, whose decentralized form resembles a montage by D. W. Griffith or Sergei Eisenstein, a "series of brief pictures following one another quickly without apparent logical order."[34] Although chronological order ultimately prevails, simultaneity seems to define the episodic action of the story.

Upper and lower classes sometimes merge, but nowhere more vividly than at Childs' during section 9. The 4:00 A.M. "crowd of poor people" gives way to the 8:00 A.M. "noisy medley of chorus girls, college boys, débutantes, rakes, *filles de joie*" (*BR*, 63). On 20 May 1919 the Gamma Psi bunch congregates there with an occasional "mouse-like figure, desperately out of place." Drab Gus Rose, embodying the latter, inconspicuously regards the scene as "a colorful circus" (*BR*, 64). He notices intoxicated Gordon Sterrett and Jewel Hudson, then Peter Himmel and Philip Dean, yet only the girl—his fellow pariah—acknowledges him. Dean scorns her, they argue, she and Sterrett flee, Himmel misbehaves. Soon "another phenomenon . . . drew admiring glances and a prolonged involuntary 'Oh-h-h!' from every person in the restaurant" (*BR*, 67). Uniting rich and poor momentarily, this is the statue of Columbus, which makes Childs' microcosmic of New York and America, where all share the same awesome legacy despite social differences.

Fitzgerald sympathized with the Left throughout his career, yet after he had introduced decentralized narration, distributing the action almost equally between upper- and lower-class figures, he abandoned that approach to return to the traditional dramatic scheme of the single protagonist and the single plot. More interested in character and individual experience than in action and public message, he would create mythical figures like Jay Gatsby and Monroe Stahr or psychological studies like Anson Hunter and Dick Diver. Twentieth-century fragmentation would become for him conceptual, not formal, and so his work would appear anachronistic beside *The Waste Land* and *The Sound and the Fury*. Nevertheless, Fitzgerald's vision of modern malaise, conveyed by what he termed "emotional bankruptcy," is equally trenchant. It begins with "May Day," when Philip Dean tells Gordon Sterrett, "You seem to be sort of bankrupt—morally as well as financially" (*BR*, 30), and it dominates the "Crack-up" articles, *Tender Is the Night*, and several stories. Given Fitzgerald's equation of the two, we should understand why, then, morally bankrupt Braddock Washington—"the richest man that ever lived" (*BR*, 87)—experiences a "financial" catastrophe in "The Diamond as Big as the Ritz."

"The Diamond as Big as the Ritz"

Fitzgerald's ambivalence toward the South in "The Ice Palace" and toward Marxism in "May Day" reflects his belief that "the test of a first-rate intelligence is the ability to hold two opposed ideas in the mind at the same time, and still retain the ability to function."[35] Several peers emphasized this dualism in his work after Fitzgerald died: for John Dos Passos, it was "a combination of intimacy and detachment"; for Malcolm Cowley, it was "double vision." They believed that Fitzgerald's simultaneous involvement in and observation of fictional situations, his playing both participating self and scribal self, helped to explain his most impressive work. Fitzgerald anticipated their "double vision" view in a 1938 letter to Frances Turnbull (see part 2, "Critical Opinions").

The observer-narrator employed in *The Great Gatsby*, which appeared intermittently from "The Pierian Springs and the Last Straw" to *The Last Tycoon*, became the author's chief means of maintaining both "intimacy and detachment." Even his felicitous third-person fiction, however, whether early or late, is also characterized by tonal distance. No less autobiographical than "The Ice Palace," whose inspiration "grew out of a conversation with a girl" (see part 2, "Critical Opinions"), and "May Day," whose Mr. In and Mr. Out were actually Scott Fitzgerald and Porter Gillespie, "The Diamond as Big as the Ritz" (1922) commences: "John T. Unger came from a family that had been well known in Hades—a small town on the Mississippi River—for several generations." Hades (that is, St. Paul, Minnesota) admired "a New England education," "the bane of all provincial places," so Unger's (that is, Fitzgerald's) "well-known" family (that is, the maternal McQuillans) sent their heir to St. Midas' School "near Boston" (that is, Newman

School near New York [*BR*, 75]), where he met Percy Washington (that is, "Sap" Donahoe). According to Arthur Mizener, Donahoe's ranch at White Sulphur Springs (the story's Fish), Montana, supplied the background for "Diamond."

Its eleven sections take the protagonist on another circular journey through alien territory, during which he becomes self-aware like Sally Carrol rather than self-destructive like Gordon Sterrett. Unger ("Hunger") begins this odyssey of enlightenment carrying "an asbestos pocket-book stuffed with money" (*BR*, 75) and is attracted to wealthy people such as the Schnitzler-Murphys; thus, we are prepared for the awe he registers over the Washingtons' fabulous chateau. That the environment victimizes such bourgeois boys the third-person narrator implies: "The simple piety prevalent in Hades has the earnest worship of the respect for riches as the first article of its creed—had John felt otherwise than radiantly humble before them, his parents would have turned away in horror at the blasphemy" (*BR*, 80). Nevertheless, the selfishness exhibited by the Washingtons, who murder their guests after enjoying them, alarms him so much he soon flees with Kismine and her sister. Then, as Marius Bewley argues in part 3, he awakens from the American dream, which, incidentally, reflects the sleep motif, possessing "the shabby gift of disillusion" (*BR*, 113).

Publishing "The Diamond as Big as the Ritz" helped disillusion Scott Fitzgerald. Consequently, his remark in *Tales of the Jazz Age*—"One . . . critic has been pleased to like this extravaganza better than anything I have written. Personally I prefer 'The Offshore Pirate' "—may be more cynical than flippant, for the "genuinely imaginative" "Diamond," which Fitzgerald really regarded as "remarkable," though requiring three weeks of effort, earned only $250 from *The Smart Set*, while the slight, if not trite, "Offshore Pirate" had appeared earlier in the lucrative *Saturday Evening Post*. Even so, his comment suggests the author shared the protagonist's obsession with opulence: "I was in that familiar mood characterized by a perfect craving for luxury, and the story began as an attempt to feed that craving on imaginary foods." This personal ambivalence or double-mindedness is kept under control by irony, Fitzgerald's means of achieving distance in third-person narratives. The result is observations like Kismine's "Think of the millions and millions of people in the world, laborers and all, who get along with only two maids" (*BR*, 99) and "There go fifty thousand dollars worth of slaves . . . at prewar prices. So few Americans have any respect for property" (*BR*, 105).

The Fitzgerald conflict between artist and hustler is reminiscent of the Twain conflict between prudence and creativity articulated in *The Ordeal of Mark Twain*, by Van Wyck Brooks, a presentation copy of which Fitzgerald underlined and annotated. The parallels between Brooks's study and Fitzgerald's story, discussed by Robert Sklar, are sometimes quite specific. For instance, referring to *The Gilded Age*, Sklar observes, "Mark Twain wrote a novel, Fitzgerald learned from Brooks, where the hero finds a mountain full of coal; Fitzgerald thereupon wrote a novella in which a Civil War veteran, prospecting in the West at exactly the same time as Mark Twain's hero, came upon a mountain full of diamonds."[36]

A tall tale in the Twain tradition, "Diamond" is an enclosed narrative framed by Hades (the Midwest), just as "The Ice Palace" was framed by Tarleton (the South) and "May Day" by two hotels. All nine internal sections occur around Fish, Montana (the West). It lacks Twain's strategies of the shrewd Westerner (narrator) versus the naive Easterner (audience) and the realistic present versus the fantastic past, but it retains the hyperbole coloring Twain's "Celebrated Jumping Frog of Calaveras County" and other exaggerated stories. Thus, the narrative is peppered with superlatives like "the most expensive and the most exclusive boys' preparatory school in the world" (*BR*, 76), "the richest man in the world" (*BR*, 77), "a diamond bigger than the Ritz-Carlton Hotel" (*BR*, 78), and "the most beautiful person he had ever seen" (*BR*, 90). Midas, Croesus, and Prometheus appear, as do El Dorado and the motion pictures. Parallels between El Dorado, the mythical country of wealth or desire sought by the conquistadores, and the diamond mountain recur: for example, the Spanish mother's "association with the Spanish conquerors of El Dorado," and the lake's association with "the holy lake of El Dorado, from which the Spanish plunderers wrested the natives' sacred treasure."[37] Recurrent also are cinematic allusions, inspiring one critic to call the style "Babylonian-Hollywood," and to detect the "implicit presence throughout of Hollywood criteria of values and taste" (see Bewley in part 3).

That Fitzgerald uses his irreal "second manner" for satiric purposes here, the Washington genealogy, as reconstructed in section 4, indicates. About their privileged background, Robert Emmet Long writes:

> Percy's father, Braddock Tarleton Washington, is the son of Fitz-Norman Washington and is descended from the stock of Washington and Lord Baltimore. All the family names have connotations of

> power and class assumption, beginning with the Norman conquerors who brought with them a system of steep class differences. Lord Baltimore, of a later period of English history, necessarily implies a charter-holding proprietor of a large tract of early America who held absolute and supreme power. Tarleton and Braddock belong to the same English tradition of lordship as it descends to the period of eighteenth-century colonialism. Both were noted for their presumptuousness—Tarleton for the barbaric cruelty of his campaigns, Braddock for his obstinacy and arrogance. Washington himself was not personally like Braddock, his commanding officer in the early colonial wars, but as a Southern, slave-owning plantation owner, he was at least implicated in proprietary interests, as they passed from England to America. Like Washington, Braddock Washington is a plantation owner. (Long, 63)

Ironically, then, America, the democratic land of the free, has always been subject to "power and class assumption," to "proprietary interests," which explains the important imprisonment/entrapment motif. Not only do we repeatedly encounter black slaves, but also encaged aviators who represent various nationalities. Once Braddock "kidnapped a landscape gardener, an architect, a designer of stage settings, and a French decadent poet" (*BR*, 98). To protect his unsurveyed "five square miles," he manipulated government "compasses . . . in the strongest magnetic field ever artificially set up" (*BR*, 81). Understandably, John Unger, like Huck Finn and subsequent American heroes, flees from such oppression.

Huck's creator may have provided Fitzgerald with the dream convention as well as the tall tale convention, though the dream convention is ancient and international rather than modern and autochthonous. *A Connecticut Yankee in King Arthur's Court* and "The Diamond as Big as the Ritz" are dreams with protagonists falling asleep at the end, the Boss through Merlin's magic and Unger to escape consciousness. The title character of *The Mysterious Stranger* claims "There is no God, no universe, no human race, no earthly life, no heaven, no hell. It is all a Dream—a grotesque and foolish dream," and the hero of "The Diamond as Big as the Ritz" believes "Everybody's youth is a dream, a form of chemical madness" (*BR*, 113). Thus, time remains vague during the later piece despite references to June, July, and August.

While considerable external evidence verifies the influence of Mark Twain on "The Diamond as Big as the Ritz," only internal evidence can establish the equally significant influence of Nathaniel Hawthorne. Leonard A. Podis, using internal evidence alone, discusses the similarities between "Diamond" and "Rappaccini's Daughter":

> In both stories the plot centers on the entrance of a young man into an enchanted, yet poisonous, environment. The young protagonists, John T. Unger and Giovanni Guasconti, both students away from home, are attracted by the magical realm they have entered, and both find themselves drawn to entrapped young women (Kismine Washington/Beatrice Rappaccini). But as the courtship proceeds, their initial captivation turns to literal captivity as the reality of their own entrapment becomes clear. In addition to the beautiful, captive daughter and the perplexed, love-stricken suitor, both stories feature a dominant, ruthless father (Braddock Washington/Dr. Rappaccini). More important, both stories involve a powerful but morally ambiguous force (wealth/science) which ideally should liberate human beings but in fact imprisons them—a force which produces evil that is attractive, even seductive. Finally, Hawthorne and Fitzgerald rely extensively on fantasy to convey the truth of their vision.[38]

Internal evidence would seem to indicate the even greater influence of another Hawthorne tale, "Young Goodman Brown," on "The Diamond as Big as the Ritz." Youthful too, Brown undertakes a circular journey through alien territory at "sunset." His forest is much gloomier than Unger's mountain, which, Manichean-like, alternates between darkness and light. In their respective hells, they encounter the devil, for Brown a grotesque protean figure, and for Unger the "Emperor of Diamonds" (*BR*, 109). These encounters with evil inculcate such disillusionment that, upon returning, Unger resumes unconsciousness and Brown becomes "a distrustful, if not a desperate man." Everything is a dream in *The Mysterious Stranger* and "youth is a dream" in "The Diamond as Big as the Ritz," so we should not be surprised when Hawthorne asks, "Had Goodman Brown fallen asleep in the forest and only dreamed a wild dream of a witch-meeting?"

He has prepared us for the allegorical implications arising from this Black Mass by the ironic title "Goodman" and the ironic name "Faith." A symbolic vocabulary similarly reverses religious expectations in "The Diamond as Big as the Ritz." Thus, Unger leaves Hades (the abode of the dead) for St. Midas' School (the rich Phrygian king beatified). Next he spends the summer at the Washington chateau, first passing through the village of Fish (Jesus), where, "under a poisoned sky," "twelve sombre and inexplicable souls" (apostles) "were beyond all religion," for "the barest and most savage tenets of even Christianity could gain no foothold on that barren rock—so there was no altar, no priest, no sacrifice; only each night at seven the silent concourse by the shanty depot, a congregation who lifted up a prayer of dim, anaemic wonder." "Had they deified any one," we learn, "they might well have chosen as their celestial protagonist" the Great Brakeman arriving on the Trans-Continental Express from Chicago (*BR*, 78).

The nine enclosed sections begin (2) and end (10) with inverted Christian allusions, the twelve disillusioned men leading to white-haired Washington as "Prometheus Enriched," "Emperor of Diamonds," a "prophet of old." In these roles, the madman expresses condescension and pride rather than supplication, for his attitude is "antithetical to prayer" when he bribes God. Sudden darkness and thunder demonstrate God's refusal. There ensues "the triumph of the day" or dawn (*BR*, 110), markedly different from the poisoned sunset of section 2. Then the wired mountain explodes, and an apocalyptic fire destroys Braddock Washington and company. Only the three young people, two of whom are lovers, survive to greet another sunset, this one "tranquil" (*BR*, 112).

If "proprietary interests" made the historical Washington, Baltimore, Braddock, and Tarleton aristocratic rather than democratic, money has likewise perverted Christianity. Its old forms remain—fish, apostle, prophet, prayer, and so forth—but now they signify their opposites. Indeed, wealth embodies the new creed Unger must revere or commit blasphemy. Now Midas is a saint, a capitalist, a priest. Bearing man's image, even God "had His price"; consequently, Braddock offers Him "the greatest diamond in the world" and "any victim He should choose" (*BR*, 109), invoking "forgotten sacrifices, forgotten rituals, prayers obsolete before the birth of Christ" (*BR*, 108). However, darkness, thunder, apocalypse, light, and love result, with their positive connotations. But revelation soon leads to disillusionment, disillusionment to unconsciousness, and "Diamond" thus terminates as ironically as it started.

"The Diamond as Big as the Ritz," like "The Ice Palace" and "May Day," is an extended, chronologically organized circular journey involving two symbolic geographical locations. All three end in flight and disillusionment, but whereas the protagonists of "The Ice Palace" and "The Diamond as Big as the Ritz" escape entrapment to become aware, Gordon Sterrett in "May Day" destroys himself. All three employ a central symbol, whether palace, statue, or diamond, that embodies an epiphany or revelation. All three are third-person narratives, with Sally Carrol Happer and John T. Unger centers of consciousness through whom the action is viewed, if not reported. All three focus on the relation between the sexes, though only Jewel Hudson and Kismine Washington can be considered femmes fatales and Harry Bellamy and Gordon Sterrett *hommes manqués*. All three attack urban, industrialized capitalist society, preferring the American past to the American present.

Differences as well as similarities mark Fitzgerald's early triumphs, making each a unique achievement among much otherwise mediocre fiction. None seems genuinely innovative except "May Day," where, through decentralized form, he prefigures Dos Passos, Faulkner, and other native writers. Even so, Fitzgerald exhibits a mastery of various established techniques during the apprenticeship that makes us question the notion of development in his case. For example, the realistic "Ice Palace" juxtaposes psychic landscapes and employs iterative imagery almost as skillfully as does *The Great Gatsby*, while the fantastic "Diamond as Big as the Ritz" is a tall tale worthy of Mark Twain, a reversed allegory worthy of Nathaniel Hawthorne.

All the Sad Young Men

Fitzgerald wrote the nine stories in *All the Sad Young Men* (1926), his third collection of short stories published by Scribner, between September 1922 ("Winter Dreams") and April to August 1925 ("The Rich Boy"). Eight of the twenty stories previously published between September 1922 and February 1926 in magazines such as *Redbook, Metropolitan, Hearst's International, American Mercury, McCall's,* and *Liberty* were republished here, but only one, "Gretchen's Forty Winks," was a *Saturday Evening Post* selection.

On 1 June 1925 the author wrote his editor, Maxwell Perkins, saying the new book's offerings "were so good" he had "had difficulty . . . selling them." "The Rich Boy" was a "serious story and very good"; "Winter Dreams" was a "sort of 1st draft of the Gatsby idea"; "Rags Martin-Jones and the Pr-nce of W-les" was "Fantastic Jazz, so good that Lorimer [*Saturday Evening Post*] and Long [*Hearst's International*] refused it"; "The Baby Party" was a "fine story"; "The Sensible Thing" was a "story about Zelda & me. All true"; "Hot & Cold Blood" was "a good story"; and, though others considered "Gretchen's Forty Winks" "my best," "it isn't." The title, Fitzgerald divulged, "is because seven stories deal with young men of my generation in rather unhappy moods." Seldom humble and ever publicity-conscious, he added that the jacket should show "transition from his early exuberant stories of youth which created a new type of American girl and the later and more serious mood which produced *The Great Gatsby* and marked him as one of the half dozen masters of English prose now writing in America" (*Dear Scott*, 112–13).

This collection—like *Flappers and Philosophers*, where "The Ice Palace" appeared with seven mediocre stories, and *Tales of the Jazz Age*, where "May Day" and "The Diamond as Big as the Ritz" appeared with eight stories ranging from good ("The Jelly-Bean") to bad ("Mr. Icky")—contains both popular and serious fiction. Indeed, its selections are almost evenly distributed between commercial pieces ("The Baby Party," "Rags Martin-Jones and the Pr-nce of W-les," "The Adjuster," "Hot and Cold Blood," "Gretchen's Forty Winks") and artistic pieces ("The Rich Boy," "Winter Dreams," "Absolution," "The Sensible Thing")—perhaps explaining why the book became a critical as well as a financial success. The first three artistic pieces are major achievements first published, respectively, by *Red Book*, *Metropolitan*, and *American Mercury*.

Because the stories in *All the Sad Young Men* were composed so soon after those in *Tales of the Jazz Age*, they often repeat techniques and themes present in the earlier volume. The subject matter is still autobiographical; for example, "The Sensible Thing" is a "true" story about the Fitzgeralds. Two narrative voices—the omniscient, or third person unrestricted, and the central intelligence, or third person restricted—dominate, sometimes as juxtaposed points of view, though "The Rich Boy," which opens the collection and which succeeded *The Great Gatsby* in 1925, uses the observer-narrator "The Pierian Springs and the Last Straw" had developed. Fitzgerald evokes a Western setting (Dakota) in "Absolution" and a Southern setting (Tennessee) in "The Sensible Thing"; otherwise, he focuses on New York City, rendered realistically rather than symbolically. Again, chronological progression orders the present and the present emerges from a past— repository of youth, illusion, and romance—that several characters try to escape, the rich *boy* excepted. These characters fantasize in *All the Sad Young Men*, yet their creator never employs his "second manner"; only Dr. Moon, who embodies "five years," seems unreal. Surprise endings and reversals persist, for instance, when Rags Martin-Jones weds, Louella Hemple changes, Jim Mather lends money, George Tompkins breaks down. Now somewhat simpler plots occur inside structures averaging four to five mechanical divisions, the longest story being "The Rich Boy" (eight sections) and the shortest, "The Baby Party" (one section). Irrelevant scenes and circular journeys have disappeared, but framed narratives remain. Now all the protagonists are males representing a spectrum of socioeconomic classes—Anson Hunter, the upper; Rudolph Miller, the lower—with middle-class individuals most pervasive. Frequently they begin as *hommes manqués*, then become monetarily successful and emotionally resilient like Dexter Green and George O'Kelley. Their nemesis, the femme fatale, is well-off, though less stereotypical than previously. Thus, Judy Jones, whose name connotes ordinariness, ends up the faded wife of a brutish husband, while Jonquil Cary, whose "picturesque fragility" commands "adolescent worship," elects to do "the sensible thing." Prefigurations of Gatsby, they acquire wealth, Dexter through the laundry business and George through construction; yet, having risen from rags to riches, they lose the girl.

Such technical and thematic similarities should prepare us for the resemblances between "Rags Martin-Jones and the Pr-nce of W-ales" (*All the Sad Young Men*) and "The Offshore Pirate" (*Flappers and Philosophers*). Both focus on a young, beautiful, narcissistic, spoiled, and insolent heiress. Ardita Farnham had remained aboard ship off Florida, while Rags Martin-Jones later disembarks at New York. Unconventional rebels, the first smokes cigarettes and "won't tolerate the parental attitude from anybody," whereas Rags wears a monocle and considers her fellow Americans dull. They demand that rich suitors Toby Moreland (alias Curtis Carlyle) and John M. Chestnut exhibit imagination (the "gallant gesture"). This the two men do by staging clever stratagems that involve disguise and deception and which produce love and marriage. What Milton Hindus says about "The Offshore Pirate" applies as well to "Rags Martin-Jones and the Pr-nce of W-les": "To be specific, a story such as 'The Offshore Pirate,' . . . despite the fact that it has no memorable meaning or message and is therefore either unnoticed or despised by most readers, is so delightful and dreamlike a fantasy that it stands no more in need of intellectual justification than a beautiful piece of music or certain lyric poems."[39]

Though none of the other four commercial stories in *All the Sad Young Men* bears such striking parallels to any single apprentice piece, their marriage motif had already been anticipated by "Head and Shoulders," "The Cut-Glass Bowl," "The Curious Case of Benjamin Button," and "The Lees of Happiness." These earlier works showed considerable variety, but not so Fitzgerald's 1926 counterparts, for the latter exploit stock characters in stock situations. Formulaic, "The Baby Party," "The Adjuster," "Hot and Cold Blood," and "Gretchen's Forty Winks" only appear to be different.

In "The Baby Party," for example, thirty-eight-year-old John Andros gets into a fistfight with neighbor Joe Markey because of his infant daughter Ede's aggressiveness and his immature wife Edith's hysteria during the baby party next door. Later, the men make up, and later still, John admonishes Edith and cradles Ede. The nuclear family appears again in "The Adjuster," where the Charles Hemples belong to "that enormous American class who wander over Europe every summer, sneering rather pathetically and wistfully at the customs and traditions and pastimes of other countries, because they have no customs or tradition or pastimes of their own." A "vile housekeeper," bored Luella wants "excitement," not caring "what form it takes or what I pay for it, so long as it makes my heart beat," she tells the mysterious intruder Dr. Moon. Her husband collapses and her baby dies; then Moon, representing time and advocating responsibility, converts this malcontent of twenty-three to a "grown up" of twenty-eight. "The Adjuster" ends idyllically, for the Hemples are now at home with their two other children. Selfish Jaqueline Mather of "Hot and Cold Blood" criticizes husband Jim: "You're—eternally—being *used!* I won't stand it! I thought I married a man—not a professional Samaritan who's going to fetch and carry for the world." Afterward, he changes radically, refusing to lend money or even give up his subway seat. When the girl beside him on the train faints, Jim coincidentally discovers she is Jaqueline, now pregnant, and becomes magnanimous again. Another newly married fellow, ambitious Roger Halsey, labors day and night to succeed in the advertising business while Gretchen, Roger's lazy Southern wife—"a bright-colored, Titian-haired girl, vivid as a French rag doll"—dates fun-loving interior decorator George Tompkins. He separates them and, to win the crucial Garrod account, drugs his wife and steals her shoes. "Gretchen's Forty Winks" concludes ironically with the exponent of the "balanced life," Tomkins, breaking down and workaholic Halsey "never looking better."

In all four stories, husbands and wives are combative characters. "The Baby Party" pits normal John Andros against neurotic Edith; "The Adjuster" pits wise Dr. Moon against foolish Luella Hemple; "Hot and Cold Blood" pits generous Jim Mather against selfish Jaqueline; and "Gretchen's Forty Winks" pits industrious Roger Halsey against indolent Gretchen. These pairs have been wed on average about three years and most often possess a child who suffers danger or destruction. The protagonist-husband, as the mature man (father figure), teaches the antagonist-wife, as the immature woman (daughter figure), how to grow up, either through criticism or example. Sometimes he employs a clever stratagem—Charles Hemple engages Moon and Roger Halsey incapacitates Gretchen—but always after being victimized he regains control, and reconciliation results. Fitzgerald's more or less happy endings often involve this simplistic reversal, the assertive antagonist growing submissive and the passive protagonist triumphant.

Superficially, "Absolution," "Winter Dreams," "The Sensible Thing," and "The Rich Boy" resemble these mediocre tales, for they too feature male protagonists, ranging in age, however, from eleven (Rudolph Miller) to thirty (Anson Hunter), and functioning in a wider variety of settings, which include Dakota, Minnesota, Tennessee, and New York. Because these stories were composed just before or right after *The Great Gatsby* and so bear thematic and technical resemblances to the novel, this artistic group may be called the *Gatsby* cluster, whose focus, incidentally, is unrequited love rather than marriage.

During April 1924 Fitzgerald apprised Perkins, "Much of what I wrote last summer was good but it was so interrupted that it was ragged & in approaching it from a new angle I've had to discard a lot of it—in one case 18,000 words (part of which will appear in the Mercury as a short story)" (*Dear Scott*, 69). "Absolution," eliminated from *The Great Gatsby*, as was "May Day" from *The Beautiful and Damned*, sold for a pittance when slick magazines were paying the author twenty-five hundred dollars per potboiler. Ten years later he informed critic John Jamieson, "It might interest you to know that a story of mine, called 'Absolution,' in my book *All the Sad Young Men* was intended to be a picture of [Gatsby's] early life, but that I cut it because I preferred to preserve the sense of mystery" (*Letters*, 509).

"Winter Dreams" was also a "sort of 1st draft of the Gatsby idea," but no more so than "The Sensible Thing"—a "story about Zelda & me" composed fourteen months later (November 1923). Whereas Southerner Jonquil Cary of "The Sensible Thing" represents Zelda Sayre, Fitzgerald's new wife, Midwesterner Judy Jones of "Winter Dreams" represents Ginevra King, his old sweetheart. They both prefigure Daisy Fay/Buchanan, while Scott Fitzgerald/Dexter Green/George O'Kelley prefigure James Gatz/Gatsby.

Of the four stories comprising the cluster under consideration, only "The Rich Boy" was published after *The Great Gatsby*.[40] Like Daisy Fay/Buchanan of the fifty-thousand-word novel, protagonist Anson Hunter of the seventeen-thousand-word novelette was based on a person Fitzgerald knew well. In a letter to Ludlow Fowler—Scott's Princeton classmate, his best man, his faithful mourner—Fitzgerald said, "I have written a fifteen thousand word story about you called *The Rich Boy*—it is so disguised that no one except you and me and maybe two of the girls concerned would recognize, unless you give it away, but it is in large measure the story of your life, toned down here and there and simplified. Also many gaps had to come out of my imagination. It is frank, unsparing but sympathetic and I think you will like it—it is one of the best things I have ever done" (*Correspondence*, 152). Except perhaps for "Babylon Revisited," "The Rich Boy" has always been regarded as the greatest Fitzgerald short story. Its critical success may be attributed mostly to the technique of the observer-narrator, borrowed from *The Great Gatsby*, though the Tom Buchanan figure rather than the James Gatz figure is the observed character here, while an anonymous narrator takes over the Nick Carraway role. As in *Gatsby*, both are Ivy Leaguers whose tale unfolds in New York.

Between December 1919, when the author was twenty-three, and August 1925, when he was still just twenty-eight, he wrote six of his major stories, three of which were novelettes, and his masterful novel *The Great Gatsby*. Few other American prose artists had metamorphosed so abruptly from apprentice to professional. And, among contemporaries, only Hemingway, who published *In Our Time*, *The Sun Also Rises*, *Men without Women*, and *A Farewell to Arms* between 1925 and 1929, and Faulkner, who published *Sartoris*, *The Sound and the Fury*, *As I Lay Dying*, *Sanctuary*, *Light in August*, and *Absalom, Absalom!* between 1929 and 1936, wrote so much superior fiction in such a brief period; but then neither Hemingway nor Faulkner functioned simultaneously as our most celebrated popular writer.

"Absolution"

"Absolution" (1924) was written during June 1923, soon after the 1922 Egoist Press edition of James Joyce's *Dubliners*, including "Araby" among its fifteen stories, came out. Fitzgerald ranked the Joyce collection among the "great English classics." On the back cover of his copy he wrote: "I am interested in the individual only in his rel[ation] to society. We have wondered [*sic*] in imaginary lonliness [*sic*] for a hundred years."

The adolescent protagonist-narrator of Joyce's "Araby," who lives in the house on "blind end" North Richmond Street, is sexually drawn to a young woman residing across the street from him. She represents glamour, while his aunt and uncle (surrogate parents) and other adults represent the drab reality characteristic of Roman Catholic Dublin. The girl cannot go to the "splendid bazaar" called "Araby," so the protagonist journeys alone to bring her back something. When the train finally arrives at the "magical" place, however, "nearly all the stalls were closed"; darkness and churchly silence prevail as two men count money. The quester, suddenly aware, considers himself "a creature driven and derided by vanity."

This bazaar may well be the source of the amusement park in "Absolution": "It's a thing like a fair, only much more glittering. . . . But don't get up close . . . because if you do you'll only feel the heat and the sweat and the life" (*BR*, 150), Father Schwartz ("Black") explains to eleven-year-old Rudolph Miller. Thus Joyce's metaphor for romance becomes "Fitzgerald's metaphor for the active secular world, variously described as an amusement park, carnival, circus, or the 'world's fair,' which appears in his notebooks, in all of the novels, and in several stories."[41]

Another *Dubliners* selection, "The Sisters," influenced "Absolution" even more than "Araby" did, though these two stories by no means exhaust the effect the older Irish writer made on his young American disciple.[42] "The Sisters" employs first-person narration and "Absolution" the central-intelligence. Consequently, though both methods make us privy to the thoughts and feelings of their respective adolescent and child protagonists, "The Sisters" achieves greater intimacy and immediacy. It nevertheless approximates the detachment omniscience lends to even limited third-person fictions like "Absolution," since "The Sisters" is told by the man his own youthful hero will become. Whether authorial or temporal, this detachment produces irony.

Whereas "The Sisters" juxtaposes two scenes to a narrative carried by the protagonist's perambulations, "Absolution" uses a split scene to frame the past. Sections 2, 3, and 4 of the Fitzgerald story are sandwiched between sections 1 and 5. Section 1 commences and section 5 culminates with a view of the Swedish girls (along with, in 5, their young men) and the Dakota wheat outside Father Schwartz's window, but the main body of both 1 and 5 treats the same scene, focused on Father Schwartz and Rudolph Miller simultaneously. In 1, the child tells the priest, who is experiencing such an "agony" of longing over those Swedish girls that his mind has run down "like an old clock" (*BR*, 136), that he, Rudolph, has "committed a terrible sin" (*BR*, 137). During 5, Father Schwartz, having heard his informal confession and having become cognizant of the child's beauty, crazily replies, "When a lot of people get together in the best places things go glimmering" (*BR*, 148), as if seeking help. Finally, pastor absolves parishioner of "apostasy," then collapses, crying, "Oh, my God!," whereupon his already terrified visitor flees the house "in a panic."

Sections 2, 3, and 4 treat Rudolph's "terrible sin," or, more accurately, sins. "On Saturday, Three Days Ago" (as the section 2 heading reads), Carl Miller, an immigrant freight agent and Roman Catholic devotee, sends son Rudolph to confession, where the latter admits he had listened while two boys and one girl said "immodest things" that inspired "a strange, romantic excitement" (*BR*, 140), and had lied about lying. This formal confession causes him an "agony" reminiscent of the torment the priest experienced with the Swedish girls, and so he resolves to "avoid communion the next day" (*BR*, 141), but Mr. Miller thwarts him.

The main theme of both Joyce's "The Sisters" and Fitzgerald's "Absolution" is adult betrayal. The earlier story contains one scene laid at the house of the nameless protagonist-narrator's aunt and uncle and one at the house of the recently deceased Rev. James Flynn, during which several adults discuss his clerical mentor before the silent boy. In the first scene, a family friend, who is described as a "tiresome old red-nosed imbecile," directs some veiled remarks toward him about the deleterious effects individuals like Father Flynn must have on children. When this fool suggests, "Let a young lad run about and play with lads of his own age," the boy's uncle responds, "That's my principle, too . . . That's what I'm always saying to that Rosicrucian there." In the second scene, we move from the male to the female world, as boy and aunt arrive at "the house of mourning." After one Flynn sister, Nannie, steers them toward the "dead-room," where the deceased priest is holding a chalice, they return downstairs, where the aunt and another Flynn sister, Eliza, discuss the whole sad affair, Eliza concluding with the tale of the broken chalice—"They say it was the boy's fault"—and how this affected Father Flynn's mind. Throughout the women are passive and rather absurd, the aunt having failed to protest male aggressiveness earlier and now the unintentional puns of Eliza sounding as ridiculous as the garments of Nannie look.

Adult betrayal in the Fitzgerald story is a less complicated, less subtle theme than in the Joyce model, for Carl Miller merely bullies Rudolph. He takes the child "by the neck," and so the child goes to church; he beats the child savagely, and so the child attends communion; he repents, then pokes the child "to sit up," and so the child receives the wafer. Meanwhile, Mrs. Miller demonstrates "nervous ineffectuality" (*BR*, 145).

Both authors epitomize the tyranny of grown-ups through priestly "fathers." In "The Sisters," this tyranny is implicit: we learn that Father Flynn, who had educated the adolescent narrator, was "queer," and that the adolescent narrator, who had caused the chalice to be broken, was resentful, observing, for instance, that he "let his tongue lie upon his lower lip—a habit which had made me feel uneasy." Significantly, the first, as paralytic, appears before the second, as dreamer, "to confess something," and the second "absolve[s] the simoniac."

This homosexual motif recurs in "Absolution." In section 5, where there occurs the inaccurately worded motto *"Sagitta Volante in Dei"* ("An arrow flying into God"),[43] Father Schwartz unconsciously reveals his own sensual nature: he is drawn toward the "beautiful little boy with eyes like blue stones, and lashes that sprayed open from them like flower-petals" (*BR*, 148). Here, priest absolves parishioner when he says, "Stop worrying about last Saturday. Apostasy implies an absolute damnation only on the supposition of a previous perfect faith"; and parishioner absolves priest when the parishioner's "own inner convictions were confirmed. There was something ineffably gorgeous somewhere that had nothing to do with God" (*BR*, 149). Though the child's "eyes are contrasted with the priest's cold, watery eyes suggesting two kinds of vision, one almost unnaturally bright, the other almost unnaturally faded" (Long, 74), they are secret sharers, as the similarity of their first names, Adolphus and Rudolph, suggests.

Sexual repression, symbolized by the loneliness and restrictiveness of the Church and its environs, drives the Fathers Flynn and Schwartz mad. Both "Araby" and "Absolution" oppose to this death force the life force. In Joyce's story, the girl inspires love *and* lust in her admirer, who, as a Catholic youngster, worships her with "strange prayers." In "Absolution," literary descendant Rudolph Miller guiltily worries about certain commandments and imagined "sexual offenses," though he "had never committed adultery, nor even coveted his neighbor's wife" (*BR*, 138). A similar guilt troubles "Absolution's" priest. When the story begins, the "shrill laughter" of the Swedish girls is dissonant and "the Dakota wheat . . . terrible" to Father Schwartz, who ultimately collapses. There follows a lyrical finale emphasizing the natural images that characterize the framework of the tale and that threaten the frustrated prelate:

> Outside the window the blue sirocco trembled over the wheat, and girls with yellow hair walked sensuously along roads that bounded the fields, calling innocent, exciting things to the young men who were working in the lines between the grain. Legs were shaped un-

der starchless gingham, and rims of the necks of dresses were warm
and damp. For five hours now hot fertile life had burned in the
afternoon. It would be night in three hours, and all along the land
there would be these blonde Northern girls and the tall young men
from the farms lying out beside the wheat, under the moon. (*BR*,
151)

One commentator has pointed out that "Father Schwartz . . . is always presented in images of enclosure, contrasted with the 'open world
of wheat and sky.' The two places where he is seen are his 'haunted
room' and the confessional booth" (Long, 73; see part 3). This applies
to Father Flynn as well, for Joyce associates him with virtually identical
confinement: he had inhabited a "little dark room" at the rear of "the
little house" and a "confession-box" when alive; when dead, he occupies the coffin inside "the dead-room." Confinement imagery marks
not only both priests but both protagonists as well. "The sisters' " adolescent takes "my usual chair in the corner" and dreams "in the dark
of my room," while the Fitzgerald boy enters "the large coffin set on
end" to confess (*BR*, 138) and visits the kitchen, or "centre of the
house" (*BR*, 143).

Whereas paralysis best defines the hostile environment of Joycean
Dublin, solitariness evokes the austere landscape of the later "lost
Swede town" (*BR*, 148). Its drugstore and main street also recall Stephen Crane's "The Blue Hotel," whose title location stands "alone on
the prairie." Like Crane's Fort Rompers, Nebraska, Fitzgerald's Ludwig, [North?] Dakota, embodies a crude Western microcosm. People
are trapped here much as in the symbolic labyrinth of "The Ice Palace"
or the symbolic cage of "The Diamond as Big as the Ritz."

Because these young protagonists find their surroundings intolera-
ble, they create fantasy worlds. The nameless narrator of "The Sisters"
dreams about "some land where the customs were strange," perhaps
Persia; and later, during "Araby," the syllables of that word "cast an
Eastern enchantment" over the hero. "Absolution," like *The Great
Gatsby*, invokes the age-old hero myth. In the story, Rudolph, who feels
superior to his father, refuses to believe that he is his son and retreats
from his environment into a world of fantasy where he becomes the
noble and romantic Blatchford Sarnemington. In the novel, Gatsby has
never accepted his parents, "shiftless and unsuccessful farm people."
He has sprung "from his Platonic conception of himself" and is "a son
of God" (*GG*, 99). He too rejects his real name, James Gatz, and in-

vents a new, more glamorous one, Jay Gatsby. He invents a fictitious background also: like his aristocratic ancestors, he has been educated at Oxford. The imagery in "Absolution" and *The Great Gatsby* is a modernized version of that of the romance or fairy tale. Blatchford Sarnemington is a character from whom "a suave nobility flowed," a character who "lived in great sweeping triumphs" (*BR*, 141). His fantasy world is full of military images: "flag," "silver pennon," "silver spurs," "crunch of leather," "troop of horsemen" (*BR*, 150). Gatsby's pursuit of Daisy is "the following of a grail" (*GG*, 149), and Daisy herself is "the king's daughter, the golden girl" who lives "high in a white palace" (*GG*, 120).[44]

Obviously, then, there are several connections between the story as a novel prologue and the novel itself: neither James Gatz nor Rudolph Miller believes he is the son of his progenitors; both create a fabulous alter ego, as Gatz becomes Jay Gatsby and Miller becomes Blatchford Sarnemington. Moreover, their lower middle-class fathers live out West and admire American railroad builder James J. Hill. And the story, like the novel, juxtaposes past and present through flashbacks while employing recurrent temporal images (for example, run-down clocks). Yet, Matthew J. Bruccoli cautions us:

> It is not certain that Rudolph Miller, the boy whose dreams of metropolitan glamour are reinforced by his encounter with the deranged priest, is Jimmy Gatz. As Fitzgerald told Perkins, "Absolution" was salvaged from a discarded version before he approached the novel from "a new angle"—by which he meant a new plot. While Miller and Gatz share a romantic disposition, there is no clear evidence that they are the same characterization from the same novel. Fitzgerald's 1922 plan was that his third novel would have a "catholic element"—which is entirely absent in *The Great Gatsby*, though central to "Absolution." (Bruccoli, 192)

In "Scott Fitzgerald—the Authority of Failure," William Troy refers to this "catholic element": "But least explored of all by his critics were the permanent effects of his early exposure to Catholicism, which are no less potent because rarely on the surface of his work. (The great exception is 'Absolution,' perhaps the finest of the short stories.)"[45] Now, some forty-five years after Troy's article first appeared, "the permanent effects" of the author's religious upbringing are better known, thanks to works like Joan M. Allen's *Candles and Carnival Lights: The Catholic Sensibility of F. Scott Fitzgerald.*

Understandably, Fitzgerald borrowed much from another lapsed Irish Catholic, his idol James Joyce, whose *Dubliners* may have supplied the conflict between sexual repression and sexual expression, which, like Joyce, Fitzgerald internalized in "Absolution" through priest-father (antagonist) and boy-son (protagonist) figures. "Araby" and "The Sisters" may also have provided the motifs of adult betrayal and perversion, as well as the inimical urban environment with its claustrophobic quarters.

Even so, Fitzgerald was no slavish imitator, since "Absolution" develops several techniques already introduced by his early triumphs. For instance, the later story depends on a structural framework that meaningfully juxtaposes present and past actions. Unlike "The Ice Palace" and "The Diamond as Big as the Ritz," which alternate geographical areas, "Absolution," which reflects the circular journey from hotel to hotel in "May Day," alternates constrictive locales of "haunted room" and church or Miller home. The Dakota of "Absolution," however, like the Manhattan of "May Day," is no less symbolic than the North versus South of "The Ice Palace" and the Midwest/East versus West of "The Diamond as Big as the Ritz."

Though radically different, "Absolution" resembles "May Day" in still another way. It avoids decentralization, yet the split focus between priest and child during sections 1 and 5 does recall the multiple perspectives conveying Fitzgerald's only major occasional tale. Otherwise, the shorter piece—similar to "The Ice Palace" and "The Diamond as Big as the Ritz"—uses the lone central intelligence, since, here too, protagonal psychology becomes all-important. If the quests for identity by Sally Carrol Happer and John T. Unger end positively and that by Gordon Sterrett negatively, Rudolph Miller's remains unresolved, as he "gave a sharp cry and ran in a panic from the house" (*BR*, 150).

Of the selections examined so far, "The Ice Palace" and "Absolution" manipulate imagery most skillfully. Not only do they present elaborate image patterns, but these patterns adumbrate thematic conflicts. Thus in "Absolution" the conflict between Eros (love, lust) and Thanatos (death) is communicated through the tension between images of openness (wheat, sky) and images of enclosure (rooms, confessional), much as the conflict between North (death-in-life) and South (life-in-death) is communicated through the tension between images of coldness and warmth in "The Ice Palace."

Besides extending techniques associated with Fitzgerald's early triumphs, "Absolution," which was published one year before *The Great*

Gatsby, prefigures that novel through various parallel phenomena, including the ancient hero myth discussed above.

"Winter Dreams"

Although "Absolution" and "Winter Dreams" (1922) form part of the *Gatsby* cluster, the qualitative differences between them are marked. "Absolution" can stand alone as a separate artwork, but "Winter Dreams"—perhaps the weakest of the eight best stories—appeals to us mainly by projecting the quintessential Scott Fitzgerald. This narrative explores virtually all of his "great and moving experiences" except "emotional bankruptcy": poor boy/rich girl, past/present, illusion/disillusion. Clinton S. Burhans comments on one: "The dream-and-disillusion motif in the story appears in varying forms and degrees from its intermittent emergence in *This Side of Paradise* to its central exploration in *The Last Tycoon;* it is Fitzgerald's major theme."[46]

As we already know, rich girl Judy Jones of "Winter Dreams" (like Jonquil Cary of "The Sensible Thing") prefigures Daisy Fay/Buchanan of *The Great Gatsby*. If Daisy's seductiveness emanates from her moneyed voice, Judy's emanates from her "radiant" smile, elsewhere termed "artificial," "convincing," "preposterous," "insincere." Seductive voices and smiles are recurrent attributes that characterize golden femmes fatales who ensnare, then abandon, suitors. Though they claim to be unhappy, popular Daisy exudes gaiety and athletic Judy vitality. The "vast carelessness" used to describe the one also describes the other. This sometimes produces physical violence, when, for example, Daisy kills Myrtle Wilson in the most gruesome of the novel's many automobile accidents, or when Judy, the child, abuses nurse Hilda, and Judy, the adult, plays reckless golf. Finally, these destructive women are, like Daisy's friend Jordan Baker, "incurably dishonest."

Several details of their lives bear close resemblance. Both "live in a house over there on the island" (*BR*, 122), but, more specifically, "Judy's home was lifted from the magazine text of the story and written into *The Great Gatsby*" for the Fay residence (Bruccoli, 174). They marry similar men. Anticipating Tom Buchanan, Lud Simms "has gone to pieces"; "he drinks and runs around." Buchanan may be more bigoted and brutal, yet Simms too "treats [his wife] like the devil" (*BR*, 134). Ironically, Judy, no less than Daisy, loves and forgives her reprobate husband, though only Judy becomes domestic and faded in the process.

Poor boy Dexter Green of "Winter Dreams" (like George O'Kelley of "The Sensible Thing") prefigures James Gatz/Jay Gatsby. Thus, Dexter's background foreshadows Rudolph's and Gatsby's, at least superficially. His mother's name "had been Krimplich. She was a Bohemian of the peasant class and she had talked broken English to the end of her days." Moreover, "he had been born in Keeble, a Minnesota village fifty miles farther north, and he always gave Keeble as his home instead of Black Bear Village" (*BR*, 123). There are also notable dissimilarities among these parallels. For example, Mr. Miller, a "freight-agent," and Mr. Gatz, a "shiftless and unsuccessful" farmer, represent the lower class, while Mr. Green, "who owned the second best grocery-store in Black Bear" (*BR*, 142), is a middle-class figure. The first two admire James J. Hill, but, evidently, the last does not. Dexter and Gatsby rise from rags to riches, Dexter remaining honest (caddy, then laundry tycoon) and Gatsby becoming dishonest (fisherman, then bootlegger). The former attended some famous old Eastern university (compare Yale graduates Nick Carraway and Tom Buchanan), whereas the latter makes the spurious claim of having been "educated at Oxford" (*GG*, 65). Both were officers, yet only Gatsby excelled at war, when even "little Montenegro" decorated him (*GG*, 66). And both are affiliated with bodies of water: for Dexter, Black Bear Lake, whose peninsula echoes "songs of last summer and of the summers before" (*BR*, 121); and, for Gatsby, Little Girl Bay on Lake Superior as well as Long Island Sound, whose peninsula likewise echoes "yellow cocktail music" (*GG*, 40) and "Vladimir Tostoff's *Jazz History of the World*" (*GG*, 50).

Though much has been made of the similarities between the protagonists of "Winter Dreams" and *The Great Gatsby*, their differences carry more weight. These arise principally from the novel's mythopoeic dimension, which the story lacks. Consequently, Rudolph Miller/James Gatz, having rejected his actual lower-class parents for the fanciful upper-class alter ego Blatchford Sarnemington/Jay Gatsby, becomes a hero less in the formal sense of protagonist than in the conceptual sense of demigod or knight. Faithful to this legendary notion, Fitzgerald deliberately concealed many biographical details so that Gatsby inspires "romantic speculation" (*GG*, 44) among both acquaintances and readers. The author also included considerable hero-myth and fairy-tale imagery, as we already know: from the hero myth come "Wise Old Man" (Dan Cody) and "Queen Goddess" (Daisy Fay) figures, ironically rendered; through Nick Caraway, we experience the "return," when the quester arrives home bearing wisdom ("boon" or "elixir"); and, finally, Gatsby's pursuit of Daisy, fraught with trials, covers dangerous, dreamlike terrain, the faraway East—epitomized by that grotesque valley of ashes—which Nick considers distorted, West Egg resembling some scene out of El Greco. These monomythic elements remove *The Great Gatsby* from one place and one time, as if the tale, celebrated for ages in song, folklore, and literature, were part of our Western psyche.

Contrariwise, plainly labeled Dexter *Green* (compare Judy *Jones*) neither rejects his parents nor creates another identity. Despite realizing "he was newer and stronger," Dexter maintains "the set patterns," since he constitutes only "the rough, strong stuff from which [the privileged few] eternally sprang" (*BR*, 123). Meantime this materialist does not want "association with glittering things and glittering people," but "the glittering things themselves." Unaffected by models like Franklin, Alger, and Hill, and unaided by millionaires like Cody, he, even more than Gatsby, is a self-made man. When Judy asks, "Who are you, anyhow?" he replies, "I'm nobody . . . My career is largely a matter of futures"; and when she continues, "Are you poor?" he responds, "No . . . I'm probably making more money than any man my age" (*BR*, 124). Without hero-myth or fairy-tale imagery, Dexter's "winter dreams" appear rather pedestrian: "He became a golf champion and defeated Mr. T. A. Hendrick in a marvellous match played a hundred times over the fairways of his imagination. . . . Again, stepping from a Pierce-Arrow automobile, like Mr. Mortimer Jones, he strolled frigidly into the lounge of the Sherry Island Golf Club—or perhaps, surrounded by an admiring crowd, he gave an exhibition of fancy diving from the spring-board of the club raft" (*BR*, 115).

George O'Kelley of "The Sensible Thing" (written shortly after "Winter Dreams") resembles Dexter Green. Middle-class too, he also attends a prestigious Eastern school (the Massachusetts Institute of Technology), where he studies engineering. George pursues Jonquil Cary in Tennessee (that is, Zelda Sayre in Alabama), just as Dexter pursues Judy Jones in Minnesota (that is, Ginevra King in Illinois). These girls motivate them to make money, but O'Kelley, who temporarily gives up construction for insurance, more nearly approximates Fitzgerald, once another impoverished New Yorker holding an alien job to earn enough to get married. Both become successes and both lose ultimately conventional femmes fatales. This loss surprises neither. Dexter "had wanted Judy Jones ever since he was a proud, desirous little boy" (*BR*, 125), yet always knew "he could not have her" (*BR*, 132). His real loss, like George's, was leaving "the country of illusion, of youth, of the richness of life" (*BR*, 135). We learn that "much . . . ecstasy" vanished during "Winter Dreams," a story rife with "the words *ecstasy* and *ecstatic*" (Long, 68).

Dexter, who has acquired "reserve," surrenders only "part of himself to . . . unprincipled" Judy, while Gatsby allows every abstract ideal and dream to become incarnated in the notorious Daisy. In his efforts down East to win her—"gleaming like silver, safe and proud above the hot struggles of the poor" (*GG*, 150)—he becomes another Trimalchio, the vulgar, ostentatious multimillionaire of Petronius Arbiter's *Satyricon*.[47] Gatsby cannot copy, far less achieve, the qualities, particularly the grace, he attributes to the people across the bay. His garish residence, his cream-colored car, and his pink suit are gauche; his attempts at formality, ridiculous.

On the other hand, Dexter has no trouble imitating the rich: for instance, "when the time had come for him to wear good clothes, he had known who were the best tailors in America" (*BR* 123). Albeit self-pitiers, neither the protagonist of "Winter Dreams" nor the protagonist of "The Sensible Thing" abandons self-control: after unsuccessful courtships, "hard-minded" Dexter marries Irene and stoical George chooses Peru. These realists survive because they accept the inevitable, while Gatsby, the romantic, perishes because he remains faithful to Daisy despite her many betrayals. Commonsensical Dexter and George lack the mythopoeic stature Gatsby embodies even as a fool. No wonder his experience is tragic, theirs merely pathetic.

The only thing mythopoeic about the Dexter Green story is a pattern of cyclical time that would normally establish renewal. Like E. E. Cummings's "anyone lived in a pretty how town," the four seasons recur: we encounter fall, winter, April, spring, fall, October, November on the first two pages, and, in section 4, "summer, fall, winter, spring, another summer, another fall" (*BR*, 127). Moreover, Dexter's various encounters with Judy, which help Fitzgerald structure the narrative, typically occur in warm weather, just as his dreams typically occur in the cold. Yet regenerative cyclical time is undermined by degenerative chronological time. Very elaborate and sometimes contradictory, this parallel pattern takes Dexter from age fourteen to age thirty-two, or from illusion (spiritual life) to disillusion (spiritual death).

Conversely, *The Great Gatsby*, whose temporal scheme also juxtaposes past, present, and future, but less complicatedly, less confusedly, sustains renewal through iterative imagery and symbolism. Its structure substitutes recurrent parties for recurrent encounters, and so adds a social element to what was just private. The presence of the circular monomythic quest—"separation," "initiation," "return"—indicates that "timelessness" is pivotal here.

Absent from Fitzgerald's finest work, including the seven other major short fictions, is an authorial voice that tells us how to read the story. As Gerald Pike points out (see part 3), it asks that we remember various narrative circumstances and implicitly that we disregard any structural inadequacies here. A characteristic passage in this voice reads: "This is not his biography, remember, although things creep into it which have nothing to do with those dreams he had when he was young. We are almost done with them and him now. There is only one more incident to be related . . . and it happens several years farther on" (*BR*, 133).

Self-consciousness in "Winter Dreams" is authorial; it suggests, therefore, how inadequately Fitzgerald composed the story, perhaps because "Winter Dreams" was in his view only a "sort of 1st draft of the Gatsby idea." In that novel, self-consciousness became narratorial, as first-person observer Nick prepares the way for rich boy Anson Hunter's anonymous biographer. These educated confidants, though amateur writers, *seem* to have more skill than the professional creator of "Winter Dreams." For modern storytellers like Fitzgerald, if not for later metafictionists, the storytelling motif was managed best when presented objectively.

This comparative analysis of "Winter Dreams" and *The Great Gatsby* illustrates the distance an artist may travel in three years. Both works reveal striking similarities, but the differences are larger. With regard to content, "Winter Dreams" lacks the mythopoeic dimension of *Gatsby,* or even "Absolution"; with regard to craft, it conveys time and focus less efficaciously. However, Dexter Green's tale, which treats the author's few "great and moving experiences" and so represents him quintessentially, ranks among his most memorable achievements.

"The Rich Boy"

In *The Rhetoric of Fiction* Wayne C. Booth discusses dependable versus undependable raconteurs:

For practical criticism probably the most important of these kinds of
distance is that between the fallible or unreliable narrator and the
implied author [that is, the "official scribe," the "second self"] who
carries the reader with him in judging the narrator. . . . If he is discovered to be untrustworthy, then the total effect of the work he
relays to us is transformed. . . . For lack of better terms, I have
called a narrator reliable when he speaks for or acts in accordance
with the norms of the work (which is to say, the implied author's
norms), unreliable when he does not. . . . But difficult irony is not
sufficient to make a narrator unreliable. Nor is unreliability ordinar-
ily a matter of lying, although deliberately deceptive narrators have
been a major resource of some modern novelists. . . . It is most
often a matter of what James calls inconscience; the narrator is mistaken, or he believes himself to have qualities which the author de-
nies him.[48]

Understanding Booth's distinctions is essential to an appreciation of
the critical controversy that has long raged over narratorial fallibility in
The Great Gatsby and its spin-off, "The Rich Boy" (1926).

Milton R. Stern represents one camp. He asseverates, "Most readers
have found Nick to be a reliable narrator," since the latter meets
Booth's criteria of speaking or acting "in accordance with the norms of
the work" and the implied author. This nonduplicitous observer becomes "educated . . . step by step" like us. For Stern, "the book
makes no sense—if Carraway is repudiated."[49]

Gary J. Scrimgeour represents what Stern calls "the persistent mi-
nority" of critics who take the opposite view, regarding Nick as an
unreliable prig. Their opinion arises from "the critical mode of the
moment, in which all first-person narrators are presumed guilty until
proven innocent," and is compounded by their awareness of "Fitzgerald's debt to Conrad" (Stern, 191). Thus, Scrimgeour argues, "When
a narrator is also a character, with all that this implies of personality,
individuality, and responsibility, we readers are forced to be more alert.
We must question the accuracy of the narrator's account. When he
makes judgments, we have to decide whether his special interests betray the truth and whether the meaning of each particular event and of
the whole fable differs from the interpretation he offers."[50] Basing his
analysis on a comparison of *The Great Gatsby* and Conrad's *Heart of
Darkness*, Scrimgeour concludes that although "we are intended to see
Carraway both as a reliable narrator and as a character learning from

experience," he is neither. Why? "Careless technique and cloudy thinking"! (Scrimgeour, 79, 80).

Composition of "The Rich Boy" commenced during April 1925, the month *The Great Gatsby* was published, so the fact that it too uses the first-person observer-narrator should not surprise us. Nor should we be surprised that several critics now regard Anson Hunter's anonymous biographer as unreliable. Patrick D. Murphy writes, "Like the protagonist whose story he relates, the narrator fails to learn the lesson, choosing appearance and pretence over inner development and honest moral judgment. Thus, Fitzgerald doubly subverts the moment-of-crisis story: the protagonist fails to change and the narrator fails to learn from the protagonist's failure."[51]

This assertion, like that of James L. W. West III and J. Barclay Inge in part 3, is easily countered. That "The Rich Boy's" inflexible protagonist "fails to change" is the point; that the ironic narrator "fails to learn" is untrue. Such irony does not necessarily make him unreliable. Moreover, so many "I" voices have recounted information and reported conversations without being present that these strategies, though perhaps unfortunate, are commonplace. Brian Way expresses no misgivings about them, as the story projects "the sustained pressure of a fine moral intelligence." What he calls "tone"—"dispassionate, sober, analytical"[52]—echoes the Fitzgerald letter to Fowler: "It is frank, unsparing but sympathetic." Then, too, we should remember that none of the author's other observer-narrators strikes most critics as essentially unaware or unreliable.

The issue of centrality accompanies the issue of reliability in both "The Rich Boy" and *The Great Gatsby*. West and Inge imply that, should we find the story's anonymous spokesman untrustworthy, he would become elevated to the level of coprotagonist with Anson Hunter. If that were the case, though, "The Rich Boy" would be a simple class conflict instead of a complex psychological study. Yet West, Inge, and other commentators hold that view, however little evidence there is to support it.

The narrator's anonymity does not automatically disqualify him as protagonist: unnamed storytellers like the lawyer in Melville's "Bartleby, the Scrivener" have been chief characters before. Nor is he automatically disqualified by the title, which focuses on Hunter, since many titles, including "Bartleby" and *Gatsby*, draw attention to the ostensible rather than the real "hero." His relative insignificance lies elsewhere. For one thing, Fitzgerald offers virtually no information about him, past or present. The narrator refers only to the "small and medium-sized houses" of "my . . . youth" (*BR*, 153). He says he met Anson in 1917, just after Anson had departed from Yale, and they were reunited as "young officers" at Pensacola (*BR*, 154).

Their subsequent meetings impress us as perfunctory, with two exceptions. The first is worth quoting:

> I was working in New York that spring, and I used to lunch with him at the Yale Club, which my university was sharing until the completion of our own. I had read of Paula's marriage, and one afternoon, when I asked him about her, something moved him to tell me the story. After that he frequently invited me to family dinners at his house and behaved as though there was a special relation between us, as though with his confidence a little of that consuming memory had passed into me. (*BR*, 165)

The second important encounter between observer and observed occurs aboard the *Paris* headed abroad. Anson, now thirty (like Nick), introduces the narrator to another anonymous person, the girl with the red tam, who then consumes nearly all of Anson's time. The narrator explains: "I don't think he was ever happy unless some one was in love with him . . . to nurse and protect that superiority he cherished in his heart" (*BR*, 187).

So ends a tale during which the observed confides in the observer while the observer, through references to "me," "you," "we," and "us," confides in the audience. As "that superiority" suggests, these latter confidences are opinionated. Fitzgerald's narrator defends this at the outset: "The only way I can describe young Anson Hunter is to approach him as if he were a foreigner and cling stubbornly to my point of view. If I accept his for a moment I am lost—I have nothing to show but a preposterous movie" (*BR*, 153). Consequently, we learn how Hunter and the rich "are different from you and me," they being "soft where we are hard, and cynical where we are trustful" (*BR*, 152). Aside from making subjective pronouncements, the narrator reveals few, if any, personal traits.

Unlike Jay Gatsby, the title figure of "The Rich Boy" is also its protagonist. We are given considerable biographical data about him, especially about the eight or so years the narrative emphasizes. We hear of Anson Hunter's childhood, his Yale career, his war service, his love life, his Wall Street activities, his family, his travels. The target of an

in-depth psychological examination, Anson possesses several sometimes incongruous aspects, mixing "solidity and self-indulgence . . .
sentiment and cynicism" (*BR*, 160). He combines popularity and loneliness, cruelty and helpfulness, vitality and sadness, according to the
narrator, who insists, "Begin with an individual, and before you know
it you find that you have created a type; begin with a type and you
find that you have created nothing. . . . There are no types, no plurals.
There is a rich boy, and this is his and not his brother's story" (*BR*,
152).

"Literary in college" (*GG*, 4), Nick Carraway, another perfect confidant, is a self-conscious narrator too, at one point mentioning "what
I have written so far" (*GG*, 56), yet, contrary to the anonymous raconteur of "The Rich Boy," he embodies active participation more than
passive observation. This earlier middle-class outsider with Ivy League
credentials inverts Gatsby's quest, for Nick—a second Young Man
from the Provinces—flees both femme fatale and Eastern wealth. Or-
dinary biographer of his extraordinary neighbor, the individuated and
flexible bond salesman matures through scrutinizing the vague and
static bootlegger during their summer together. Therefore, Nick becomes Fitzgerald's real hero while the title figure remains only the ostensible hero. Romantic quester perishes, but realistic quester returns
home (the Midwest), ironically completing the monomythic journey
whose circularity confirms life. Horatio-like, he must reveal Gatsby's
history to our "harsh world," and so the novel, if not the story, has a
discernible major motive.

John A. Higgins faults Fitzgerald for including too much summary
in "The Rich Boy." The story is a chronicle rather than a drama, however, and thus lacks the plot elements—conflict, crisis, climax—necessary to the theatrical novel preceding it. Though summary and scene
are not as well balanced in the Hunter tale, Anson dominates several
scenes replete with dialogue: for instance, at Hempstead, at Palm
Beach, at Port Washington, at the Plaza Hotel, at Rye. Only at sea does
the narrator also participate.

"The Rich Boy" is a framed fiction, its prologue (section 1) and
epilogue (section 8) focused on the relationship between chronicler and
chronicled. Because the enclosed sections (2–7) also concern their relationship, the framework lacks the tonal contrast, the symbolic meaning, and the dramatic impact that the juxtaposed landscapes of "The
Ice Palace," "The Diamond as Big as the Ritz," and *The Great Gatsby*

achieve. Peter Wolfe believes that the novella "has two competing designs":

> In the first, Part I is a prologue, written as a narrative, and Part VIII is a dramatic epilogue; the action extends from Part II to Part VII. The competing design, breaking the story at its halfway point at the end of Part IV, introduces moral commentary. Each of the story's two halves ends with a combined birth and death. . . . The meaning of his failure hits home in Part VIII, a coda or reworking of earlier elements in his wasted life. This reworking gives the combined birth-and-death of part VIII much more force than that of Part IV, which occupied but two paragraphs. (Bryer, 246).

Clearly, the implied author, not the observer-narrator (whether reliable or unreliable, central or peripheral) created these "competing designs," just as he alternated Gatsby's activities between Manhattan and Long Island, while "The Rich Boy," more nearly resembling "May Day" in this respect, focuses only on the first location. Here, too, characters wander aimlessly about, with Anson strolling from the Yale Club "up Madison Avenue and over to Fifth" (*BR*, 169) in one sequence, and visiting the Plaza Hotel, Edna's house, a Fifty-third Street nightclub, and Fifth Avenue (again) in another. Near Central Park, he remembers that "his name had flourished" in the city over "five generations" and had become permanently "identified . . . with the spirit of New York" (*BR*, 177).

All the Sad Young Men is well named, since virtually all the inclusions do, indeed, treat "young men of my generation in rather unhappy moods." Throughout the commercial pieces, they are sad because their wives are neurotic, foolish, and indolent, but during the serious ones (except for "Absolution"), they suffer unrequited love. Other familiar elements are repeated: the autobiographical background and biographical foreground; the mixed third-person perspective; the framed narrative; the middle-class emphasis; the varied settings. Characters still lead fantasy lives, but now the author, whose simpler plots require fewer divisions, almost never invokes his "second manner." Whereas *Flappers and Philosophers* and *Tales of the Jazz Age* contain three major stories together, *All the Sad Young Men* alone boasts the same number. These constitute the *Gatsby* cluster, yet remain independent works of art.

Taps at Reveille

During the nine years between *The Great Gatsby* and *Tender Is the Night* (1934), Scott Fitzgerald published fifty-odd stories. Eighteen, or twice the amount of any previous collection, appeared in *Taps at Reveille* (1935). All but three—"Crazy Sunday" (*American Mercury*), "The Night at Chancellorsville" (*Esquire*), and "The Fiend" (*Esquire*)—were *Saturday Evening Post* contributions. He did not include such superior pieces as "One Trip Abroad" and "The Swimmers"; nor did he include "Jacob's Ladder" because, as he wrote actress Lois Moran, "I found that I had so thoroughly disemboweled ['Jacob's Ladder'] of its best descriptions for 'Tender Is the Night' that it would be offering an empty shell" (*Correspondence*, 403). Although it contained two major stories ("Babylon Revisited" and "Crazy Sunday") and several good ones ("The Last of the Belles" and the Basil Duke Lee selections), the volume elicited mixed reviews and sold only a few thousand copies.

That *Taps at Reveille* is continuous with the previous Scribner collections becomes obvious when we glance at "The Last of the Belles." Not only does the story conclude the Tarleton trilogy by reintroducing Sally Carrol Happer of "The Ice Palace" and Nancy Lamar of "The Jelly-Bean," but it extends themes and techniques often manifested in Fitzgerald's fiction since the apprentice work. Among these are femme fatale/*homme manqué*, rich girl/poor boy, first-person observer, North vs. South, and lost youth.

Ostensible protagonist Ailie Calhoun was the pure "Southern type" because "she had the adroitness sugarcoated with sweet, voluble simplicity, the suggested background of devoted fathers, brothers and admirers stretching back into the South's heroic age." Consequently, "there were notes in her voice that ordered slaves around, that withered up Yankee captains." Numerous World War I officers futilely pursue Georgia's nineteen-year-old blonde—a fictional counterpart of Alabama's Zelda. When an aviator commits suicide over the girl, "her brow went up in what can only be described as mock despair." Ailie is later engaged to "a man in Cincinnati" and "a man from Savannah."

Throughout these abortive liaisons, the word "sincere" recurs, meaning only "some special way she wanted to be regarded" rather than "constancy," for "she felt most security with men . . . who were incapable of passing judgments on the . . . aristocratic heart."

A "white pillared veranda" indicates that the last belle is affluent as well as aristocratic. Ailie's ingrained snobbishness surfaces during an encounter with Lieutenant Earl Schoen and Kitty Preston. She asserts that Schoen "looked like a street-car conductor," then poses her "breeding" against the "commonness" of the other girl. Snobbish too, the Harvard-educated narrator concedes "natural grace" and a "magnificent body" to Schoen, yet considers him "illiterate" and "bumptious." He comments: "Exteriorly Earl had about everything wrong with him that could be imagined. . . . It wasn't as though he had been shiny and poor, but the background of mill-town dance halls and outing clubs flamed out at you—or rather at Ailie." Less an *homme manqué* than most other suitors, Schoen accepts rejection stoically by terming the Southern siren "too much of a highbrow for me."

Just as Ailie is one among many central women in *Taps at Reveille*, the real protagonist, twenty-three-year-old Andy, is one among many first-person narrators. He loves the last belle throughout their relationship; she does not love him "that way at all," and so never kisses, much less marries, the Northerner who "became her confidant instead." Presumably about unrequited love, this tale is actually about the observer-participant's fondness for what Ailie embodies. He admits loving Tarleton in section 1, and, in section 2, he nostalgically recreates his final night there fifteen years ago:

> We drove through pine woods heavy with lichen and Spanish moss, and between the fallow cotton fields along a road white as the rim of the world. We parked under the broken shadow of a mill where there was the sound of running water and restive squawky birds and over everything a brightness that tried to filter in anywhere—into the lost nigger cabins, the automobile, the fastnesses of the heart. The South sang to us—I wonder if they remember. I remember— the cool pale faces, the somnolent amorous eyes and the voices.

Later Andy muses, "I suppose that poetry is a Northern man's dream of the South."

Just as Ailie embodies the South, the South embodies the "midsummer world of my early twenties, where time had stood still." The story ends tragically with Fitzgerald's narrator searching amid refuse for his vanished youth. He concludes, "All I could be sure of was this place that had once been so full of life and effort was gone, . . . and that in another month Ailie would be gone, and the South would be empty forever."

The title *Taps at Reveille* neatly sums up the transitional nature of the fourth and last Scribner collection, since "taps" suggests movement backward to the illusioned world culminating in *The Great Gatsby*, while "reveille" suggests movement forward to the disillusioned world culminating in *Tender Is the Night*. Both worlds are prefigured by short satellite fictions, but the *Tender* group is more extensive; Anthony Bryant Mangum has classified its seventeen pieces variously under "European Setting," "Character Study," and "General Cluster."[53] Four were selected for *Taps at Reveille*: "Two Wrongs," "Majesty," "One Interne," and "Babylon Revisited." "One Interne," a marginal story, is not discussed here; "Babylon Revisited" receives separate treatment in the next section.

Both "Two Wrongs" and "Majesty" were composed in 1929 when Fitzgerald was writing *Tender Is the Night*, and they explore motifs germane to the novel. For instance, "Two Wrongs," like other stories from this period, treats an older man (twenty-six-year-old Bill McChesney) courting a younger woman (eighteen-year-old Emmy Pinkard), foreshadowing the affair between Dick Diver and Rosemary Hoyt. After Bill marries Emmy, as Dick marries Nicole Warren, vitality shifts, he becoming passive and she becoming active. He is a self-confessed "hick" who wants "to be the Marquis of McChesney," yet his rich acquaintances on Long Island and in England waste his energy. Eventually, diseased Bill, heading West toward death, must leave Emmy behind at their Manhattan residence alive and well. He has lost control through dissipation; she has acquired character through work.

For Arthur Mizener, the "emotional bankruptcy" McChesney suffers was "the most pervasive idea [Fitzgerald] ever had."[54] Fitzgerald himself implies as much in his essay "Handle With Care," where he describes his own "crack-up" as "an over-extension of the flank, a burning of the candle at both ends; a call upon physical resources that I did not command, like a man over-drawing at his bank. . . . a feeling that I was standing at twilight on a deserted range, with an empty rifle in my hands and the targets down" (*CU*, 77–78). Fourteen years earlier *The Beautiful and Damned*—in which the phrase "lesion of vitality" had first appeared—not only demonstrated how emotional bankruptcy resulted from personal relationships, hedonistic activities, and unsettled times (1920s prosperity, 1930s depression), but also presented its manifestations: drinking, brawling, infidelity, racial prejudice.

"Emotional bankruptcy" is most eloquently, most trenchantly dramatized in Fitzgerald's fourth novel. We are told that between the time Dick discovers Nicole "flowering under a stone on the Zürichsee" and the time he first meets Rosemary, "the spear had been blunted."[55] Dick's emotional bankruptcy, "a lesion of enthusiasm" (*TN*, 208) and "a process of deterioration" (*TN*, 283), is exhibited in ways already mentioned. There is a general physical decline, as he loses his once superb strength and energy. There is a moral decline too. He becomes sexually promiscuous, falling in love "with every pretty woman" (*TN*, 201) he sees. An argument with a taxicab driver results in a brawl that lands him in jail. He drinks heavily and develops prejudices: "He would suddenly unroll a long scroll of contempt for some person, race, class, way of life, way of thinking" (*TN*, 265). Dr. Diver degenerates from the serious, brilliant professional whose learned articles have been standard in their line, whose ambition was "to be a good psychologist— maybe to be the greatest one that ever lived" (*TN*, 130–31), to an absolute failure. He returns to America "to be a quack . . . only a shell to which nothing matters but survival as long as possible with the old order" (Fitzgerald's notes in Mizener, 309).

Similarly, when Bill McChesney of "Two Wrongs" meets obscure ballerina Emmy Pinkard, he stands on top the theatrical profession, having produced in just three years "nine shows—four big hits—only one flop." A friend observes after another three years that Bill, now married, consorts with dukes and ladies, but has "had two flops in New York." This decline continues until he becomes tubercular, while physically and mentally well Emmy, whose "fine health and vitality" sustain him, works hard to dance at the Metropolitan. Bill "was drinking too much" even before they were married; later, he becomes an abusive alcoholic.

His emotional bankruptcy, his crack-up, climaxes in section 3 of the four-part story, where he drinks several highballs, then crashes Lady Sybil's party. Two footmen bounce Bill, and a nightmarish spree ensues. Meanwhile, Emmy "had fallen down at the door of the hospital, trying to get out of the taxicab alone." She gives birth to their stillborn child.

Significantly, this climactic episode transpires in London, not New York (sections 1 and 4) or Atlantic City (section 2). Europe also provides the setting for Dick Diver's deterioration. But whereas anti-European remarks like "British ladies took to piecing themselves together out of literature" appear in only one section of "Two Wrongs," they pervade *Tender Is the Night*, whose continental aristocracy, after losing its power and prestige through World War I, has grown degenerate. There we find Lady Caroline Sibley-Biers, a "fragile" and "tubercular" Englishwoman, bearing aloft "the pennon of decadence; the last ensign of the fading empire" (*TN*, 268). There we also find Tommy Barban, half-French and "utterly aristocratic," who, as "the end product of an archaic world" (*TN*, 35), has served the cause of the nobility almost everywhere by killing Russian communists. Barban's efforts notwithstanding, the cause of the European elite is futile. Displaced and financially insolvent, it develops a penchant for wealthy Americans, a group very happy for an opportunity to mingle with it, a group typified by the Anglophile Baby Warren. McKisco's experience with the American rich, with people like the Warrens—a "ducal family without a title" (*TN*, 157)—is that they have taken from the English "their uncertain and fumbling snobbery, their delight in ignorance, and their deliberate rudeness" (*TN*, 35). Both groups are wasting away in hotels, sanitariums, tuberculosis resorts, and psychiatric clinics.

Another four-part effort anticipates *Tender Is the Night*'s international theme even more fully than "Two Wrongs." In "Majesty," Emily Castledon, "one of America's perfect types," "moved abroad, where she did various fashionable things." After "wandering the continents looking for happiness," she returns home determined to get married, but deserts William Brevoort Blair at the altar. He then weds her cousin Olive, and, like the emissaries in James's *The Ambassadors*, they are asked by one parent to bring the errant offspring back from Europe, where she has joined a "dissipated ne'er-do-well . . . Prince Gabriel Petrocobesco," recently "invited by the police to leave Paris." This "fat little fellow with an attractive leer and a quenchless thirst" had "moved around Europe for several years," sponging off Americans, though currently "even the most outlying circles of international society were closed to him." The Blairs locate Emily and her companion in Czjeck-Hansa, Petrocobesco's "native country," which he will rule. Since "Tutu" is king rather than prince now, she consents to become his wife. Subsequently, the new queen adorns a royal cavalcade possessing "the glamour shed always by the old empire of half the world, by her ships and ceremonies, her pomps and symbols." Brevoort comments, "It's all so silly," and Olive retorts, "I suppose so," while filled with "helpless adoration."

Two other stories in *Taps at Reveille*, "One Interne" and "Family in the Wind," resemble *Tender Is the Night* in their focus on the medical profession. Another pair, "A Short Trip Home" and "The Fiend," are melodramas about criminals. More noteworthy is "The Night at Chancellorsville," which like "The Fiend" illustrates Fitzgerald's exclusive style. Each of these stories, cast in one section, first ran in *Esquire*, earning the author $250, in contrast to the $3,500 the *Saturday Evening Post* paid for each of the three- to six-part stories collected in *Taps*. John A. Higgins discusses their formal properties:

> Despite its derivative nature "The Fiend" does mark the "new" Fitzgerald in that it is told briefly and almost entirely in summary, with only two short dialog scenes and a five-line epilog. Though its time span is thirty years, it contains only about 2,400 words—one-third as many as his typical *Post* story. . . . in contrast to his earlier stories he refrains from all interpretation of character and action. . . . It is here and in the ending that Fitzgerald makes use of the indirection which he so admired in Hemingway and which marks the best pieces in his late style.
>
> In structure and setting the story is stark: the monolithic plot focuses squarely on the simple revenge theme without any of the distracting minor characters or complicating incidents typical of Fitzgerald's earlier work. There is virtually no description of settings and little of characters. . . .
>
> The second *Esquire* story, "The Night at Chancellorsville" . . . maintains most of the technical changes of "The Fiend" and adds others that will become characteristic of Fitzgerald's late style. Like "The Fiend" it is quite brief (under 2,000 words) and unembellished; it relies on indirection for characterization and maintains an objective authorial attitude. In addition, the story centers on a single episode and leans heavily on dialog. (Higgins, 160–61).

When we compare the manner of these two stories with that of the Basil and Josephine offerings in the same volume—typified by an intrusive author, numerous mechanical divisions, rhetorical flourishes, multiple episodes, secondary characters, and so on—we immediately perceive *Taps at Reveille* as a collection linking Fitzgerald's inclusive and exclusive styles as well as his early and late concerns.

"Babylon Revisited"

Throughout his fictional career, Fitzgerald used both first- and third-person perspectives. *Taps at Reveille* demonstrates the alternation better than *All the Sad Young Men*, since the earlier book has only one first-person story ("The Rich Boy") whereas the later has five first-person and five third-person stories, exclusive of the third-person Basil and Josephine group.

Commenting on another familiar juxtaposition, David Toor cites lapses in narrative focus in "Babylon Revisited" (1931) when Fitzgerald "shifts from limited to omniscient" voice—lapses "concerned with the Peters," particularly Marion.[56] For instance, just one brief paragraph of direct speech separates third-person unlimited (omniscient) and third-person limited (central intelligence) paragraphs below:

> Marion shuddered suddenly; part of her saw that Charlie's feet were planted on the earth now, and her own maternal feeling recognized the naturalness of his desire but she had lived for a long time with a prejudice—a prejudice founded on a curious disbelief in her sister's happiness, and which, in the shock of one terrible night, had turned to hatred for him. It had all happened at a point in her life where the discouragement of ill health and adverse circumstances made it necessary for her to believe in tangible villainy and a tangible villain.
>
> "I can't help what I think!" she cried out suddenly. "How much you were responsible for Helen's death, I don't know. It's something you'll have to square with your own conscience."
>
> An electric current of agony surged through him; for a moment he was almost on his feet, an unuttered sound echoing in his throat. He hung on to himself for a moment, another moment. (*BR*, 222)

Narrative focus moves in this sequence from what the implied author alone can know to what his protagonist, through whose eyes we otherwise view the action, hears, then feels. Thus perspective changes, causing momentary inconsistency, not unlike first-person storytellers reporting conversations they never witnessed. Such commonplace technical "lapses," which may sometimes be unavoidable, remain undetected by most readers.

Choosing the central intelligence over the omniscient as the dominant point of view in "Babylon Revisited" represents a felicitous decision on Fitzgerald's part (as Roy R. Male points out in part 3) because it emphasizes the conflict between the solid but dull present-day Charles J. Wales and the livelier but self-destructive "good-time" Charlie Wales of the past. This psychic struggle pitting Charles against Charlie becomes dramatic through exaggerated objectification of the protagonist's divided nature, Charles embodied by responsible but narrow Marion and Lincoln (present) and Charlie by irresponsible but tolerant Lorraine and Duncan (past), with the women functioning as extreme manifestations of the two poles. (Although he refers to himself as "Charles," he is called "Charlie" throughout the story, probably because that is how people from the past still perceive him.)

Tension mounts in section 4 when Charlie lunches with Lincoln, who explains: "I think Marion felt there was some kind of injustice in it—you not even working toward the end, and getting richer and richer." He then receives a *pneumatique* from Lorraine, who reminds him, "We *did* have such good times that crazy spring, like the night you and I stole the butcher's tricycle, and the time we tried to call on the president and you had the old derby rim and the wire cane" (*BR*, 224–25). Later in section 4 the action climaxes as childless Lorraine and Duncan crash the Rue Palatine apartment of the Peters family while Charlie is paying a third and final visit. Unmistakably drunk, "They were gay, they were hilarious, they were roaring with laughter." He cannot understand how these intruders had secured the address, apparently forgetting he had left a message for them. Lorraine proposes dinner, Charlie refuses, and she says, "All right we'll go. But I remember once when you hammered on my door at four A.M. I was enough of a good sport to give you a drink" (*BR*, 227). Meanwhile, Marion has retreated, one arm protectively around her little girl, another around her little boy. Soon the section comes full circle with the men together again. Lincoln observes, "That kind of people make [Marion] really physically sick," and Charlie lies, "I didn't tell them to come here. They wormed your name out of somebody" (*BR*, 228).

If "Babylon Revisited" contains "a Catholic slant" involving "sin," "guilt," "penance," and "redemption" (Higgins, 123), this pattern was consummated before the action commences. "Reformed sinner" (*BR*, 220) Charlie first arrived in Paris three years ago. For the first eighteen months he misbehaved, until "that terrible February night" (*BR*, 223). His wife died; he went first to a sanitarium, then to Prague. During the past eighteen months Charlie has taken just one drink per day. That is not unusual, though, as "I never did drink heavily until I gave up business and came over here with nothing to do," and "my drinking only lasted about a year and a half" (*BR*, 220). Marion ignores "how hard I worked for seven years" (*BR*, 224) prior to the French debacle, he tells Lincoln, indicating that his original, responsible self had been briefly superseded by a temporary, irresponsible self.

Like "The Ice Palace," "Babylon Revisited" is a geographical journey that confirms rather than transforms identity. Both are crucibles imposed unconsciously by protagonal questers. Consequently, Charlie inquires after Mr. Schaeffer at the outset, yet makes no mention of this college pal or of Miss Quarrles at the end when he tellingly phones the Peters residence. Between these events, the past that Duncan and Lorraine symbolize is renounced once and for all. The purge begins when Charlie, who informs his daughter, Honoria, "My name is Charles J. Wales of Prague" (*BR*, 216), rejects their proposals twice during the "unwelcome" encounters of section 2, realizing that "they liked him because he was functioning, because he was serious; they wanted to see him, because he was stronger than they were now, because they wanted to draw a certain sustenance from his strength" (*BR*, 217–18). Next day, as Charlie remembers how "trite, blurred, worn away" Lorraine had appeared, "he emphatically did not want to see her" (*BR*, 225–26), and later still in section 4, where the "cagy business" about the address arises, Charlie snubs Lorraine and Duncan one final time. That he has confirmed his true nature becomes clear when he contemplates the Peters family immediately afterwards: "It was warm here, it was a home, people together by a fire. The children felt very safe and important; the mother and father were serious, watchful" (*BR*, 226). He departs, murmuring, "Goodnight, dear children" (*BR*, 229). Custody of his daughter may be denied him for six months or more, yet Charlie, turning down a drink right before the story terminates, regains Honor, if not Honoria.

This self-imposed trial or confirmation journey is bracketed by a framework, the structural form Fitzgerald adopted in six of his eight major stories. Here, the quester's return to Paris begins and ends at the Ritz bar, emblematic of American dissipation during the 1920s boom and of French desolation during the Great Depression. Opening and closing frames emphasize the past and its disastrous effects, with Charlie inquiring about former acquaintances (1) and recalling catastrophic events (5). Between these circular Ritz episodes, three additional sections and twelve additional scenes transpire linearly over "four or five days" (*BR*, 211). "Babylon Revisited," similar to "May Day," whose framework consisted of hotels, moves quickly on foot or by taxi along mazelike streets containing public places such as the Ritz bar, Bricktop's, Zelli's, the Poet's Cave, Le Grand Vatel, the Empire, and Griffons. They are juxtaposed with one private setting, the Rue Palatine apartment, where lengthy confrontations between Charlie and Marion occur in sections 1, 3, and 4. Throughout the narrative, a single bygone incident—the locking out of his wife, Helen—determines the contemporary situation.[57]

Fitzgerald's statement, "My recent experience parallels the wave of despair that swept the nation when the boom was over" (*CU*, 84), implies the lifelong identification he made between autobiographical and historical phenomena. This equation greatly enriches "Babylon Revisited" and other tales. In section 5 Charlie and barman Paul, "who in the latter days of the bull market had come to work in his own custom-built car" (*BR*, 211), hold the following conversation:

> "I heard that you lost a lot in the crash."
> "I did," and [Charlie] added grimly, "but I lost everything I wanted in the boom."
> "Selling short."
> "Something like that." (*BR*, 219)

Their exchange climaxes the narrative's numerous stock market allusions. Better than any other, "selling short" tacitly compares public financial and private moral transactions, since the first is a macrocosm of the second and the second is a microcosm of the first. Protagonist and market collapse together as inseparable entities (*crack-up* equals *crash*), emotional bankruptcy mirroring economic bankruptcy. While the world at large recovers from its Depression, Charlie occupies a sanitarium. Ironically, he and his compatriots lost more during the boom than during the crash because moral depletion transcends financial depletion. Toward the end, customer asks barman, "What do I owe you?" then thinks, "they couldn't make him pay forever" (*BR*, 230). In tandem these comments suggest two kinds of currency, one material, one spiritual.

Ruminative Charlie identifies with boom behavior after the "selling short" remark:

> Again the memory of those days swept over him like a nightmare—the people they had met travelling; then people who couldn't add a row of figures or speak a coherent sentence. The little man Helen

had consented to dance with at the ship's party, who had insulted
her ten feet from the table; the women and girls carried screaming
with drink or drugs out of public places—
   —The men who locked their wives out in the snow, because the
snow of twenty-nine wasn't real snow. If you didn't want it to be
snow, you just paid some money. (*BR*, 229)

The second paragraph, which locates an individual deed within the
context of group psychology, touches upon the bygone incident deter-
mining present action. This incident epitomizes the story's emotional
bankruptcy. Charlie and Helen "had senselessly begun to abuse each
other's love, tear it into shreds." "On that terrible February night,"
they quarrelled, she "kissed young Webb," and he angrily locked their
door. Confused Helen returned amid a snowstorm later wearing slippers. She escaped pneumonia, husband and wife reconciled, yet this
"was the beginning of the end" (*BR*, 223). Shutting her out "didn't fit
in with any other act of his life but the tricycle incident did," Charlie
admits after receiving Lorraine's note and before asking himself, "How
many weeks or months of dissipation to arrive at that condition of utter
irresponsibility?" (*BR*, 225).
   Earlier he had "realized the meaning of the word 'dissipate'—to dissipate into thin air; to make nothing out of something" (*BR*, 214).
Synonymous with emotional bankruptcy, it too has monetary connotations: "In the little hours of the night every move from place to place
was an enormous human jump, an increase of paying for the privilege
of slower and slower motion" (*BR*, 214–15). Charlie remembers "thou-
sand-franc notes given to an orchestra for playing a single number,
hundred-franc notes tossed to a doorman for calling a cab." He ironically concludes:

   It hadn't been given for nothing.
   It had been given, even the most wildly squandered sum, as an
   offering to destiny that he might not remember the things most
   worth remembering, the things that now he would always remember—his child taken from his control, his wife escaped to a grave in
   Vermont. (*BR*, 215)

Like Bill McChesney of "Two Wrongs," Charlie Wales follows the
pattern later immortalized by Dick Diver in *Tender Is the Night*—work,
success, inaction, dissipation, illness—but whereas McChesney per-

ishes and Diver vanishes, Wales recovers, indicating that the other two fictions are less optimistic than "Babylon Revisited." Why? Because Charlie, who had always worked hard, resumes his professional career in Prague after leaving the sanitarium, no doubt inspired by Honoria. Consequently, he can inform Lincoln, "I'm bringing my sister over from America next month to keep house for me. My income last year was bigger than it was when I had money" (*BR*, 213). Money is evil, then, only if unearned (for example, during the boom or with the rich), since under that condition people abandon the actual to seize upon the fantastic, snow that "wasn't real snow" (*BR*, 229). While capitalism implicitly represents the negative pole of Fitzgerald's brief masterpiece, character explicitly represents the positive pole. Old-fashioned Charlie "believed in character; he wanted to jump back a whole generation and trust in character again as the eternally valuable element. Everything else wore out" (*BR*, 214).

Besides enabling the author to internalize the conflict between the two sides of the protagonal nature, third-person limited perspective enabled him here, as in "The Ice Palace," to internalize opposing landscapes. This opposition, which previously focused on one geographical area (the North) versus another (the South), now focuses on Europe, the setting where Americans most often become emotional bankrupts. If the Charlie/Charles dichotomy was objectified by irresponsible Lorrain and Duncan and responsible Marion and Lincoln, it is also dramatized through Paris before and after the crash. They are, simultaneously, the repository of historical events and the origin of mental states.

In "May Day" Philip Dean calls Gordon Sterrett "morally as well as financially" bankrupt. His and Charlie's self-destructive circular journeys involve iniquitous urban environments that breed dissipation. Just as John Dos Passos compared New York City to ancient metropolises like Babylon, Nineveh, Athens, Rome, and Constantinople in *Manhattan Transfer*, Scott Fitzgerald's Paris resembles "Babylon Revisited." These titles reflect the centrality of metaphorical place.

The *Encyclopedic Dictionary of the Bible* tells how Babylon's rise and fall exemplified "the progressive degeneration of mankind before the time of Abraham."[58] Certainly, Babylonian confusion and degeneration characterize precrash Paris.

The last sentence of Fitzgerald's story reads, "He was absolutely sure Helen wouldn't have wanted him to be so alone" (230). This private isolation had commenced during the first Ritz bar scene, which had opened with questions: "And where's Mr. Campbell?" "And George Hardt?" To Charlie, then an exile, "the stillness . . . was strange and portentous." No longer could he see the doorman "in a frenzy of activity"; no longer could he hear multiple voices from "the once-clamorous women's room" (*BR*, 210). His loneliness is mirrored all through "Babylon Revisited" by similar postcrash desolation. Thus, "Zelli's was closed, the bleak and sinister cheap hotels surrounding it were dark; up in the Rue Blanche there was more light and a local, colloquial French crowd. The Poet's Cave had disappeared, but the two great mouths of the Café of Heaven and the Café of Hell still yawned—even devoured, as he watched, the meager contents of a tourist bus—a German, a Japanese, and an American couple who glanced at him with frightened eyes" (*BR*, 214).

Like Bill McChesney, Dick Diver, and other emotional bankrupts, Charlie Wales knows that the fruits of interconnected personal and cultural disorder are what T. S. Eliot had termed "Shape without form, shade without colour, / Paralyzed force, gesture without motion." Only he among Fitzgerald's "hollow men" will escape this death-in-life paralysis, since only he possesses "character."

"Crazy Sunday"

"Babylon Revisited" contains much autobiographical data. Honoria derives her name from the daughter of Fitzgerald companions Sara and Gerald Murphy, though she more closely resembles his own child Scottie. He did not lose Scottie after Zelda broke down (compare the sanitarium allusions), but sister-in-law Rosalind, to whom he sent the typescript, had advocated that and so became rigid Marion Peters. Many of the other stories in *Taps at Reveille* include private facts: for instance, South Carolinian Emmy Pinkard of "Two Wrongs" studies Russian ballet under Paul Makova, as Zelda Fitzgerald did under Madame Lubov Egorova, and "The Last of the Belles" narrator Andy is stationed outside Tarleton, Georgia, as officer Scott was stationed outside Montgomery, Alabama. Most apparent, perhaps, are the personal references incorporated in the Basil and Josephine stories:

> The dates during which the stories take place—the earliest in 1909 while Basil is still attending Mrs. Cary's Academy, the last in the fall he enrolls at Yale—tally exactly with Fitzgerald's life from his last

year in Buffalo to his enrollment at Princeton. White Bear Lake, where Fitzgerald spent part of his summers . . . becomes Black Bear Lake; "The Captured Shadow," the play Fitzgerald wrote and produced in 1912, is the same play Basil writes and produces the same year; the note in Fitzgerald's "Ledger," September, 1911, "Attended State Fair and took children on rollercoaster," refers to the same fair that Basil attends the same fall; even the small size of Newman Academy (actually only sixty pupils) is used in the Basil story in which St. Regis loses valiantly to Exeter. (Eble, 72)

In 1959 actress Laurette Taylor's son Dwight published an article important because it shows such real phenomena being transmuted within the context of Fitzgerald's last major story, "Crazy Sunday" (1932). Both men, who had met back East, came West to work for Irving Thalberg at MGM Studios. One day, as "the only two writers invited," they attended a Thalberg beach party. Since there had been trepidation about hiring an alcoholic, Taylor watched over his famous friend, yet the latter vanished and soon returned drunk. Taylor introduced him to Robert Montgomery, who was wearing "white riding breeches and black boots," and Fitzgerald insulted the actor, inquiring, "Why didn't you bring your horse in?" Afterward, he sang some silly canine lyrics, accompanied by Ramon Novarro after hostess Norma Shearer (Mrs. Thalberg) had supplied her dog. "The song was so inadequate to the occasion, or, indeed, to any occasion, that I could think of, that the company stood frozen in their places, wondering how to extricate themselves from an unbearable situation." Jack Gilbert and Lupe Velez hissed, then the scene took "on the quality of a nightmare where everyone seemed doomed to remain frozen in his place forever." Next morning at the studio, Fitzgerald received a telegram from Miss Shearer; it said, "Dear Scott: I think you were the nicest person at my party." He was nevertheless fired "the following Saturday." When "Crazy Sunday" finally appeared, Taylor reacted as follows:

I hied myself to the nearest newsstand and bought the magazine [*American Mercury*]. The story was by F. Scott Fitzgerald. It was about two writers who had been asked to a big party at the beach house of a famous motion picture producer. One of them gets drunk and makes a jackass of himself by singing an unsolicited song. In a carefully delineated passage at the beginning of the story, giving a description of his appearance, and an oblique reference to his famous mother, there is no mistaking the fact that this unfortunate drunk is supposed to be *me!* Scott is the Good Samaritan who takes him home. The truth is turned topsy-turvy, as in *Alice Through the Looking Glass.* To make matters worse, once Scott has convinced himself that *I* am Joel Coles, rather than he, the story opens up into a veritable flower of fantasy, in which the unruly guest has an affair with his hostess, and the motion picture tycoon is killed in an airplane accident while they are in bed together.[59]

This paragraph unconsciously implies that the Fitzgerald method of creating literature from life depended on two artistic strategies. The first, his "double vision," or what Dos Passos called the "intimacy and detachment" permitting him simultaneously to participate and to observe, has already been mentioned. The second, "composite characterization," is the related device found objectionable here. Taylor's good-natured complaint about inverting the screenwriters echoes the humorless grievance Hemingway lodged after Fitzgerald had used both himself and Zelda *and* Gerald and Sara Murphy for Dick and Nicole in *Tender Is the Night.* Hemingway argued that he had tampered with the Murphys, changed them into something different, something they were not in real life. However, Fitzgerald reminded Hemingway, long before he had attempted "composite characterization" "the feat of building a monument out of three kinds of marble was brought off" by William Shakespeare (*Letters,* 309). Figures like Joel Coles—a Taylor-Fitzgerald amalgam—reflect their own as well as their creator's experiences and emotions, giving the work added richness while preserving its objectivity.

Fitzgerald's interest in motion pictures went back at least as far as 1919, when he wrote a number of rejected scripts. Then he sold four stories to Hollywood: "Head and Shoulders," "Myra Meets His Family," "The Offshore Pirate," and "The Camel's Back." In 1923, Alan Margolies informs us, the novelist "received $10,000 for writing a treatment of *This Side of Paradise,* but the film was never made. He also wrote the titles for the 1923 film *The Glimpses of the Moon* based on Edith Wharton's novel. . . . Finally, that same year he wrote the story for the Film Guild production of *Grit*" (Bryer, 70). By the time Fitzgerald took the first of three California sojourns in January 1927 to tackle the unproduced United Artists picture "Lipstick," he had become an experienced amateur. His second trip, in the fall of 1931, when Fitzgerald abortively helped Taylor adapt *Red-Headed Woman* under Irving Thalberg, engendered "Crazy Sunday." And his last trip during July 1937 involved a large, renewed MGM contract that covered *Three Comrades* (Fitzgerald's sole screen credit), "Infidelity," *Marie Antoinette, The Women,* and *Madame Curie. Gone with the Wind, Winter Carnival,* and free-lance assignments at Paramount, Universal, Twentieth Century-Fox, Goldwyn, and Columbia followed.

Cosmopolitan, the film version of "Babylon Revisited" for which independent producer Lester Cowan paid Fitzgerald $6,000 ($1,000 for the rights and $5,000 for writing the screen version), represents Fitzgerald's last cinematic contribution. His letters to Scottie in 1940 frequently mention it, a typical comment being, "You have earned some money for me this week because I sold 'Babylon Revisited,' in which you are a character, to the pictures (the sum received wasn't worthy of the magnificent story—neither of you nor of me—however, I am accepting it)."[60] Comparing the two versions, critic Aaron Latham has observed: "The basic situation, the problem, in both stories is the same: a father separated from his daughter. But in the short story the father knows from the beginning what he wants: his daughter back. The screenplay, on the other hand, is actually the story of how the father comes to discover his need for that daughter."[61] Despite further differences—the movie's altered plot, the girl's expanded role, the camera's split focus—*Cosmopolitan* is generally considered the best Fitzgerald scenario. Eventually MGM paid Cowan $100,000 for the script and produced it in 1954 with a title borrowed from the Eliot Paul expatriate book *The Last Time I Saw Paris.* Julius J. and Paul G. Epstein were the accredited scenarists. Thus even after his death Hollywood confirmed what the creator of Pat Hobby had him declare almost fifteen years before, that "this was no art, . . . this was an industry," that "they don't want authors. They want writers—like me."

"I seem to have put all the stuff I had on Hollywood into '*Crazy Sunday*' which you couldn't use, + which is in the current *Mercury,*" Fitzgerald wrote Alfred Dashiell, editor of *Scribner's Magazine,* after his second California stay (*Correspondence,* 299). "All" was much and would be more, but though the picture business deeply affected him during the 1930s, he maintained artistic disengagement through double vision and composite characterization. Yet the critical controversy over centrality and reliability pertaining to the first-person "Rich Boy" has also marked third-person "Crazy Sunday," where Joel Coles, like Charlie Wales, functions as central intelligence.

Some analysts feel that the later story divides its focus between observer and observed. There are precedents for the centrality of either, the observer (Nick Carraway) playing protagonist in *The Great Gatsby* and the observed (Anson Hunter) playing protagonist in "The Rich Boy." Here the *Gatsby* mode prevails, with observer Coles dominant and observed Calman secondary. The story of "Crazy Sunday" revolves around the screenwriter, who is omnipresent, rather than the producer, who controls only section 3, if that. We follow him from house party in section 1 to office in section 2; to Riviera apartment, Beverly Hills mansion, and office–conference room in section 3; and to Hollywood Theater and Beverly Hills mansion in sections 4 and 5. Meanwhile he encounters Stella again, shows off, receives her telegram, witnesses Miles's psychological problems and troubled marriage, attends another potentially adulterous rendezvous, and seduces, then abandons, the newly widowed wife. Fitzgerald gives Coles a detailed background missing from Calman: "He was twenty-eight and not yet broken by Hollywood. . . . His mother had been a successful actress; Joel had spent his childhood between London and New York" (*BR*, 231). And because the implied author employs limited third-person perspective, we get the reactions as well as the actions of the screenwriter. On the other hand, even during section 3 the producer is perceived exter-nally—*and by Coles*. Their technical relationship appears thus: "Miles Calman, tall, nervous, with a desperate humor and the unhappiest eyes *Joel ever saw* [emphasis added], was an artist from the top of his curi-ously shaped head to his niggerish feet. Upon these last he stood firmly—he had never made a cheap picture though he had sometimes paid heavily for the luxury of making experimental flops. In spite of his excellent company, *one could not be with him long without realizing* [emphasis added] that he was not a well man" (*BR*, 237–38). Signifi-cantly, too, Miles dies toward the end of "Crazy Sunday," whereas Joel bitterly admits, "Oh, yes, I'll be back—I'll be back!" (*BR*, 248).

For Kenneth G. Johnston, "the key to 'Crazy Sunday'" involves its point of view because "Joel Coles provides the focus of narration, but at the very outset his trustworthiness—that is, his ability to distinguish between appearance and reality—is called into question: the son of a successful actress, 'Joel had spent his childhood . . . trying to separate the real from the unreal.'" His "blunted and uncertain perception" explains "inconsistent portrayal of character," "blurred relationships and motivations," and "structural disharmony." Joel has "lived and worked too long in a world of make-believe." Consequently, "when he comes face to face with genuine, shattering grief, he fails to recognize or to respond to it. The situation is no more real to him than a scene from a film script or a page from a fairy tale."[62] (This "world of make-believe," it should be noted, anticipates Nathanael West's grotesque novel *The Day of the Locust* [1939] by seven years in passages such as the one evoking "the sad, lovely Siamese twins, the mean dwarfs, and the proud giant" at the studio restaurant [*BR*, 237], and the one evoking "obscure replicas of bright, particular stars, spavined men in polo coats, a stomping dervish with the beard and staff of an apostle, a pair of chic Filipinos in collegiate clothes" at the Hollywood Theater [*BR*, 242].) Whereas Johnston labels Joel "the fool," Stanley Grebstein sees in his character an evolution from weakness toward strength (see part 3).

Such ambiguity does not mark Miles Calman, the observed figure that anticipates Monroe Stahr of Fitzgerald's unfinished novel, *The Last Tycoon* (1941). Both Calman and Stahr are Thalberg replicas, and both take two interrelated guises: creative genius and emotional bankrupt. The passage cited earlier depicting Miles as simultaneously incorruptible and unhealthy is the most obvious among several allusions to the predicament of the superior individual destroyed by a corrupt society, which spawns the Dave Silverstein Joel burlesques and the "old Beltzer" Stella mentions. Another passage reads: "He was the only American-born director with both an interesting temperament and an artistic conscience. Meshed in an industry, he paid with his ruined nerves for having no resilience, no healthy cynicism, no refuge—only a pitiful and precarious escape" (*BR*, 247). His "precarious escape"—the adulterous Eva Goebel affair—represents just one symptom of deterioration, for jealous Miles, who undergoes analysis, has many psychological problems, including the classical "mother complex." Nevertheless, Stella loves him enough to make Joel a "pawn in a spite game" (*BR*, 245), unaware how Joel, despite their erotic attachment, regards the Calmans when alone: Miles "even brought that little gamin [Stella] alive and made her a sort of masterpiece" (*BR*, 248). Sleeping together before the weary husband dies would seem to be vicarious on both parts.

Although Monroe Stahr embodies an artist only as Abraham Lincoln was a general, his guidance of motion pictures "way up past the range and power of the theatre" makes him "a marker in industry like Edison and Lumière and Griffith and Chaplin."[63] Concerned about the caliber of his films, Stahr immediately plans improvement after one Negro, whose children are never allowed to see movies, tells the producer they contain "no profit." Fitzgerald said *Tycoon*, unlike *Tender*, is not a "story of deterioration" (*LT,* "Notes," 141); emotional bankruptcy does enter, however. Thirty-four-year-old Stahr grows ill, on the verge of death. Having experienced a "lesion of vitality," he informs narrator Cecilia Brady he would marry her, but he feels "too old and tired to undertake anything" (*LT,* 71). Moreover, procrastination with Kathleen indicates that "his balanced judgment," on which "thousands of people depended" (*LT,* 116), is dulled. He begins to drink and even expresses the desire "to beat up Brimmer" (*LT,* 126). If Stahr's crack-up has resulted from ennui and marriage, it has also been caused by promoting older American values.

Three essays published in *Esquire* between *Tender Is the Night* and *The Last Tycoon*—"The Crack-Up" (February 1936), "Handle with Care" (March 1936), and "Pasting It Together" (April 1936)—record the nervous breakdown Fitzgerald had already fictionalized in "Two Wrongs," "Babylon Revisited," and "Crazy Sunday." That he remained a creative genius like Calman and Stahr throughout his own emotional bankruptcy is apparent from those works.

We should not be surprised, therefore, when Ruth Prigozy says the following about "Babylon Revisited" and "Crazy Sunday":

> In both stories, plot—as Fitzgerald usually conceived of it, a series of actions, each culminating in either a moment of suspense, sudden reversal, intimation of disaster, or pitch of ecstasy followed by a series of complications (he referred to it as "plot business" in his outlines)—is by comparison with the above stories virtually absent. . . .
>
> What emerges clearly in both stories is Fitzgerald's approach to scene and atmosphere: the nuanced line replaces the lengthy adjectival paragraph, and the atmosphere is always directly related to the meaning of the story. (Bryer, 122–23)

Accordingly, these last major tales are more structured than plotted. Each contains five mechanical divisions (compare "Absolution"), during which several scenes transpire. They occur as confrontations between Charlie and Marion at the Rue Palatine apartment in "Babylon Revisited" (sections 1, 3, and 4), and as encounters between Joel and Stella at various locations in "Crazy Sunday" (sections 1–5). Viewed this way, the latter's central relationship seems formally the less dramatic of the two, yet Grebstein points out that "Crazy Sunday" has only three primary scenes staged on three successive weekends (sections 1, 3, and 5), creating symmetry and closure (see part 3).

Fitzgerald's mature artistry becomes evident even by such relatively minor devices as telephone and telegraph. Charlie puts off Lorraine and Duncan in "Babylon Revisited" with promises to phone, while he reaches Lincoln twice about Honoria, whose imminent release (in section 4) is later canceled (section 5). More important, Lorraine's *pneumatique* provides exposition concerning their previous adventures. Both means of communication acquire great significance in "Crazy Sunday," where they advance the narrative and heighten the drama. Joel gets all his invitations—to the party (section 1), to the supper (2), and to the theater (3)—through them. We are thus prepared for the tense sequence of telegrams and calls carrying forward the remaining action. Several telegrams chart Miles's fatal journey: one "from South Bend saying that he's starting back" (*BR*, 243); one from Chicago saying "Home tomorrow night" (*BR*, 244); and two from Kansas City, the first saying "he dropped it" (*BR*, 245) and the second saying "the plane fell" (*BR*, 246). Some of these arrive via the telephone, which Joel uses to contact Stella's friends and physician. It is still ringing when he departs and the story ends.

The Basil and Josephine Stories

As the discussions of the essentially fictional Tarleton trilogy and the essentially nonfictional "Crack-Up" articles have indicated, Fitzgerald was given to sequential writing. The best of his various series—which also include tales about Philippe, Gwenn, and Pat Hobby—are the Basil Duke Lee and Josephine Perry stories.

Sometime in March 1928 he interrupted work on the intractable *Tender Is the Night* for these autobiographical pieces, finishing eight devoted to Basil by February 1929. The *Saturday Evening Post*, which liked successive fiction, published them between 28 April 1928 and 27 April 1929. The editors rejected a ninth story, "That Kind of Party," because, according to Arthur Mizener, they "did not care to believe . . . children of ten and eleven played kissing games." Fitzgerald changed the protagonist's name, but there were no takers elsewhere, so the story remained unpublished until the Summer 1951 issue of *The Princeton University Library Chronicle*.[64]

With *Tender Is the Night* still uncompleted, the author then created five stories about Basil's female counterpart, Josephine Perry. The *Post* published these between 5 April 1930 ("First Blood") and 15 August 1931 ("Emotional Bankruptcy"), paying Fitzgerald four thousand dollars for each story. The Josephine series takes her from "just sixteen" to "a month short of eighteen."

After seeing the first three Basil stories, Fitzgerald's editor Maxwell Perkins wrote on 28 June 1928 that he had "read them with great interest" and that he hoped there would be "some more of these stories" (*Dear Scott*, 151). Similarly, after seeing the first four, Fitzgerald's agent Harold Ober wrote on 8 August 1928: "I think you will have to write two or three more of these stories for I shall never be satisfied until I hear more about Basil, and I think everyone who reads the stories feels the same way." Ober echoed Perkins when he remarked, "They will make an exceedingly interesting book" (*As Ever*, 116).

Fitzgerald considered submitting the Basil and Josephine stories as a book in order to lower the amount of advance money he owed to Scribner, but ultimately rejected the idea, since he felt doing so before publishing *Tender Is the Night* would cheat the public and lower his reputation as a serious writer. But in May 1934, *Tender* now in print, he offered four plans for a fall volume. Plan 2 was:

> The Basil Lee stories, about 60,000 words, and the Josephine stories, 37,500—with one or two stories added, the last of which will bring Basil and Josephine together—making a book of about 120,000 words under some simple title such as "Basil and Josephine." This would in some ways look like the best commercial bet because it might be taken like Tarkington's "Gentle Julia," "Penrod," etc. almost as a novel, and the *most dangerous artistically for the same reason*—for the people who buy my books might think that I was stringing them by selling them watered goods under a false name. (*Dear Scott*, 196)

Perkins reacted positively, corresponding, "We are all strongly in favor of Plan   2. . . . I think we could surely do it with safety and I believe the book would be very much liked and admired" (*Dear Scott*, 198–99).

Soon, though, Fitzgerald replaced this scheme with a planned selection of short stories that had first appeared as early as 1926. He explained on 21 May 1934 that the Basil and Josephine tales were "not as good as I thought"; that they were "full of Tarkington" and might invite comparisons; that "they would require a tremendous amount of work and a good deal of new invention to make them presentable";

and that "their best phrases and ideas" had been used in *Tender Is the Night*. Still haunted by the "watered goods" fear, Fitzgerald elaborated:

> I have not quite enough faith in the Business Department to believe that they would not exploit it to some extent as a novel . . . and any such misconception would just ruin what position I have reconstituted with the critics. The ones who like "Tender" would be disgusted; the ones who were baffled by it or dislike my work would take full advantage to goose-pile on me. It's too damn risky and I am too old for such a chance and the penalty might be too high. What it amounts to is that if it is presented as a novel it wrecks me and if it were presented as short stories then what is the advantage of it over a better collection of short stories? (*Dear Scott*, 199)

Fitzgerald's misgivings are understandable. He hoped *Tender Is the Night* (published on 12 April 1934), his first full-length piece of fiction since *The Great Gatsby* (1925), would revive his reputation for serious long fiction. By 1934 most readers knew of him only as a popular writer who contributed stories like the Basil and Josephine series to the *Post* and other mass circulation magazines. These readers might very well regard a book of Basil and Josephine as "watered goods." Fitzgerald— who considered the short story, with its hackwork connotations and its literal potboiling function in his life, as a less "artistic" and "serious" genre than the novel—was thus uneasy. When *Taps at Reveille* appeared in March 1935, it included only five Basil stories ("The Scandal Detectives," "The Freshest Boy," "He Thinks He's Wonderful," "The Captured Shadow," and "The Perfect Life") and three from the Josephine sequence ("First Blood," "A Nice Quiet Place," and "A Woman with a Past"). Three additional Basil stories ("A Night at the Fair," "Forging Ahead," and "Basil and Cleopatra") were later reprinted by Arthur Mizener in *Afternoon of an Author* (1957). Not until 1971, with the publication of *The Basil and Josephine Stories*, did the two series become one comprehensive collection. Now they may be discussed as finished sequences rather than scattered selections.[65]

To think the Basil and Josephine stories novelistic is not far-fetched, for both series reflect the longer genre in the way *Winesburg, Ohio* does. Each portrays a central figure among recurrent acquaintances experiencing growth dependent on time and place, while playing sociosexual roles. If we heed Fitzgerald's comment about planning additional stories, "the last of which will bring Basil and Josephine together," we will want to read them juxtaposed.

That he saw the Basil material as a cohesive, carefully plotted unit is indicated by the presence among the F. Scott Fitzgerald Papers at Princeton of a chart pertaining to these stories. The characters are arranged under headings like "St. Paul," "school," "male," and "female," and the eight *Post* pieces are outlined.[66] Obviously, the author designed the work to dramatize the protagonist enduring setbacks "to achieve self-control through an understanding of his own assets and liabilities of personality."[67] The measure of success toward attaining this goal demonstrates how interdependent thematically and structurally the various episodes become. Matthew J. Bruccoli has shown that all but "The Captured Shadow" employ "a duplicate action structure in which Basil is involved twice in substantially the same situation." The boy's second response varies from the first, and accordingly the reader knows whether maturation has occurred. Thus, in "That Kind of Party," we find two parties; in "The Scandal Detectives," two Hubert Blair encounters; in "A Night at the Fair," two visits to the fair; in "The Freshest Boy," two train rides; in "He Thinks He's Wonderful," two dates; in "The Perfect Life," two conversations with Jobena Dorsey; in "Forging Ahead," two statements by Mrs. Lee; and in "Basil and Cleopatra," two country club scenes.

Three dominant motifs run through these adventures: gentleman burglar, athletic prowess, and the automobile, whose romantic promise and social prestige emerge. This last is introduced in "A Night at the Fair," where Basil and Riply watch enviously as Speed Paxton, escorting some beautiful blonde, powers a Blatz Wildcat. It reappears in "He Thinks He's Wonderful," where Basil knows "the great thing . . . was to own an automobile," and where, at the end, he borrows his grandfather's electric and takes Imogene Bissel along. In "The Perfect Life" Basil meets Jobena Dorsey, who occupies the first "long, low, English town car" he had ever seen. Finally, in "Forging Ahead" the symbol surfaces again when Basil confesses to Minnie Bibble, "I haven't got a car."

Of the recurrent characters linking the stories, Ermine Gilberte Labouisse Bibble remains the most important. She charms Basil in "He Thinks He's Wonderful." Then, in "Forging Ahead," Rhoda Sinclair casually mentions his unfortunate reputation, and, because two stories have intervened, we wonder why the phrase "he thinks he's wonderful" is repeated. After Minnie comes back, we realize the remark was a foreshadowing device. The return is thematically necessary, for we must observe Basil's second response to a similar situation in order to discover whether he has changed. And, almost immediately, the disparity becomes clear: when Minnie challenges him to kiss her, he jumps up panicky, thinking he "couldn't possibly kiss her like this—right at once. It was all so different and older than a year ago." Here, Basil's new dream of success, as it has been developed in "The Captured Shadow" and "Forging Ahead," has come into conflict with his old romantic dreams, which the Minnie of "He Thinks He's Wonderful" represents. By the end of "Forging Ahead," Basil is still unable to choose, and his "moments of foresight alternated with those when the future was measured by a day." The opening passages of "Basil and Cleopatra" clearly express his continued fascination with Minnie. But at the conclusion of that story Basil's maturation has reached a significant point. This is made apparent in the final paragraph:

> There was a flurry of premature snow in the air and the stars looked cold. Staring up at them he saw that they were his stars as always—symbols of ambition, struggle and glory. The wind blew through them, trumpeting that high white note for which he always listened and the thin-blown clouds, stripped for battle, passed in review. The scene was of an unparalleled brightness and magnificence, and only the practiced eye of the commander saw that one star was no longer there.

A "commander" now, Basil possesses a "practiced eye" that tells him that Minnie (and what she stands for) is just one of several stars. Because the other stars, which signify male "ambition, struggle and glory," are still his, Basil, whose middle name conveys nobility, emerges triumphant, escaping the fate of Amory Blaine, Anthony Patch, Jay Gatsby, Dick Diver, and Monroe Stahr, all victimized by females. Why? Because Basil possesses the vitality this passage from "He Thinks He's Wonderful" claims for him: "He lay on his bed, baffled, mistaken, miserable but not beaten. Time after time, the same vitality that had led his spirit to a scourging made him able to shake off the blood like water not to forget, but to carry his wounds with him to new disasters and new atonements—toward his unknown destiny." Would even vitality have been enough, however, had Basil, an aristocrat of the world of spirit, and Josephine, an aristocrat of the world of matter, come together as Fitzgerald once planned?

If Basil's symbolic triumph is unusual in Fitzgerald's work, many other aspects of both series are not. One such aspect is his view of and emphasis on social class. When he reviewed *Penrod and Sam* for a 1917 issue of *The Nassau Literary Magazine*, Fitzgerald observed, "Mr. Tarkington has done what so many authors of juvenile books fail to do: he has admitted the unequaled snobbishness of boyhood and has traced the neighborhood social system which, with Penrod and Sam at the top, makes possible more than half the stories."[68] These words apply just as accurately to Fitzgerald's own juvenile stories, for his Basil series captures "the neighborhood social system" and the Josephine sequence "unequaled snobbishness." But Tarkington focuses on such matters, while Fitzgerald places them in a larger context. "Only comfortable," Basil embodies the insecure American middle class; "almost very rich," Josephine embodies the insulated American upper class. Two stories—one about each—show that their author thought class even more a psychological than an economic condition.

After Basil's mother loses several thousand dollars in "Forging Ahead," her son must earn money or attend the drab state university instead of glamorous Yale. He consults Horatio Alger's *Bound to Rise*, then seeks a job. At newspaper offices, doorkeepers, office boys, and telephone girls insult him; at the Great Northern car shops, his efforts are criticized, his overalls stolen, and his services terminated. As a last resort, Basil visits great-uncle Benjamin Reilly, who insinuates, "Your mother can't afford to send you, eh?" and "Spent all her money?" Working for Reilly Wholesale Drug Company means becoming an unappealing cousin's constant companion and seeing little of the desirable Minnie Bibble. Though "Forging Ahead" ends on a happy note with his mother solvent and Basil engaged to Minnie, he has been spiritually damaged by his precarious social position.

"A Snobbish Story" bears a double-edged ironic title, since soon after its poor artist expresses contempt for the wealthy, their representative, Josephine, flees the sordidness he exemplifies. Having unceremoniously approached her during the Lake Forest tennis tournament, handsome, shabby reporter-turned-playwright John Boynton Bailey takes her to the little theater that is considering his play, *Race Riot*. She finds out he is married, but accepts a part. Bailey meets Mr. Perry and the latter offers financial support for the play, only to have the local constable interrupt with the news that Bailey's wife has tried to kill herself. Josephine quickly abandons him, deciding "that any value she might have was in the immediate shimmering present—and thus . . . she threw in her lot with the rich and powerful of this world forever."

Like a good deal of Fitzgerald's fiction, the Basil and Josephine stories are about those who dominate life through sexual magnetism. If, like Tarkington, he portrayed snobbishness and the neighborhood social system in his juvenile stories, he also added an important ingredient: the adolescent's growing awareness of sex and its power. Usually in Fitzgerald's fiction, the theme of sexual magnetism involves a victorious upper-class female and a vanquished middle-class male who define each other as if they were alter egos. With Basil and Josephine, though, the rejecter fails and the rejected succeeds because ambitious Josephine functions exclusively among men—"the only thing she cared about in the world was being in love and being with the person she currently loved"—while ambitious Basil intermittently manages to transcend the feminine universe. Since Josephine's conquests produce ultimate defeat and Basil's seeming defeats lead to potential triumph, the juxtaposition of the two sequences is ironic.

Without any future, without any destiny, Josephine is also without any moral sense. "A Nice Quiet Place" concludes when she compromises her sister's groom just before the wedding as an excuse to return to Island Farms and Sonny Dorrance. Basil behaves badly too, but invariably suffers private remorse. In "That Kind of Party," where he commits "insolence and forgery" and assaults "both the crippled and the blind," he chants several *Now I lay mes* and *Our Fathers;* in "The Scandal Detectives," after waylaying Hubert Blair, he feels "morally alone"; and in "The Captured Shadow," when he exposes little Ham Beebe to the mumps for selfish private reasons, he cannot savor his public success.

Development within the Basil series, then, is toward increased maturity, but with Josephine it is more a matter of awareness. And, if the Basil stories are linked by similar scenes that show Basil often responding differently, the Josephine sequence features the main character going through the same basic situation five times, with the same results on all but one occasion. The only change that occurs is in her growing understanding of what has happened. In each story, Josephine ignores men who desire her and instead pursues a handsome, glamorous outsider she ultimately wins, only to discover she doesn't want him. It is in her comprehension of why she doesn't want him that the development within the series occurs. The single exception to this pattern, "A

Part 1

Woman with a Past," shows Josephine for the first time seeking a man, Dudley Knowleton, and failing. Here, and in the last story, "Emotional Bankruptcy," she evidences considerable understanding of her dilemma. From Knowleton, Josephine learns, "There were two kinds of men, those you played with and those you might marry." This leads to the femme fatale's "first mature thought": "One mustn't run through people, and, for the sake of a romantic half-hour, trade a possibility that might develop."

Yet the final recognition doesn't take place until "Emotional Bankruptcy." After she has experienced nothing when she repeats the same old pattern and runs through several men on a Princeton weekend, Josephine meets the perfect man, Edward Dicer, but even *his* kisses are meaningless. "What have I done? What have I done?" she wails, realizing that "one cannot both spend and have," and that "the love of her life had come by, and looking in her empty basket, she had found not a flower left for him—not one." To convey such depletion, Fitzgerald initially introduced the title phrase, though many concomitant symptoms expressed through earlier and later male protagonists are absent. That phrase, defined in Josephine's cry of dismay, could well describe her series as a whole; but because only the first three pieces were published in *Taps at Reveille*, its readers were unable to view the important culmination of her gradual disintegration. Likewise, the Basil series is thematically incomplete without "Forging Ahead" and "Basil and Cleopatra," omitted from the same collection.

Josephine has some theatrical experience (midsummer vaudeville) and seeks more (*Race Riot*), yet she is even less the prospective artist than the confirmed moralist. Basil represents both. His imagination and conscience are attributable to a special middle-class background. Evidently fatherless after "That Kind of Party," and spoiled by a mother who remains prominent throughout, he grows egotistical, as such titles as "The Freshest Boy" and "He Thinks He's Wonderful" and such epithets as "conceited," "Bossy," "ultraconfidant," and "stuck-up" suggest. Basil the egotist manipulates things with considerable skill, organizing a party, terrorizing a friend, eluding a date, directing a play, avoiding a dance, preventing a marriage. Since egotism and its servant manipulation have often made him unpopular and penitent, however, he eventually perceives that "others had wills as strong as his, and more power." What he does not perceive, but what the stories imply, is that egotism become a sense of self and manipulation become a sense of design are creative tools. Indeed, Basil has already

100

employed them when composing "The Book of Scandal," which records "deviations from rectitude on the part of . . . fellow citizens." Whereas Josephine will probably remain a mere narcissistic schemer, Basil could well metamorphose into a professional playwright. His series, then, might constitute the author's portrait of the artist as a young man.

Although *Taps at Reveille* does not cohere as well as the other Scribner collections, it has generally been considered the best volume of Fitzgerald stories published during his lifetime. *Flappers and Philosophers*, *Tales of the Jazz Age*, and *All the Sad Young Men* are much shorter books, so, understandably perhaps, even the third collection, whose "The Rich Boy," "Winter Dreams," "Absolution," and "The Sensible Thing" we have examined, contains fewer good stories. Not only does *Taps* give us several superior stories, including "The Last of the Belles," and "The Freshest Boy," but two major achievements, "Babylon Revisited" and "Crazy Sunday." Higgins voiced received critical opinion when he called "Babylon" Fitzgerald's "one virtually flawless contribution to the canon of the American short story" (Higgins, 121).

Transitional, *Taps at Reveille* looks backward to the romantic 1920s through "The Last of the Belles" (composed November 1928)—replete with femme fatale, *homme manqué*, North versus South, and lost youth—and forward to the realistic 1930s through the *Tender Is the Night* cluster (composed 1929–32)—replete with emotional bankruptcy. The inclusive style persists in the Basil and Josephine stories, where intrusive third-person narrator, elaborate mechanical divisions, rhetorical flourishes, multiple episodes, and secondary characters abound, yet we also get "The Fiend" and "The Night at Chancellorsville" (composed September and November 1934), which are brief, stark, indirect, and objective, and "Babylon Revisited" and "Crazy Sunday" (composed December 1930 and January 1932), which are more structured than plotted. This exclusive style began as far back as *The Great Gatsby* (1925) and "Outside the Cabinet-Maker's" (composed December 1927). It will soon depict tragic producer Monroe Stahr and comic writer Pat Hobby, Hollywood figures descended from Bill McChesney, Charlie Wales, Miles Calman, and the other emotional bankrupts populating *Taps at Reveille*.

Posthumous Collections

"The Rough Crossing" and "One Trip Abroad"

According to Jackson R. Bryer, "Fitzgerald wrote 178 short stories; 146 of them were published during his lifetime; 18 have been published since his death; 14 remain unpublished" (Bryer, xi).[69] Only forty-six were collected in *Flappers and Philosophers, Tales of the Jazz Age, All the Sad Young Men*, and *Taps at Reveille*. All but a handful of the rest appeared posthumously in *The Stories of F. Scott Fitzgerald*, edited by Malcolm Cowley (1951); *Afternoon of an Author*, edited by Arthur Mizener (1957); *The Pat Hobby Stories*, with an introduction by Arnold Gingrich (1962); *The Apprentice Fiction of F. Scott Fitzgerald, 1909–1917*, edited by John Kuehl (1965); *The Basil and Josephine Stories*, edited by Jackson R. Bryer and John Kuehl (1973); *Bits of Paradise*, edited by Matthew J. Bruccoli (1974); and *The Price Was High*, also edited by Bruccoli (1979).

Introducing *Afternoon of an Author*, Mizener commented, "Because the distinction between fiction and nonfiction is not, in Fitzgerald's case, of major significance, I have not tried to distinguish between the two in making the selections for this book" (*AA*, 5). Thus he included such borderline pieces as "Afternoon of an Author" and "Author's House" with more or less clear-cut stories and essays. These borderline pieces, epitomized by the "Crack-Up" sequence, which appeared first in *Esquire* (1936), then in *The Crack-Up*, edited by Edmund Wilson (1945), are considered to be essentially nonfictional throughout this study. Wilson's collection, like *F. Scott Fitzgerald: A Miscellany*, edited by Matthew J. Bruccoli and Jackson R. Bryer (1971), contains both imaginative and factual selections.

Several superior stories from the *Tender Is the Night* cluster were excluded from *Taps at Reveille* because they contributed directly to the novel. We will recall, for example, Fitzgerald's statement about "Jacob's Ladder" that he "had so thoroughly disemboweled" the "best descriptions" that including it "would be offering an empty shell."[70] Yet "Jacob's Ladder" (1927) is not just a precursor of *Tender Is the Night*, but an independently effective creation. Higgins made this assessment of the work:

> His first *Post* story with an unhappy ending, it is a *Pygmalion*-like tale of Jacob, a thirty-three-year-old rich man who propels Jenny, a beautiful sixteen-year-old slum waif, to movie stardom, only to find after he has fallen in love with her that her love for him has passed; she has fallen in love with a Hollywood man. Jacob must content himself at the end with watching her flickering image in a movie house. . . .
>
> From a standpoint of artistry "Jacob's Ladder," though it cannot be ranked among Fitzgerald's finest pieces, is probably the best of his stories yet uncollected [see *Bits of Paradise*]. The dialog returns to crackling realism after the woodenness of his recent pot-boilers. Moreover, it is used to convey emotion and reveal character rather than merely to propel the plot. (Higgins, 96, 97)

Even better than "Jacob's Ladder" are two other *Post* satellite fictions, "The Rough Crossing" (1929) and "One Trip Abroad" (1930), which were collected in *The Stories of F. Scott Fitzgerald* and *Afternoon of an Author,* respectively. They share much besides the Fitzgeralds' stormy marriage as refracted through the Smiths and the Kellys.

Reminiscent of "May Day," both begin portentously, suggesting a large, somewhat ominous context. "The Rough Crossing" opens:

> Once on the long, covered piers, you have come into a ghostly country that is no longer Here and not yet There. . . . The past, the continent is behind you; the future is that glowing mouth in the side of the ship; this dim turbulent alley is too confusedly the present. . . . A last odd idea that one didn't really have to come, then the loud, mournful whistles, and the thing—certainly not a boat, but rather a human idea, a frame of mind—pushes forth into the big dark night.

And "One Trip Abroad" begins:

> In the afternoon the air became black with locusts, and some of the women shrieked, sinking to the floor of the motorbus and covering their hair with traveling rugs. The locusts were coming north, eating everything in their path, which was not so much in that part of the world; they were flying silently and in straight lines, flakes of black snow.

These passages prepare us for Fitzgerald's identification between the storm within and the storm without, the expressionistic technique of objectifying the internal in the external world, as do "The Ice Palace" (psychic/geographic), "Babylon Revisited" (private/public), and other works. "Rough Crossing" protagonists Adrian and Eva Smith, whose marriage suddenly turns bad, experience "the wildest hurricane on the North Atlantic in ten years." The "Catholic slant" ("sin," "guilt," "penance," "redemption") shaping Rudolph Miller of "Absolution" and Charlie Wales of "Babylon Revisited" emerges again when Eva, being punished over "sins and omissions," propitiates the storm: "It was Adrian's love that was demanded of her. Deliberately she unclasped her pearl necklace, lifted it to her lips—for she knew that with it went the freshest, fairest part of her life—and flung it out into the gale." Later Adrian rescues his wife, and later yet they become reconciled after the storm subsides. "One Trip Abroad" protagonists Nelson and Nicole Kelly are less fortunate, since their storm, during which "the mountains and the lake disappeared completely; the hotel crouched . . . amid tumult and chaos and darkness," reveals them "alone together." These storms dramatize the disorder inherent in broken marriages. Moments of crisis, they eventually pass, reuniting the first couple and dooming the second. The fact that the Smiths and the Kellys are creative as well as procreative—Adrian writes, Nelson paints, Nicole sings—does not alter fate.

Whereas the Italian liner represents only the original of many evanescent locations in "One Trip Abroad," the English liner of "The Rough Crossing" constitutes its sole setting. International associations—American passengers, British crew, French destination—make the English liner microcosmic. At the Italian liner's bar, "groups . . . leaned desperately on one another," one of whose "gay crowd . . . disappeared permanently into the Atlantic," an event recalling the Carton death on the English liner in "The Rough Crossing."

"The Rough Crossing's" tightly plotted interaction among a quartet consisting of the Smiths, Betsy D'Amido, and Stacomb Butterworth is confined to the English liner over a six-day period, but the loosely plotted interaction among several people in "One Trip Abroad" takes the Kellys far and wide over about a three-year period. If the unities prepare us for the return of coherence in the earlier story, their absence prepares us for further disarray in the later effort. Obviously, then, form reflects content here, as in other successful Fitzgerald fictions.

That Nelson and Nicole, unlike Adrian and Eva, possess no certain destination, the author implies through one uniquely self-conscious passage stressing his familiar reliance on place: "This is the story of a trip abroad, and the geographical element must not be slighted. Having visited North Africa, Italy, the Riviera, Paris and points in between, it was not surprising . . . the Kellys should go to Switzerland. Switzerland is a country where very few things begin, but many things end."[71]

The contention "Every place is the same. . . . the only thing that matters is who's there" is borne out in their travels. Cynical friend Oscar Dane claims Nelson and Nicole's cronies have "sifted down through Europe like nails in a sack of wheat, till they stick out of it a little into the Mediterranean Sea." "International society" he continues, "is just about as hard to enter nowadays as the public rooms at the Casino." "Society" signifies the Europeans "peppered with Americans" whom the Kellys have known after abandoning the Americans "salted with Europeans." One member, Count Chiki Sarolai, resembles Prince Gabriel Petrocobesco of "Majesty": "He was an attractive relic of the Austrian court, with no fortune or pretense to any, but with solid social and financial connections in France. His sister was married to the Marquis de la Clos d'Hirondelle, who, in addition to being of the ancient noblesse, was a successful banker in Paris. Count Chiki rove here and there, frankly sponging, rather like Oscar Dane, but in a different sphere." Having a penchant for Americans, he gravitates toward the Kellys and their apartment, which the count and his valet occupy while Nicole gives birth. They are invited to one Seine canal-boat party ostensibly thrown by the De la Clos d'Hirondelles, but actually charged against Nelson. Then their noble guest steals Nicole's jewel box and absconds.

At another party, aboard the T. F. Golding yacht, "seven different nationalities" attend. There, somebody remarks that the English are "doing a sort of dance of death," which echoes what happened more than two years before in Sorrento, where "the English owned the hotel. They were aged, come South for good weather and tranquility. . . . Could people be content to talk eternally about the weather, promenade the same walks, face the same variant of macaroni . . . month after month?" The Kellys' single British connection, General Sir Evelyne and Lady Fragelle, was "brief and unpleasant," as Lady Fragelle had loudly objected to their swimming costumes. Subsequently, a battle over the electric piano between her and Nelson terminated with the

Part 1

American couple angrily departing. Foreigners remain negligible during "The Rough Crossing," so "the rows of stiff, disciplined men and women" at the sea burial merely seem "British and sad."

The Kellys, like Bill McChesney, Charlie Wales, and other emotional bankrupts, behave badly in Europe. For instance, following the Golding luncheon, Nicole overhears husband and closest friend Noel Delauney exchange intimacies. She hurls a vase toward him that hits the French woman; then she attacks Nelson, who, out of self-defense, inadvertently strikes Nicole's eye and she falls, sobbing. The Kellys later make up: "Nicole accepted his explanations, not because they were credible, but because she wanted passionately to believe them."

Masculine promiscuity and feminine violence had already marked "The Rough Crossing." Its thirty-one-year-old husband pursues teenage Betsy D'Amido, "a dark little [American] beauty" with an Italian name. She is "the pretty girl of the voyage," infatuated with Adrian for some time now. They kiss and become both tennis partners and constant companions. Reacting to this cruel "breach of the contract," Eva throws away her pearls, collapses at dinner, wanders about aimlessly, and insults a medical stewardess.

These irresponsible actions, which prefigure those of McChesney and Wales, occur when the characters are drunk. We learn that the Smiths "'never wanted to see a cocktail again' after leaving America—but they had forgotten the staccato loneliness of ships, and all activity centered about the bar." Abandoned Eva makes repeated pilgrimages there, though "she wasn't used to so much drinking." Finally, the doctor says, "I've given orders that she is not to have any more to drink on this ship." Even more restless and bored than the Smiths, the Kellys soon increase their wine consumption in Europe. They draw up "a conscientious list of the places they wouldn't visit any more"—bars, nightclubs, early-morning clubs, summer resorts—yet "when one went out one generally drank." Nelson "was not a drunk, he did nothing conspicuous or sodden, but he was no longer willing to go out socially without the stimulus of liquor." If Eva grew physically ill during her rough crossing, so too do the Kellys during their one trip abroad. Nicole has two operations, while he develops jaundice, and thus they join "the obese, the wasted, the crippled and the broken of all nationalities who filled the hotel."

Both American couples appear privileged and compatible at the outset. Eva "had never tried to bind Adrian, never needed to—for they were serious people, with all sorts of mutual interests and satisfied with

106

each other." As a successful playwright, he is a celebrity; as a talented and charming twenty-six-year-old woman, she is "precious to everyone who knew her." Similarly, the Kellys are among the well-adjusted, fortunate few. Though Nelson and Nicole "had passed lonely youths," once he inherits $500,000 the newlyweds look forward to studying art and music abroad. Fitzgerald offers this description in section 1:

> They were in their twenties, and there was still a pleasant touch of bride and groom upon them. A handsome couple; the man rather intense and sensitive, the girl arrestingly light of hue in eyes and hair, her face without shadows, its living freshness modulated by a lovely confident calm. Mr. and Mrs. Miles did not fail to notice their air of good breeding, of a specifically "swell" background, expressed both by their unsophistication and by their ingrained reticence that was not stiffness. If they held aloof, it was because they were sufficient to each other.

This superficial harmoniousness has led critics like Sergio Perosa to complain, "The motivations in these two stories are often insufficient, the psychological explanations are inadequate."[72] However, closer analysis contradicts this claim: in fact, "it was in the hope that there was some . . . real compensation for the lost, careless confidence of twenty-one, that [the Smiths] were going to spend a year in France." After their "long *seven-year* dream" (emphasis added), Adrian, whose antennae immediately feel out the shipboard world, no doubt pursues Betsy because of the conventional seven-year itch. He is flattered by "the deference with which she neglected the young men and bent her politeness on him." To Adrian, nothing "felt so young and fresh as her lips. She was all new and immaculate." There ensues Fitzgerald's familiar transference of vitality: "Her youth seemed to flow into him. . . . he had discovered something that he had thought was lost with his own youth forever." If recapturing the past inspires Adrian's flirtation, responding to that inspires Eva's drunkenness. Both actions are psychologically valid.

The motivation in "One Trip Abroad" is predictable, echoing other *Tender* cluster stories: as in the fiction of Henry James, European decadence corrupts American innocence. What Fitzgerald adds to the international theme centers on the conflict between work and pleasure, responsibility and irresponsibility, character and emotional bankruptcy. The seeds of self-indulgence were planted during the Kellys' lonely youths: "When I was young," Nicole says, "my father had asthma and I had to live in the most depressing health resorts with him for years; and Nelson was in the fur business in Alaska and he loathed it; so when we were free we came abroad." Inheriting a fortune hastens their deterioration, which the author traces over more than three married years.

The dramatic device of analogous or parallel characterization enables Fitzgerald to represent in Liddell and Cardine Miles what Nelson and Nicole Kelly might become. The older and younger American couples meet "on the edge of the Sahara" just after "One Trip Abroad" commences. Though Mr. and Mrs. Miles are "bored with themselves" and are "somewhat worn away inside by fifteen years of a particular set in Paris," they exhibit "undeniable style, even charm." These "formally sophisticated and frankly snobbish" world travelers take the inexperienced Kellys to the Café of the Ouled Nails, where the foursome watches wildly sensual belly dancing. When Nicole learns that the Berber girls will perform "Oriental style," or wearing only jewelry, she leaves despite Liddell's assertion, "We're here to see the real customs and manners of the country; a little prudishness shouldn't stand in our way." He and his wife foreshadow Duncan Schaeffer and Lorraine Quarrles of "Babylon Revisited."

Nicole follows "another young American woman" out of the café. This woman and her husband had already been discussed by the Kellys:

> "I passed that couple in the hall just now."
> "Who—the Mileses?"
> "No, that young couple—about our age—the ones that were on the other motorbus, that we thought looked so nice, in Bir Rabalou after lunch, in the camel market."
> "They did look nice."
> "Charming," she said emphatically; "the girl and man, both. I'm almost sure I've met the girl somewhere before."
> The couple referred to were sitting across the room at dinner, and Nicole found her eyes drawn irresistibly toward them.

Always nameless, "that young couple" appears throughout the narrative as a déjà vu phenomenon. Three years after Algeria and at the time of the Delauney incident, they are "harder-looking," the husband "dissipated." In the Café de Paris, these doppelgängers also experience "something strident and violent," for the wife's face is "pale now, and distorted with anger." Their final manifestation occurs during the climactic storm. Afterward, Nicole

> inspected the face closely. It was an inquisitive face, she saw at once, possibly calculating; the eyes, intelligent enough, but with no peace in them, swept over people in a single glance as though estimating their value. "Terrible egoist," Nicole thought, with a certain distaste. For the rest, the cheeks were wan, and there were little pouches of ill health under the eyes; these combining with a certain flabbiness of arms and legs to give an impression of unwholesomeness. She was dressed expensively, but with a hint of slovenliness, as if she did not consider the people of the hotel important.

Nelson did not like *him* either: "I ran into the man in the bar. . . . His face is so weak and self-indulgent that it's almost mean—the kind of face that needs half a dozen drinks really to open the eyes and stiffen the mouth up to normal." Soon these "two dark forms" join the Kellys in "the dark garden." With a shock of recognition, Nicole cries, "They're us! They're us!," reversing the comical conclusion of "The Rough Crossing":

> "Who do you suppose those Adrian Smiths on the boat were?" he demanded. "It certainly wasn't me."
> "Nor me."
> "It was two other people," he said, nodding to himself. "There are so many Smiths in this world."

"The Swimmers" and "Outside the Cabinet-Maker's"

"The Swimmers" (1929; collected in *Bits of Paradise*) also mirrors *Tender Is the Night*. The American abroad is Henry Clay Marston, obviously named after Kentucky statesman Henry Clay (1777–1852). Both are Southerners, with Marston descended from seven generations of ancestors that include one grandfather "who freed [the] slaves in '58, fought from Manassas to Appomattox, knew Huxley and Spencer as light reading, and believed in caste only when it expressed the best of race." This background resembles that of Dick Diver, for his great-grandfather had been governor of North Carolina; he numbers Mad Anthony Wayne among his predecessors; and his father came north following the Civil War. Diver still has cousins in Virginia and feels at home in Westmoreland County. Like him, Marston learns the morality Edward Fitzgerald (born in 1853 near Rockville, Maryland) bequeathed his son Scott: "honor, courtesy, and courage."

These pre–Civil War values counter European corruption throughout "The Swimmers," where Choupette betrays her American husband. Discovering the adultery, he breaks down, but later, infused with energy symbolized by swimming and provided by a nameless eighteen-year-old fellow-Virginian—"that perfect type of American girl"— Marston outfoxes the materialistic lovers, disproving their theory "money is power" and winning back his children. No emotional bankrupt, he survives.

The story, Fitzgerald's most patriotic short fiction, perceptively juxtaposes native versus foreign manners. Two proximate passages are illustrative:

> He knew that she wanted the children only because without them she would be suspect, even *déclassée*, to her family in France; but with that quality of detachment peculiar to old stock, Henry recognized this as a perfectly legitimate motive.

> Americans, he liked to say, should be born with fins, and perhaps they were—perhaps money was a form of fin. In England property begot a strong place sense, but Americans, restless and with shallow roots, needed fins and wings.

Because "The Swimmers" is both a brilliant comparative analysis of two cultures and a highly contrived piece of fiction, it has elicited mixed reactions. Robert Sklar, who investigates the effect of Spengler on Fitzgerald, echoes Eble and anticipates Bruccoli when he calls "The Swimmers" "neglected" and "undervalued," "the most important precursor to *Tender Is the Night*" (Sklar, 236, 238). Conversely, Higgins regards the story as having "negligible worth," a combination of "rickety plot" and "significant passages" demonstrating "Fitzgerald's chronic inability to fuse good matter with good form" (Higgins, 113, 114). Negative, too, Prigozy writes:

> Any reading of the stories I have cited reveals that Fitzgerald had not found a replacement for a love story to serve as the center of a work. He still relied heavily on the plot twist, the sudden reversal

of fortune brought about by an external agent. He continued to pad lifeless plots with overblown romantic rhetoric, or by now hackneyed movielike scenic descriptions. And he could not create sympathetic and believable characters, only wooden stereotypes. The most serious problem was that his gift for narrative flow, the perfect distancing of author from subject, had virtually disappeared. (Bryer, 120)[73]

The author himself best described the major flaw of "The Swimmers" in a letter to Harold Ober that considers "the hardest story I ever wrote" as "too big for its space." Ober replied, "I have just read THE SWIMMERS and I think it is the ablest and most thoughtful story you have ever done" (*As Ever,* 142).

Successful or not, this fractious tale exemplifies the kind of thing the *Post* would pay four thousand dollars to publish. The long four-part narrative covers more than four years, alternating between Europe (especially Paris) and the United States (especially Richmond, Virginia). Considerable exposition appears: Henry's Southern ancestry, his past life, his family, his position at the Calumet Tobacco Company. Simultaneously, a rather elaborate plot unfolds, with his discovering the illicit relationship between Choupette and Charles, suffering temporary paralysis, trying to save the "thoroughbred" American girl, learning how to swim, returning home, meeting the girl again, confronting the adulterers, securing the children, taking less lucrative employment overseas, and encountering the girl one last time.

More contrived than any other scene, the motorboat episode of section 3 transpires when husband, wife, and lover discuss their situation as they "drift, without will or direction through the bright water" toward Hampton Roads. Lover tells husband: "I received a letter from Paris that puts the matter in a new light. It is a statement by a specialist in mental diseases, declaring you to be of unsound mind, and unfit to have the custody of children. The specialist is the one who attended you in your nervous breakdown." After recounting "this scurvy trick," Charles contends, "Money is power." Coincidentally, their battery becomes dry and the engine goes dead. Fortuitously, neither Charles nor Choupette can swim, we learn while the tide takes them out to sea. Soon Marston announces: "If you'll write and sign about two hundred words at my dictation, I'll swim to the lighthouse and get help." The deceitful pair thereby "relinquished all lien on the children." Then, placing this document and the doctor's certificate in a heretofore unmentioned "oiled-silk tobacco pouch," resourceful Marston makes "the longest swim he had ever tried."

All four principals are stereotypes, as Fitzgerald confirmed by calling Henry "a Virginian of the kind . . . prouder of being Virginians than of being Americans"; Choupette, "a wise little Provençal girl"; Charles, "one of the richest men in Virginia"; and the young thoroughbred, "that perfect type of American girl." Even so, these people, who constitute the conventional love triangle/quartet, appear believable enough, if not very complex. Though the central intelligence figure evokes sympathy, Henry Marston is too often identified with the implied author. For instance, we hear Fitzgerald's voice in rhetorical flourishes like the conclusion of "The Swimmers": "France was a land, England was a people, but America, having about it still that quality of the idea, was harder to utter—it was the graves at Shiloh and the tired, drawn, nervous faces of its great men, and the country boys dying in the Argonne for a phrase that was empty before their bodies withered. It was a willingness of the heart."

Such rhetorical flourishes, which convey lofty sentiments in elaborate sentences, are often bombastic, too pompous for the occasion that inspired them. Conveyed through a central intelligence or by an intrusively omniscient narrator and voiced at two or three juxtaposed locations over considerable chronological time, Fitzgerald's purple passages occur in all the major stories except "Absolution," "Babylon Revisited," and "Crazy Sunday." This particular one was probably written to please the patriotic *Post*, but others were also designed for the mass circulation magazines rather than for himself, since he felt "shaping" and "pruning" were essential to good writing. Thus the author followed two sprawling novels with the selective *Gatsby*, and the expansive *Tender Is the Night* with the compact *Last Tycoon*.

What Fitzgerald meant by shaping and pruning is well-illustrated through the neglected minor masterpiece, "Outside the Cabinet-Maker's" (1928; collected in *Afternoon of an Author*). It has one setting where a simple action occurs: three individuals, nameless, as if viewed distantly—"the man," "the lady," "the little girl"—park "at the corner of Sixteenth and some dingy-looking street" that lacks further urban specification; there "the lady got out." After she enters the cabinet-maker's shop on this "fine November day," presumably to purchase the vague object the French dialogue implies is a secret gift for her six-year-old, "Daddy" spins his impromptu yarn about Fairy Princess, Ogre, King, Queen, and Prince, whose parts, plus others, are enacted by passersby. The lady interrupts him once, calling down "from the upper story," "He's busy. . . . Gosh, what a nice day!" Two unnumbered breaks ensue, then she reappears to bring the narrative full circle before "they drove off." Before the first break, this typical spare descriptive paragraph appears: "The little girl looked. It was a flat in back of a shop. Curtains masked most of its interior, but there was a faint stir behind them. On one window a loose shutter banged from back to forth every few minutes. Neither the man nor the little girl had ever seen the place before."

The embedded fairy-tale narrative receives more development than the basic arrival-departure structure of the framework story. Father tells daughter than an Ogre has entrapped the Fairy Princess in the flat behind the shop and has imprisoned the King and Queen "ten thousand miles below the earth"; that her release depends upon three stones: "The Prince has already found one stone in President Coolidge's collar-box. He's looking for the second in Iceland. Every time he finds a stone the room where the Princess is kept turns blue"; that the King and Queen are now free and the King, along with Witch, soldiers, and fairies, is presently involved; that one soldier will "put . . . ice on the Ogre's head and freeze his brains so he can't do any more harm."

This yarn reflects an incident from the near past recorded in *Sara and Gerald* by the Murphys' daughter Honoria: "One particular evening, Scott said he had an exciting plan for the three of us, and he took two lead soldiers from his pocket. He told us there was to be a party for Scottie, the Fitzgeralds' four-year-old daughter, at which one of the soldiers, who was secretly a prince, would attempt to rescue a princess he intended to marry. The princess, he explained, was being held prisoner by a wicked witch in a castle, which was guarded by a dragon."[74]

When Scott and Zelda Fitzgerald performed this sketch at the Villa America, it confirmed a dramatic bent that had been manifested in his work since childhood. Through dialogue, the self-effacing author objectifies the emotional relationship between father and daughter in "Outside the Cabinet-Maker's" and "Babylon Revisited," both of which invoked the detached exclusive style. Matching exchanges from the two stories are indicative. "Outside the Cabinet-Maker's" reads:

"Who is the lady?"
"She's a Witch, a friend of the Ogre's."

Part 1

The shutter blew closed with a bang and then slowly opened again.

"That's done by the good and bad fairies," the man explained. "They're invisible, but the bad fairies want to close the shutter so nobody can see in and the good ones want to open it."

"The good fairies are winning now."

"Yes." He looked at the little girl. "You're my good fairy."

And "Babylon Revisited" reads:

"Daddy, I want to come and live with you," she said suddenly.

His heart leaped; he had wanted it to come like this.

"Aren't you perfectly happy?"

"Yes, but I love you better than anybody. And you love me better than anybody, don't you, now that mummy's dead?"

"Of course I do. But you won't always like me best, honey. You'll grow up and meet somebody your own age and go marry him and forget you ever had a daddy."

"Yes, that's true," she agreed tranquilly. (*BR*, 218)

Without the last line, the second exchange might strike us as sentimental.

This same irony also characterizes "Outside the Cabinet-Maker's," where, toward the end, we understand the meaning of previous events for the man, now "old enough to know that he would look back to that time—the tranquil street and the pleasant weather and the mystery playing before the child's eyes, mystery which he had created, but whose luster and texture he could never see or touch any more himself." This melancholy realization is soon undercut by a truncated denouement that occurs after "they drove off." Now the little girl becomes raconteur: "And there's the Ogre's body in that yard. . . . The King and Queen and Prince were killed and . . . the Princess is queen." Daddy reacts "rather impatiently" because "he had liked his King and Queen," commenting, "You had to have a heroine." Then, one final paragraph matter-of-factly identifies her gift and records the isolation all three family members inevitably experience: "The lady thought about the doll's house, for she had been poor and had never had one as a child, the man thought how he had almost a million dollars and the little girl thought about the odd things on the dingy street that they had left behind."

114

"Financing Finnegan" and The Pat Hobby Stories

"Outside the Cabinet-Maker's" was published in 1928, yet most instances of the exclusive style occurred after 1934 when"Fitzgerald began publishing autobiographical articles in *Esquire*." According to Bruccoli: "At first [he] sent Gingrich stories that were not placeable in 'family magazines'—'The Fiend' and 'The Night before Chancellorsville.' . . . Between 1934 and 1940 Fitzgerald sold forty-four articles and stories to *Esquire*—eight of which appeared posthumously in 1941."[75] Several submissions were superior (for example, "The Long Way Out," "The Lost Decade," and "Three Hours between Planes"), but the best was "Financing Finnegan," published by *Esquire* (January 1938) and collected by Malcolm Cowley (*Stories*).

Composed a little more than two years before Kenneth Littauer and Maxwell Perkins received Fitzgerald's synopsis of *The Last Tycoon*, this story anticipates his fifth novel insofar as it revives the first-person observer technique. Here the storyteller is an anonymous "old professional" who shares the same agent and publisher with another writer, Finnegan. They are opposites, for the observer refers to "my own conscientious if uninspired literary pursuits," while "facile flow" and "ready wit" mark his alter ego's work. Since Finnegan, "the perennial man of promise in American letters," made words that "glowed and coruscated," "sentences, paragraphs, chapters" that "were masterpieces of fine weaving and spinning," no wonder the mediocre and unacquainted narrator wishes he "could write like that." The life led by Finnegan seems no less colorful than the craft practiced by him, a versatile craft producing diverse literary genres: novel, play, story. Fitzgerald's mythical Irishman fosters rumors like the anecdote about the half-empty swimming pool or the remarks about heart disease and cancer. At one point, we learn this charming adventurer "had walked off into a snow-storm when the food supply gave out, and the Arctic had claimed another sacrifice of intrepid man," but soon a cablegram arrives from Oslo, reading, "Am miraculously safe here." After the narrator investigates such stories, he claims, "They're mostly as false as the half-empty pool. That pool was full to the brim."

"I broke the clavicle of my shoulder, diving," Fitzgerald told Perkins on 19 September 1936 (*Dear Scott*, 230), unintentionally disclosing the autobiographical fact behind Finnegan's accident. Autobiographical, too, is the money motif introduced through the title word "Financing."

Slowly, it grows apparent that most of the Irishman's visits to agent Cannon (that is, Harold Ober) are for loans. While discussing Finnegan with their Fifth Avenue publisher (that is, Scribner), the narrator cannot believe a telegram George Jaggers (that is, Maxwell Perkins) opens: "*With fifty I could at least pay typist and get haircut and pencils.*" Then Jaggers admits breaking his private rule, "I take [the money] out of my own pocket." The investment made by publisher and agent "had reached a sum so considerable that Finnegan belonged to them"; indeed, they have become the writer's insurance beneficiaries. But having paid these debts, Finnegan still asks Cannon to "*wire passage money for four people and two hundred extra.*"

The comic irony, which runs all through "Financing Finnegan," is well illustrated when the narrator lends the agent two hundred dollars "never shown to my credit" just before the agent receives this request. Dependent on distance, such irony stems partly from the first-person observer, since it promotes double vision, with the antithetical self viewing the essential, if exaggerated self, as in *The Great Gatsby*, where stable Nick Carraway is fascinated by flamboyant James Gatz.

Composite characterization represents a second means toward detachment. For George Monteiro, who reminds us that Fitzgerald and Hemingway, like the observer and the observed, were Scribner authors together, Finnegan embodies both. Their story may be construed "as Fitzgerald's qualified 'answer' to Hemingway's 'Snows [of Kilimanjaro]' in much the same way the latter constituted Hemingway's sniping 'answer' to Fitzgerald's original 'Crack-Up' pieces, also published in *Esquire*" (Bryer, 291). Monteiro further observes, "Fitzgerald was of course never entirely taken in by Hemingway's public self. In 'Financing Finnegan,' instead of having him go on an African safari or to a civil war fought on an international scale, Fitzgerald has Finnegan concoct a harebrained scheme to explore the Arctic wastes of the North Pole in the company of three Bryn Mawr anthropologists, three 'girls'" (Bryer, 295).

Subsequently, Monteiro credits Fitzgerald with "considerable prescience" for imagining "the disappearance and assumed death of the literary lion and his equally remarkable reappearance," because later Hemingway would "'die' in Africa (twice in a matter of days) only to come walking out of the jungle large as life." And, the critic adds, "to anyone familiar with Hemingway's telegraphic epistolary style . . . Finnegan's cablegram from Oslo, unlike the telegram that materializes early in the story (which is vintage Fitzgerald) is pure Hemingway" (Bryer, 297).

"Financing Finnegan" contains three allusions to the Hollywood both Fitzgerald and Hemingway despised. Two—the call Cannon awaits and the narrator's statement, "I had just got a thousand dollars advance for a venture in Hollywood"—set up the oddly personal third: "so far there's only been a short story about the polar expedition, a love story. Perhaps it wasn't as big a subject as he expected. But the movies are interested in him—if they can get a good look at him first and I have every reason to think that he will come through. He'd better." This reference concludes Fitzgerald's tall tale, yet, since *Esquire* started publishing his series about Hollywood scenarist Pat Hobby (who also happens to be an impecunious Irishman) exactly two years later, it would appear that "Financing Finnegan" inspired additional treatment.

Printed by *Esquire* between January 1940 and May 1941, the seventeen Pat Hobby stories were not collected until 1962. Arnold Gingrich, *Esquire* publisher and Fitzgerald's friend, introduced the Scribner edition, asserting:

> But this volume is more than a collection of previously uncollected stories. For while its several episodes were originally published as a series of separate sketches, Fitzgerald began thinking of them, after the first three were written, as a collective entity. Almost every time he wrote another, he would reconsider the order of their appearance in print and as long as he lived he kept revising them, just before their publication. Some were revised up to four times. The revisions were in some instances caused by considerations of the interdependence of the various parts in constituting the overall delineation of the character of Pat Hobby.[76]

The Scribner edition concludes with an appendix showing the revisions Fitzgerald made on "A Patriotic Short," probably his finest Hobby story. Though these revisions arrived too late for the magazine to incorporate, they demonstrate how carefully he emended material that paid only $250.

It and the other sixteen pieces are the best-known instances of Fitzgerald's exclusive style. They contain from one to five parts and range from twelve hundred to twenty-six hundred words. The Hollywood studio Pat calls home, even though he works there infrequently, represents the single most dominant setting. Not many characters appear during the individual episodes, but those who do stand for the entire motion picture industry: producers, directors, actors, actresses, writers, agents, secretaries, policemen, and so on. Unlike the Basil and Josephine casts, only a few individuals recur—for example, Jack Berners (producer) and Louie (studio bookie). The coming and going of most suggests the impermanence of Hollywood. The episodes, which are defined by their titles,[77] "turn on the attempts of [the protagonist] to work his way into some kind of a writing job" (Eble, 143). The time period covered is as circumscribed as the studio setting, and these attempts usually take but a day or two in Hobby's forty-ninth year. They are presented through a combination of narration and dialogue. Functional rather than figurative, the prose passages emphasize action over description. Simple sentences have replaced convoluted ones and rhetorical flourishes evident in inclusive fictions like "The Swimmers" do not occur. This paragraph from "'Boil Some Water—Lots of It'" is typical:

> Once Pat had been a familiar figure at the Big Table; often in his golden prime he had dined in the private canteens of executives. Being of the older Hollywood he understood their jokes, their vanities, their social system with its swift fluctuations. But there were too many new faces at the Big Table now—faces that looked at him with the universal Hollywood suspicion. And at the little tables where the young writers sat they seemed to take work so seriously. As for just sitting down anywhere, even with secretaries or extras— Pat would rather catch a sandwich at the corner.

Clipped dialogue quickly ensues:

> "I'm working on a medical," he said. "I need some help."
> "A medical?"
> "Writing it—the idea about a doc. Listen—let me buy you lunch. I want to ask you some medical questions."
> The nurse hesitated.
> "I don't know. It's my first day here."
> "It's all right," he assured her, "studios are democratic; everybody is just 'Joe' or 'Mary'—from the big shots right down to the prop boys."

Nowhere does the difference between Fitzgerald the putter-inner and Fitzgerald the leaver-outer become more evident than in the degree of self-consciousness each employs. Such authorial comments as "this is the story of a trip abroad" are common in his saturated fiction, but scarce in his selective fiction. Only one self-conscious assertion occurs in "Financing Finnegan"—"that is afield from this story"—and one in the Pat Hobby series—"we perceive it through the red-rimmed eyes of Pat Hobby"—while "Outside the Cabinet-Maker's" avoids autoreferentiality altogether. Thus Kenneth Eble observes: "These stories are remarkable for their almost complete detachment from feeling and therefore, from the affective impulse of most of Fitzgerald's previous fiction. We do not sympathize with or condemn Pat Hobby, and we are not expected to. Nor, despite the continuing satire of Hollywood people and manners, are we aroused to feel strongly about either the people or the place" (Eble, 143). Comic irony, which often accompanies detachment here, is produced when the author alternates limited and unlimited third-person foci, as, for example, at the beginning of section 3 in "Pat Hobby and Orson Welles":

> To those grouped together under the name "talent," the atmosphere of a studio is not unfailingly bright—one fluctuates too quickly between high hope and grave apprehension. Those few who decide things are happy in their work and sure that they are worthy of their hire—the rest live in a mist of doubt as to when their vast inadequacy will be disclosed.
> Pat's psychology was, oddly, that of the masters and for the most part he was unworried even though he was off salary.

Sergio Perosa has articulated the most serious charge leveled at the Hobby sequence: "There is no narrative development from one moment to another, but rather a repetition of a few basic actions, similar in substance and often predictable, in a limited context of different situations" (Perosa, 150).[78] These actions, these situations involve failure, about which Fitzgerald proclaimed himself the authority. In the Pat Hobby stories, we discover alcoholism, gambling, broken marriages, and poverty. Pat, whose "apartment lay athwart a delicatessen shop," wears shabby clothes, drives an old car, borrows money, and works intermittently for $250 per week instead of regularly for $2,000, as in the past. He does not behave well, stealing material, betraying people, and trespassing on property. In the ironically titled "Pat Hobby's Christmas Wish," he even attempts to blackmail producer Harry Gooddorf with spurious evidence supplied by Harry's rejected lover, Helen Kagle. "The Rat" with the bad eyes "was a writer but he had never written much, nor even read all the 'originals' he worked from, because it made his head bang to read much. But the good old silent days you got somebody's plot and a smart secretary and gulped benzedrine 'structure' at her six or eight hours every week. The director took care of the gags. After talkies came he always teamed up with some man who wrote dialogue. Some young man who liked to work." Twenty-odd years of experience and thirty-odd credits later, Hobby remains an inefficient and incapable hack. One morning the only thing he does "except a little changing around of lines so he could claim them as his own" is invent "a single imperative sentence, spoken by a doctor": "'Boil some water—lots of it.'"

Eble's contention that "these stories are remarkable for . . . almost complete detachment" notwithstanding, the affective impulse does occasionally appear. Thus when Pat Hobby, "script writer," and Phil Macedon, "once the star of stars," argue because the latter refuses "to acknowledge . . . they were old acquaintances," both old-timers land in jail, where Pat recalls their tenuous past relation. He is discharged after a sobriety test, but his 1933 automobile—"lately become the property of the North Hollywood Finance and Loan Co."—will not run, so a police sergeant offers to take him home. This nostalgic exchange, which arouses our sympathy because it contrasts previous affluence and present indigence, transpires:

"Where do you live?" he asked as they started off.

"I don't live anywhere tonight," said Pat. "That's why I was driving around. When a friend of mine wakes up I'll touch him for a couple of bucks and go to a hotel."

"Well, now," said Sergeant Gaspar, "I got a couple of bucks that ain't working."

The great mansions of Beverly Hills slid by and Pat waved his hand at them in salute.

"In the good old days," he said, "I used to be able to drop into some of those houses day or night. And Sunday mornings—"

"Is that all true you said in the station," Gaspar asked, "—about how they put him in the hole?"

"Sure it is," said Pat. "that guy needn't have been so upstage. He's just an old-timer like me."

"A Patriotic Short" juxtaposes "the glamorous past" and the vulgar present more effectively and more movingly than any other Hobby fiction. Allusions to the swimming pool Pat had possessed during "those fat days of silent pictures" frame the one-part narrative, which ends on an emotional note: "He bent down over his desk, his shoulders shaking as he thought of that happy day when he had had a swimming pool." Between these allusions, material about Pat's current $250 assignment, *True to Two Flags*, regarding "the career of General Fitzhugh Lee who fought for the Confederacy and later for the U.S.A. against Spain—so it would offend neither North nor South," punctuates his recollection of former glories. He proposes, "We could have this Fitzhugh Lee in love with a Jewish girl. He's going to be shot at curfew so she grabs a church bell—," but producer Jack Berners rudely dismisses such melodrama: "If you thought up this tripe to please me you're losing your grip." Pat then remembers "a certain day over a decade ago in all its details, how he had arrived at the studio in his car driven by a Filipino in uniform; the deferential bow of the guard at the gate which had admitted car and all to the lot, his ascent to that long lost office which had a room for the secretary and was really a director's office."

Sandwiched among subsequent *True to Two Flags* passages is another treasured recollection, the one concerning the first visit an American president ever paid any Hollywood studio: "His memory of the luncheon was palpitant with glamor. The Great Man had asked some questions about pictures and had told a joke and Pat had laughed and laughed with the others—all of them solid men together—rich, happy and successful. . . . Ah he was proud of pictures then—of his position in them—of the President of the happy country where he was born." Soon Pat, near the water cooler, sees several executives approaching with "the girl of the year, the It girl, the Oomph girl, the Glamour Girl, the girl for whose services every studio was in violent competition." Though they exchange looks, her "party seemed to walk right through him—so that he had to take a step back against the wall."

Scott Fitzgerald and Pat Hobby share various characteristics and circumstances, yet the novelist resembles the scenarist even less than he does the flamboyant Finnegan. The real person was as impecunious as either fictional mask when he composed the Hobby sequence, which, ironically, "except for odd studio jobs . . . constituted [the] only certain source of income in those last two years" (*PH*, xxii). He, too, had owned a used car, signed over insurance, paid off debts. Unlike Hobby or Finnegan, however, Fitzgerald, suffering from tuberculosis and heart disease, struggling against alcoholism, and starting *The Last Tycoon*, managed to keep his daughter, Scottie, in Vassar College and his wife, Zelda, in Highland Hospital. Is it any wonder, then, that, "tired of being Scott Fitzgerald," he recommended diverse noms de plume to Gingrich: John Darcy, John Blue, Paul Elgin? And is it any wonder that he wrote Perkins about reissuing *Gatsby* almost exactly seven months before his death on 21 December 1940: "But to die, so completely and unjustly after having given so much. Even now there is little published in American fiction that doesn't slightly bare [*sic*] my stamp—in a small way I was an original" (*Dear Scott*, 261)?

Conclusion

To understand Fitzgerald's art, one must be cognizant of the technical and thematic patterns that pervade his best efforts. Only *The Great Gatsby* seemingly incorporates them all, but they appear in other significant works as well. Focusing on the major stories, with sidelong glimpses at some of his other superior fiction, both long and short, let us recapitulate the permanent achievement of this author.

Fitzgerald was an autobiographical writer and thus needed distancing devices to minimize his subjective involvement in his fiction. Accordingly, he often invoked the first-person observer point of view, which he had introduced at prep school. "The Pierian Springs and the Last Straw," his most impressive college story, employs a persona that anticipates subsequent observer-narrators in *The Great Gatsby*, "The Rich Boy," "The Last of the Belles," "Financing Finnegan," and *The Last Tycoon*. About Cecilia, the sympathetic "biographer" of Monroe Stahr, Fitzgerald commented:

> This love affair is the meat of the book—though I am going to treat it, remember, as it comes through to Cecilia. That is to say by making Cecilia, at the moment of her telling the story, an intelligent and observant woman, I shall grant myself the privilege as Conrad did, of letting her imagine the actions of the characters. Thus, I hope to get the verisimilitude of a first person narrative, combined with a Godlike knowledge of all events that happen to my characters. (*LT*, Notes, 139–40)

Elsewhere in his notes Fitzgerald stated: "Cecilia is the narrator because I think I know exactly how such a person would react to my story. She is *of* the movies but not *in* them. . . . So she is, all at once, intelligent, cynical, but understanding and kindly" (*LT*, Notes, 138).

Another device that permitted him to blend intimacy and detachment was composite characterization, whereby fictional figures fused traits from more than one actual person. Often, if not always, a protagonist would combine the author and some close friend: Dwight Taylor contributed to Joel Coles in "Crazy Sunday," Gerald Murphy to Dick Diver in *Tender Is the Night,* Ernest Hemingway to Finnegan in "Financing Finnegan." Fitzgerald wrote Sara Murphy regarding this not long after he had defended his theory of "building a monument out of three kinds of marble" against Hemingway's objections: "In my theory, utterly opposite to Ernest's, about fiction, i.e., that it takes half a dozen people to make a synthesis strong enough to create a fiction character—in that theory, or rather in despite of it, I used you again and again in *Tender*" (*Letters,* 423).

The imaginative combination of first-person observer Carraway and composite character Gatsby, who together represented Fitzgerald's divided nature, explains why *The Great Gatsby* appears to be so impersonal, while the two earlier novels are solipsistic. Double vision, possible only when the author employs such objective correlatives as observer-narrator and composite characterization, produces the tragicomic irony marking *Gatsby* and other similar fictions. For example, in "The Rich Boy, in which an anonymous narrator (fictionalized Scott Fitzgerald) records the life of Anson Hunter (fictionalized Ludlow Fowler), the following ironic passage occurs: "He had an instinctive and rather charitable knowledge of the weaknesses of men and women, and, like a priest, it made him the more concerned for the maintenance of outward forms. It was typical of him that every Sunday morning he taught in a fashionable Episcopal Sunday-school—even though a cold shower and a quick change into a cutaway coat were all that separated him from the wild night before" (*BR,* 164).

It must be remembered, however, that though the first-person observer was used in two of Fitzgerald's five novels and in some of his good minor stories, only "The Rich Boy" among the eight major short fictions uses this perspective. Most others are told via alternate unlimited and limited third-person foci, a union he seems to have been working toward during college when he shifted from the omniscient voice of the prep school fiction to a Jamesian central intelligence. This method also allowed him to wed "the verisimilitude of a first person narrative" and "a Godlike knowledge." Retaining omniscience meant the raconteur knew more than any first-person observer, while adding a central intelligence enabled Fitzgerald to minimize authorial intrusiveness, both important considerations for the self-indulgent young writer.

Now events were perceived, not voiced, by a character whose protagonal role seemed less ambiguous than that of the observer-narrator.

Not only did pyschological reactions remain pivotal, but main characters might transcend the static choice between realistic storyteller and romantic hero. Protagonal diversity therefore distinguishes the major stories exclusive of the first-person "Rich Boy" and the multiple-focused "May Day," with a Southern belle featured in "The Ice Palace," a Midwestern student in "The Diamond as Big as the Ritz," a laundry executive in "Winter Dreams," a Catholic child in "Absolution," a businessman in "Babylon Revisited," and a scenarist in "Crazy Sunday."

Internalizing narration through first-person observers and third-person consciousnesses helped Fitzgerald merge private and public phenomena, so that the microcosmic individual would reflect the external world and the macrocosmic group would reflect the personal psyche. Consequently, Charlie Wales's mental depression mirrors the historical Great Depression and vice versa.

Geographical locations, which are often urban, contain symbolic significance in Fitzgerald. The violent Manhattan of "May Day" is even more Babylonian than the decadent Paris of "Babylon Revisited." Illusions born in pretentious Black Bear [St. Paul], Minnesota ("Winter Dreams"), or obscure Ludwig, [North?] Dakota ("Absolution"), die in callous Hollywood, California ("Crazy Sunday"). Arguably the most versatile prose landscapist among modern American authors, Fitzgerald far surpasses giants like Hemingway, whose settings tend to be international, and Faulkner, whose settings tend to be local, by treating every important national area. Furthermore, no one rivals him in juxtaposing these regions for thematic purposes. "The Diamond as Big as the Ritz" alone covers Hades (the Midwest), St. Midas' School (the East), and Fish, Montana (the West). The personal conflict between Sally and Harry in "The Ice Palace" becomes externalized through antithetical places, the South representing her life-oriented inertia and the North his death-oriented energy, while in *The Great Gatsby* the East destroys the older indigenous qualities hinterland characters possess. For Gatsby and for us, the transcendental, the spiritual, can be found only out West, despite "the bored, sprawling, swollen towns beyond the Ohio, with their interminable inquisitions" (*GG*, 177), out "where the dark fields of the republic rolled on under the night" (*GG*, 182). *Tender Is the Night* and its satellite stories demonstrate that the Jamesian international theme is hardly less central to Fitzgerald's fiction than to Hemingway's. The expatriate couple of "One Trip Abroad," who anticipate the Divers, are as decadent as the lost generation of *The Sun*

Also Rises in their restless movement from spot to spot. Although less successful, "The Swimmers" more directly juxtaposes European and American landscapes.

Besides psychosymbolic meaning, landscape juxtaposition supplies coherence, since dichotomous geographical locations make possible circular journeys—the most effective structural mode Fitzgerald employed. Thus, South (Georgia) frames North (Minnesota) in "The Ice Palace," while Midwest (Mississippi River town) frames West (Montana) in "The Diamond as Big as the Ritz." Since these stories depend on monomythic return, they are essentially positive, Sally Carrol Happer reaffirming her Southern heritage and John T. Unger escaping annihilation with his girlfriend Kismine. They also entail irony, for both protagonists, like many another Fitzgerald hero or heroine, become disillusioned questers. Such bittersweet experiences reach their apotheosis in *The Great Gatsby*, where a nameless "Middle Western city" (St. Paul) frames a designated Eastern one (New York). Here, observer Nick goes home and survives, but observed Gatsby stays away and perishes.

When journeys involve only one geographical area, circularity is achieved through recurrent locales. "May Day" (Manhattan) and "Babylon Revisited" (Paris) commence and conclude at public establishments, the first shifting between antipodal hotels after its abstract prologue and the second reverting back to the same bar—public places that bracket similar settings like Delmonico's and Childs' or Le Grand Vatel and Griffons. The limited private place characterizes the more circumscribed rural milieu projected by "Absolution." In Ludwig the world outside ("Swede girls," "Dakota wheat"), which may be seen from a window, literally encloses the world inside ("haunted room"). All three stories end irresolutely, as the death of Gordon Sterrett, the flight of Rudolph Miller from the madness of Father Schwartz, and the failure of Charlie Wales have ambiguous implications.

Occasionally, temporal juxtaposition accompanies spatial juxtaposition for structural purposes. "Absolution," the discarded prologue to *The Great Gatsby*, illustrates this. What happened "*On Saturday, Three Days Ago*" constitutes a long flashback narrated one afternoon while the outside world emanates omnipresent sunshine (compare "May Day"). Not unexpectedly, the Chinese box arrangement of past within present within timelessness reflects the novel's strategy whereby the present (the Midwest) enframes the past (the East), but invokes mythical rather than natural phenomena.

Fitzgerald more commonly uses temporal juxtaposition *during* the narrative. "Babylon Revisited" is as impressive as *Gatsby* when it comes to implying how the past motivates or even determines the present. Anterior references dominate both the Ritz bar framework and the framed material. The story begins:

> "And where's Mr. Campbell?" Charlie asked.
> "Gone to Switzerland. Mr. Campbell's a pretty sick man, Mr. Wales."
> "I'm sorry to hear that. And George Hardt?" Charlie inquired.
> "Back in America, gone to work."
> "And where is the Snow Bird?" (*BR*, 210)

From here on, prior events gradually unfold: the protagonist's drinking and spending, his alcoholism and pranks, his market losses and hospitalization, his recovery and return. These events, which culminate with the crucial snowstorm episode, rival the present action in importance.

Though such temporal juxtaposition may be considered modern, Fitzgerald's commitment to chronological order suggests a more traditional bent that derives from the dual emphasis on character (biography) and country (history), besides an obsession over youth that inspired Hemingway's comment about Fitzgerald having confused growing up with growing old. At any rate, "The Ice Palace" transpires between summer and spring; "May Day" between 9:00 A.M. 19 May and 9:00 A.M. 20 May; "The Diamond as Big as the Ritz" takes one summer; "Absolution" one half hour; "Babylon Revisited" four or five days; "Crazy Sunday" three Sundays. "Winter Dreams" and "The Rich Boy" are even better examples because they record their subjects' lives from fourteen to thirty-two and from seven to thirty, respectively. His linear time bias may explain why Fitzgerald felt the "great fault" of *Tender Is the Night* was "that the *true* beginning—the young psychiatrist in Switzerland—is tucked away in the middle of the book" (*Dear Scott*, 251). Later, he rearranged the novel to open with Dick's antecedent existence and noted, "the *final version* of the book as I would like it."[79]

If Fitzgerald the dramatist could juxtapose places and Fitzgerald the fictionist could juxtapose times, Fitzgerald the poet could juxtapose images. Iterative imagery, which represents yet another instrument of coherence, enriches all his best efforts. As early as "The Ice Palace" it becomes evident. There, the North/South opposition is rendered by complex patterns of conflictive but interrelated allusions that encompass canine/feline, masculine/feminine, Scandinavian/Latin, snow god/ sun god, and energy/inertia. Anticipating *The Great Gatsby*—a magnificent prose poem—"Absolution" contains considerable romance imagery, but its focus is military. Unlike the novel, the story poses images of openness (wheat, sky) against images of enclosure (room, confessional). Dominant symbols usually accompany Fitzgerald's image patterns, symbols like the green light (*Gatsby*) and the amusement park ("Absolution"). These symbols elsewhere include ice palace, Columbus statue, diamond mountain, and Babylon.

The stress Fitzgerald put on the classical battle of the sexes confirms that his art is fundamentally conventional. To dramatize the masculine-feminine conflict, Fitzgerald introduced two archetypal characters: the *homme manqué* and the femme fatale. These types were fully developed before he became a professional writer, as "The Pierian Springs and the Last Straw," which prefigures *Gatsby,* suggests. Its George Rombert–Myra Fulham relationship adumbrates more than James Gatz–Daisy Fay, however, for inadequate men and destructive women are also paired in novels like *The Beautiful and Damned* and *Tender Is the Night* and short works like "May Day," "The Jelly-Bean," "The Last of the Belles," and the Josephine stories. The *homme manqué* and the femme fatale each bears certain generic similarities revolving around masculine passivity and feminine aggressiveness, with male victim and female victimizer often drawn from the upper classes. But not all of Fitzgerald's youthful protagonists represent the American aristocracy, since we encounter several middle-class parvenus like Dexter Green and John T. Unger. However, his fascination with social manners in a loosely stratified class system remains a constant from the "Thought-book" to *The Last Tycoon*. Even so, Fitzgerald the psychologist often resisted such mechanical stereotypes: thus, Sally Carrol Happer is victimized, while her Tarleton cronies Ailie Calhoun and Nancy Lamar remain victimizers; and though Gordon Sterrett is destroyed by Jewel Hudson, Anson Hunter abandons one girlfriend after another. Several men emerge triumphant through resourcefulness in the battle of the sexes, just as several women seem to be vital rather than destructive.

Conventional too is the centrality of the male protagonist, as the five Fitzgerald novels illustrate. Despite his agent Harold Ober's tax claim that Fitzgerald's stories were inappropriate to women's magazines, the author, who published in *Collier's, McCall's, Liberty, Woman's Home*

Companion, Harper's Bazaar, and *Redbook,* had already narrated some *Post* selections through female eyes, among them "The Ice Palace" and the Josephine pieces. This perspective culminates in Cecilia Brady's re-creation of Monroe Stahr.

Almost every important hero or heroine up to and including Basil and Josephine grows disillusioned. In Fitzgerald, youth frequently means innocence and illusion, the period when imagination, unfettered by a knowledge of reality and the limitations it imposes, operates freely. The romantic young see the world as mysterious, as containing infinite possibilities. Because of their naïveté, they can experience beauty and wonder without the disturbing knowledge that the beautiful and the wonderful are transitory, or worse yet, disguises for ugliness and evil. Typical of many others is this passage from one Basil story: "Quivering at every scene, sight or tune, he wanted to be blasé and calm. Wretchedly he felt the whole world of beauty pour down upon him like moonlight, pressing on him, making his breath now sighing, now short, as he wallowed helplessly in a superabundance of youth for which a hundred adults present would have given years of life."

This adolescent response to beauty and wonder does not depend solely on sexual stimulation, since such feelings can also be elicited by dance, play, or football game, by going to New York, by walking alone through moonlight. Yet juvenility must end, innocence become experience, illusion entail disillusion: "It is in the twenties that the actual momentum of life begins to slacken, and it is a simple soul indeed to whom as many things are as significant and meaningful at thirty as at ten years before."[80]

When Fitzgerald emphasized illusion per se over its realization, he betrayed his own romantic heritage: from Goethe's Faust, who was damned after asking the "beautiful moment" to "Linger, thou art so fair"; from Browning, who wrote that "A man's reach should exceed his grasp, / Or what's a heaven for"; from Robert Louis Stevenson, who suggested that "To travel hopefully is a better thing than to arrive." If illusion materializes, the ideal gets lost in the real, the eternal in the mortal. For instance, marriage, which caps love, embodies one common form of disillusionment.

According to Fitzgerald, authors have a limited number of themes (see part 2). His first major idea, lost illusion, metamorphosed into his second, emotional bankruptcy. Just as the earlier climaxed in *The Great Gatsby,* the later climaxed in *Tender Is the Night,* though dissolute figures like Gordon Sterrett, Anthony Patch, and Tom Buchanan had already appeared. The term, used to name a 1931 Josephine piece, was explicated by the "Crack-Up" articles. Lesions of vitality leading to emotional bankruptcy often occur within vampiric marriages. They produce predictable symptoms, which Fitzgerald transferred from his life with Zelda to his work: drinking, brawling, promiscuity, prejudice, ennui. If unrealistic illusions reflect the optimistic 1920s, emotional bankruptcy aptly depicts the pessimistic 1930s. Both "great and moving experiences" when conveyed through sophisticated fictional techniques—observer-narrator and central intelligence, composite characterization, psychosymbolic landscapes, circular journeys, temporal juxtaposition, iterative imagery, archetypal figures—help to explain how Scott Fitzgerald came to write his few immortal tales.

Notes to Part 1

1. *F. Scott Fitzgerald in His Own Time: A Miscellany*, ed. Matthew J. Bruccoli and Jackson R. Bryer (Kent, Ohio: Kent State University Press, 1971), 270; subsequently referred to in the text as *Miscellany*.

2. *The Letters of F. Scott Fitzgerald*, ed. Andrew Turnbull (New York: Scribner, 1963), 206; subsequently referred to in the text as *Letters*.

3. *Dear Scott/Dear Max: The Fitzgerald-Perkins Correspondence*, ed. John Kuehl and Jackson R. Bryer (New York: Scribner, 1971), 70; subsequently referred to in the text as *Dear Scott*.

4. Quoted in *The Stories of F. Scott Fitzgerald*, ed. Malcolm Cowley (1951; reprint, New York: Macmillan Scribner Classic, 1986), xix; subsequently referred to in the text as *Stories*.

5. Matthew J. Bruccoli, *Some Sort of Epic Grandeur: The Life of F. Scott Fitzgerald* (New York: Harcourt Brace Jovanovich, 1981), 323.

6. *As Ever, Scott Fitz–*, ed. Matthew J. Bruccoli (Philadelphia: Lippincott, 1972), 36; subsequently referred to in the text as *As Ever*.

7. Henry Dan Piper, *F. Scott Fitzgerald: A Critical Portrait* (New York: Holt, 1965), 481.

8. *Correspondence of F. Scott Fitzgerald*, ed. Matthew J. Bruccoli and Margaret M. Duggan (New York: Random House, 1980), 557; subsequently referred to in the text as *Correspondence*.

9. Ellen Kimbel, "The American Short Story: 1900–1920," in *The American Short Story: 1900–1945*, ed. Philip Stevick (Boston: Twayne, 1984), 41.

10. Thomas A. Gullason, "The 'Lesser' Renaissance: The American Short Story in the 1920s," in *The American Short Story*, 79.

11. Sherwood Anderson, *A Story Teller's Story*, ed. Ray Lewis White (1924; reprint, Cleveland: Case Western Reserve University Press, 1968), 255, 262.

12. This review, "How to Waste Material: A Note on My Generation," appeared later in *Afternoon of an Author*, ed. Arthur Mizener (Princeton, N.J.: Princeton University Library, 1957), 117–22. The quotations have been taken from the Mizener version. Subsequently referred to in the text as *AA*.

13. *The Notebooks of F. Scott Fitzgerald*, ed. Matthew J. Bruccoli (New York: Harcourt Brace Jovanovich, 1978), 158; subsequently referred to in the text as *Notebooks*.

14. Lionel Trilling, *The Liberal Imagination* (New York: Doubleday Anchor, 1950), 241.

15. *The Short Stories of F. Scott Fitzgerald: New Approaches in Criticism*, ed. Jackson R. Bryer (Madison: University of Wisconsin Press, 1981), xi–xii.

16. *Thoughtbook of Francis Scott Key Fitzgerald*, ed. John Kuehl, *Princeton University Library Chronicle* 26, no. 2 (Winter 1965). My discussion is taken from this source; so, too, are the quotations, which retain the author's punctuation, capitalization, etc. Elsewhere I have used "[*sic*]" to indicate incorrect usage. Reprinted as a limited edition book in 1965.

17. As quoted in *The Apprentice Fiction of F. Scott Fitzgerald, 1909–1917*, ed. John Kuehl (New Brunswick, N.J.: Rutgers University Press, 1965). All quotations for the juvenile stories, as well as much of my discussion, are taken from this source. Matthew J. Bruccoli has edited *F. Scott Fitzgerald's "Ledger"* (Washington, D.C.: NCR Microcard Editions, 1973).

18. Andrew Turnbull, *Scott Fitzgerald* (New York: Scribner, 1962), 259.

19. This story, with my analysis, was also published under the title "A Note on the Begetting of *Gatsby*," *University: A Princeton Magazine*, no. 21 (Summer 1964): 26–32.

20. *The Great Gatsby* (1925; reprint, New York: Macmillan Scribner Classic, 1986), 1; subsequently referred to in the text as *GG*.

21. "The Mystery of the Raymond Mortgage" had introduced this character, and, since the piece unintentionally burlesqued nineteenth-century detective fiction, Edgar Allen Poe and Sir Arthur Conan Doyle probably inspired its use. "The Room with the Green Blinds" was the single other prep-school story narrated from this point of view. Later, Fitzgerald's understanding of the first-person observer as narrator would be increased by his reading of Joseph Conrad and Willa Cather.

22. Patricia Waugh, *Metafiction: The Theory and Practice of Self-Conscious Fiction* (London: Methuen, 1984), 136.

23. Kenneth Eble, *F. Scott Fitzgerald* (New York: Twayne, 1963), 55.

24. All eight stories appear in *Babylon Revisited and Other Stories* (New York: Macmillan Scribner Classic, 1987); subsequently referred to in the text as *BR*.

25. Scott Donaldson, "Scott Fitzgerald's Romance with the South," *Southern Literary Journal* 5 (Spring 1973): 8.

26. See section 4 of "Scott Fitzgerald's Critical Opinions" in part 2 for the evolution of "The Ice Palace" as described by his letter to *The Editor* of June 1920. My own discussion of the story is an abridged and revised version of "Psychic Geography in 'The Ice Palace,'" which appeared in Jackson R. Bryer's *The Short Stories of F. Scott Fitzgerald: New Approaches to Criticism* (Madison: University of Wisconsin Press, 1982), 169–79.

27. Edwin Moses, "F. Scott Fitzgerald and the Quest to 'The Ice Palace,'" *CEA Critic* 36 (January 1974): 12.

28. See Tahita N. Fulkerson, "Ibsen in 'The Ice Palace,'" *Fitzgerald/Hemingway Annual* (1979): 169–71.

29. John A. Higgins, *F. Scott Fitzgerald: A Study of the Stories* (Jamaica, N.Y.: St. John's University Press, 1971), 55.

30. *Tales of Grimm and Andersen*, ed. Frederick Jacobi, Jr. (New York: Random House, 1952), 412.

31. In this 1931 letter to Maxwell Perkins, Fitzgerald claimed "credit for naming" "the Jazz Age."

32. See Colin S. Cass, "Fitzgerald's Second Thoughts about 'May Day'": A Collation and Study," *Fitzgerald/Hemingway Annual* (1970): 69–95.

33. Anthony J. Mazella, "The Tension of Opposites in Fitzgerald's 'May Day,'" *Studies in Short Fiction* 14 (Fall 1977): 379–80.

34. C. Hugh Holman, *A Handbook to Literature*, 4th ed. (Indianapolis: Bobbs-Merrill, 1980), 277.

35. F. Scott Fitzgerald, "The Crack-Up," in *The Crack-Up*, ed. Edmund Wilson (1945; reprint, New York: New Directions, 1956), 69; subsequently referred to in the text as *CU*.

36. Robert Sklar, *F. Scott Fitzgerald: The Last Laocoön* (New York: Oxford University Press, 1967), 142. Henry Dan Piper wrote in the *Fitzgerald Newsletter* 8 (Winter 1960): "F, like Hemingway and many another of that generation, was a lifelong admirer of the fiction of Mark Twain. . . . [W]e find him writing Edmund Wilson in 1921 [*CU*, 256] that he has just finished reading Albert Bigelow Paine's three-volume biography of Mark Twain and thinks it 'excellent.' He was a member of the Mark Twain Society."

37. Robert Emmet Long, *The Achieving of "The Great Gatsby": F. Scott Fitzgerald, 1920–1925* (Lewisburg, Pa.: Bucknell University Press, 1979), 63, 64.

38. Leonard A. Podis, "Fitzgerald's 'The Diamond as Big as the Ritz' and Hawthorne's 'Rappaccini's Daughter,'" *Studies in Short Fiction* 21 (1984): 244.

39. Milton Hindus, *F. Scott Fitzgerald: An Introduction and Interpretation* (New York: Holt, 1968), 106.

40. *The Great Gatsby* was published 10 April 1925, and "The Rich Boy," which was accepted by *Red Book* for $3,500 once the *Post* had rejected it, was published January/February 1926. Composed and extensively revised the previous spring and summer, "The Rich Boy" might be considered a *Gatsby* spinoff. The novelette should also have been a novel, according to *All the Sad Young Men* dedicatee Ring Lardner (see *Correspondence*, 191).

41. Joan M. Allen, *Candles and Carnival Nights: The Catholic Sensibility of F. Scott Fitzgerald* (New York: New York University Press, 1978), 100.

42. In my article "A la Joyce: The Sisters Fitzgerald's Absolution" (*James Joyce Quarterly* 2, no. 1 [Fall 1964]: 2–6), which provided the basis for the present discussion, I wrote, "By now it is common knowledge that when Scott Fitzgerald met James Joyce at a Sylvia Beach dinner party during July of 1928 he threatened to jump out of the window in honor of Joyce's genius and drew a picture in Miss Beach's copy of *The Great Gatsby* showing himself kneeling

beside the master who has a halo on and whom Miss Beach asserts Fitzgerald 'worshiped.'" Although "A la Joyce" had been printed fifteen years before, Kenneth Cushman stated in "Scott Fitzgerald's Scrupulous Meanness: 'Absolution' and 'The Sisters'" (*Fitzgerald/Hemingway Annual*, 1979), "The debt owed by 'Absolution' to Joyce's 'The Sisters,' the first story in *Dubliners*, has never been noticed."

43. If Fitzgerald meant "an arrow flying into God," the phrase should be *Sagitta volante in Deum*. J. I. Morse, in the *Fitzgerald/Hemingway Annual* (1972): 321–22, however, argues that this is a spelling rather than a grammatical error. According to Morse, Fitzgerald intended to write *Sagitta volante in die*, as he did later in "Sleeping and Waking," an allusion taken from Psalm 90, reading "the arrow that flieth in the day."

44. My comments on *The Great Gatsby* and "Absolution" in the present chapter, as well as on *Tender Is the Night* and *The Last Tycoon* in subsequent chapters, are indebted to my article "Scott Fitzgerald: Romantic and Realist," *Texas Studies in Literature and Language* 1 (Autumn 1959): 412–26.

45. William Troy, "Scott Fitzgerald—Authority of Failure," in *F. Scott Fitzgerald: A Collection of Critical Essays*, ed. Arthur Mizener (1945; reprint, Englewood Cliffs, N.J.: Prentice-Hall, 1963), 23–24.

46. Clinton S. Burhans, Jr., "'Magnificently Attune to Life': The Value of 'Winter Dreams,'" *Studies in Short Fiction* 6 (Winter 1969): 412.

47. *The Great Gatsby*'s galley proofs bear the title *Trimalchio*.

48. Wayne C. Booth, *The Rhetoric of Fiction* (Chicago: University of Chicago Press, 1961), 158–59.

49. Milton R. Stern, *The Golden Moment. The Novels of F. Scott Fitzgerald* (Urbana: University of Illinois Press, 1970), 191, 194, 193.

50. Gary J. Scrimgeour, "Against *The Great Gatsby*," *Twentieth Century Interpretations of "The Great Gatsby*," ed. Ernest H. Lockridge (Englewood Cliffs, N.J.: Prentice-Hall, 1968), 71, 79, 80.

51. Patrick D. Murphy, "Illumination and Affection in the Parallel Plots of 'The Rich Boy' and 'The Beast in the Jungle,'" *Papers on Language and Literature* 22 (1986): 407.

52. Brian Way, *F. Scott Fitzgerald and the Art of Social Fiction* (London: Arnold, 1980), 85.

53. Anthony Bryant Mangum, "The Short Stories of F. Scott Fitzgerald: A Study in Literary Economics" (Ph.D. diss., University of South Carolina, 1974), Appendix C.

54. Arthur Mizener, *The Far Side of Paradise* (Boston: Houghton Mifflin, 1949), 70.

55. *Tender Is the Night* (1934; reprint, New York: Macmillan Scribner Classic, 1986), 201; subsequently referred to in the text as *TN*.

56. David Toor, "Guilt and Retribution in 'Babylon Revisited,'" *Fitzgerald/Hemingway Annual* (1973): 156.

57. In an essay titled "When the Story Ends: 'Babylon Revisited,'" Carlos Baker discusses "the double theme of freedom and imprisonment, of locking out and locking in" (Bryer, 269).

58. *Encyclopedic Dictionary of the Bible*, trans. Louis F. Hartman, C.S.S.R. (New York: McGraw-Hill, 1963), 2478.

59. Taylor's article, "Scott Fitzgerald in Hollywood," originally appeared in *Harper's*, March 1959, 67–71. In the same year Putnam reprinted it in his book *Joy Ride* as the chapter entitled "This Side of Malibu," the source cited here. The block quotation is taken from pp. 249–50 and the quotations preceding it from pp. 240, 242, 244–45, 246, and 248.

60. *Letters to His Daughter*, ed. Andrew Turnbull (New York: Scribner, 1963), 103; Subsequently referred to in the text as *Daughter*.

61. Aaron Latham, *Crazy Sundays: F. Scott Fitzgerald in Hollywood* (New York: Viking, 1970), 251.

62. Kenneth G. Johnston, "Fitzgerald's 'Crazy Sunday': Cinderella in Hollywood," *Literature/Film Quarterly* (Summer 1978): 215, 216, 220.

63. *The Last Tycoon* (1941; reprint, New York: Macmillan Scribner Classic, 1986), 28; subsequently referred to in the text as *LT*.

64. See the *Princeton University Library Chronicle* 12, no. 4 (Summer 1951): 167–80. In his brief introductory note just quoted, Arthur Mizener says the story belongs chronologically second among the Basil fictions. However, a comparison of details with the "Ledger" notations unmistakably locates "That Kind of Party" in 1907, thus putting it first. Of the Basil series, only this one and "The Scandal Detectives" treat the period encompassed by the "Thoughtbook."

65. See *The Basil and Josephine Stories*, ed. Jackson R. Bryer and John Kuehl (New York: Scribner 1973). My discussion of these stories is a revised version of the introduction to this book. "The Freshest Boy," which most critics regard as the best Basil story, appears with the eight major short fictions previously discussed and "The Long Way Out" in *Babylon Revisited and Other Stories*.

66. The outline reads as follows:

I	Scandal Detectives	(Age 14)	Gentleman Burglar
II	A Night at the Fair	(" 14)	Long Pants
III	The Freshest Boy	(Age 15)	Fresh–New York
IV	He Thinks He's Wonderful	(" 15)	Conceit–Talking
V	The Captured Shadow	(" 15)	1st Success
VI	The Perfect Life	(" 16)	Priggishness
VII	Forging Ahead	(" 16)	Work
VIII	Basil and Cleopatra	(" 17)	Love

67. For this and subsequent insights, see Matthew J. Bruccoli's unpublished thesis "'A Handful Lying Loose'—a Study of F. Scott Fitzgerald's Basil Duke Lee Stories" (University of Virginia, 1955).

68. Review of Tarkington's *Penrod and Sam, Nassau Literary Magazine* 72 (January 1917): 291–92; see *Miscellany,* 113–14.
69. Subsequently, a previously unpublished story, "The Vanished Girl" (retitled "A Full Life"), was published in the *Princeton University Library Chronicle* 49, no. 4 (Winter 1988) with James L. W. West III's introduction. This story had been "discovered" by Ruth Prigozy, who wrote about it in "The Unpublished Stories: Fitzgerald in His Final Stage," *Twentieth Century Literature* 20, no. 2 (April 1974):79–80.
70. In *The Composition of "Tender Is the Night": A Study of the Manuscripts* (Pittsburgh: University of Pittsburgh Press, 1963), Matthew J. Bruccoli observes on page 127:

> In the story—as in *Tender Is the Night*—the man had previously failed to reciprocate the girl's passion, and now he is jealous of her young suitor. "Jacob's Ladder" includes a scene in which the man visits a movie location on which the actress is working, where he is annoyed by a would-be Valentino named Raffino. Nicotera, the Latin lover in *Tender Is the Night*, is named Raffino in this draft. Several speeches in Chapter 20—for example, Rosemary's comment about having sex appeal in the rushes—are taken from the story.

71. Zelda was hospitalized first at the Valmont, then at Prangins clinic in Switzerland, following her 1930 breakdown in Paris.
72. Sergio Perosa, *The Art of F. Scott Fitzgerald* (Ann Arbor: University of Michigan Press, 1965), 101.
73. Bryer's collection also contains "'The Swimmers': Paris and Virginia Reconciled" by Melvin J. Friedman, which reviews critical reactions to this controversial work and discusses its various motifs.
74. Honoria Murphy Donnelly with Richard N. Billings, *Sara and Gerald* (New York: Holt, 1982), 26. The Murphys are alluded to in the story: "L'un des Murphys était comme ça." Not only does fairy-tale imagery permeate "Absolution," *The Great Gatsby,* and other works, but it may also be found in Fitzgerald's notebooks, where he writes, "The two basic stories of all times are *Cinderella* and *Jack the Giant Killer*—the charm of women and the courage of men."
75. *The Price Was High: The Last Uncollected Stories of F. Scott Fitzgerald,* ed. Matthew J. Bruccoli (New York: Harcourt Brace Jovanovich, 1981), 710; subsequently referred to in the text as *Price.*
76. *The Pat Hobby Stories,* intro. Arnold Gingrich (New York: Scribner, 1962), ix; subsequently referred to in the text as *PH.*
77. In sequence, they read: "Pat Hobby's Christmas Wish," "A Man in the Way," "'Boil Some Water—Lots of It,'" "Teamed with Genius," "Pat Hobby and Orson Welles," "Pat Hobby's Secret," "Pat Hobby, Putative Fa-

ther," "The Homes of the Stars," "Pat Hobby Does His Bit," "Pat Hobby's Preview," "No Harm Trying," "A Patriotic Short," "On the Trail of Pat Hobby," "Fun in an Artist's Studio," "Two Old-Timers," "Mightier Than the Sword," and "Pat Hobby's College Days."

78. Despite Gingrich's claim that Fitzgerald intended the Hobby sequence to be "a collective entity" with interdependent parts, Thomas E. Daniels feels "that Fitzgerald intended each individual story as an entity in itself by his obvious attempt to include in each story all the background material necessary for an understanding of each story—therefore the repetition." Consequently, "the Pat Hobby stories are better as individual units than as a series. When presented as a series there is too much repetition of character, setting, and devices Fitzgerald found necessary to tie the stories together." See "Pat Hobby: Anti-Hero," in *Fitzgerald/Hemingway Annual* (1973): 138.

79. See Fitzgerald's copy of *Tender Is the Night*, Fitzgerald Papers, The Princeton University Library. In 1952 Scribner published a new version of the novel edited by Malcolm Cowley reflecting this scheme.

80. *The Beautiful and Damned* (1922; reprint, New York: Scribner, 1988), 169.

Part 2

THE WRITER

Introduction

This part consists of a revised and expanded version of an article of mine originally published in *Modern Fiction Studies*. Fitzgerald's critical opinions, culled from the published writings, letters, notebooks, and other sources, fall into four categories. The first section introduces Fitzgerald, the self-conscious craftsman who advocated and practiced "shaping" and "pruning." Then follows material devoted to the role poetry and originality play in developing a great style. The need for morality and the tension between "subjectivity" and "objectivity" occupy the third section. Though the views this and the other sections express cover both story and novel, I have added several final paragraphs regarding the short form alone, their focus an important letter that traces the evolution of "The Ice Palace."

"Scott Fitzgerald's Critical Opinions" not only proves how well the author understood the craft of fiction, but demonstrates how articulate he was in expressing that knowledge. See *F. Scott Fitzgerald On Writing*, edited by Larry W. Phillips (Scribner, 1985), as a useful supplement to my discussion.

Scott Fitzgerald's Critical Opinions

Scott Fitzgerald wrote for money more mediocre fiction than any other American author of similar stature except, perhaps, Mark Twain. He deeply regretted this. In 1924 he informed Edmund Wilson, "I really worked hard as hell last winter—but it was all trash and it nearly broke my heart" (*CU*, 264–65). A little later he observed to John Peale Bishop, "I've done about 10 pieces of horrible junk in the last year . . . that I can never republish or bear to look at—cheap and without the spontaneity of my first work" (*CU*, 267–68). Nor was he ever happy about his Hollywood experiences, for he found turning out scenarios even more trying than turning out potboilers.

When on 20 May 1940 he told Maxwell Perkins, "I just couldn't make the grade as a hack—that like everything else, requires a certain practised excellence" (*Dear Scott*, 261), Fitzgerald underrated himself, since he ranked well above the average slick writer. He maintained otherwise because he wanted to be an artist, not just a hired drudge like the fictitious Pat Hobby. Fitzgerald approached his serious efforts, his "labors of love," with intelligence and perception. He did indeed "slave over every sentence" to avoid the charge of "fatal facility" (*AA*, 181).

I

Fitzgerald laid great stress upon the writer's need of self-conscious *craft*. In 1938 he commented, "Some people seem to look on our time as a sort of swollen Elizabethan age, simply crawling with geniuses. The necessity of the artist in every generation has been to give his work permanence in every way by a safe shaping and a constant pruning, lest he be confused with the journalistic material that has attracted lesser men" (*Letters*, 571–72).

Revised and expanded by the author from the original version of his essay published in *Modern Fiction Studies* 7 (Spring 1961): 3–18. © 1961 by Purdue Research Foundation, West Lafayette, Indiana. Reprinted by permission.

The intensity with which he held the conviction that form and economy are essential to good writing is well illustrated by his attitude toward Thomas Wolfe, who poured himself out, cultivating "every stray weed found in the garden." The real artist, the craftsman, must be selective: "That is where talent comes in to distinguish between the standard blooms which everyone knows and are not particularly exciting, the riotous and deceitful weeds, and that tiny faint often imperceptible flower hidden in a corner which, cultivated à la Burbank, is all it will ever pay us to cultivate whether it stays small or grows to the size of an oak" (*Letters*, 592). Wolfe marshaled his material in a "gawky and profuse way" and as a result was only "half-grown artistically." In his copy of *Of Time and the River* Fitzgerald wrote, "All this has been about as good as Dodsworth for chapter after chapter," and "trite, trite, trite, trite, page after page after page." Replying to Fitzgerald's advice that he be a more selective artist, Wolfe said, "A great writer is not only a leaver-outer but also a putter-inner," citing Shakespeare, Cervantes, and Dostoevsky as evidence (*CU*, 314). Though this did not mitigate his antagonism toward the sprawling novel, Fitzgerald admitted that Wolfe had escaped "the cardinal sin" of writing a dead work.

Most native authors were similarly negligent about craftsmanship because they too were obsessed by content. Thus, in "How to Waste Material," Fitzgerald complained, "Ever since Irving's preoccupation with the necessity for an American background, for some square miles of cleared territory on which colorful variants might presently arise, the question of material has hampered the American writer. For one Dreiser who made a single minded and irreproachable choice there have been a dozen like Henry James who have stupid-got with worry over the matter, and yet another dozen who, blinded by the fading tail of Walt Whitman's comet, have botched their books by the insincere compulsion to write 'significantly' about America" (*AA*, 117). He went on to say that even now, when a usable past has been discovered and "the foundations have been laid," our authors are still more interested in subject matter than craft. They focus on the American farmer, American cities, American politics, business, and society, and since this is a "literary gold rush," they can find no time to be artists. The material gets "turned out raw and undigested" (*AA*, 118).

Two men, Fitzgerald believed, shared the responsibility for the current manifestations of this long-existing indigenous literary sickness. One was H. L. Mencken, whom he praised on his own merits but condemned as bad for young writers. "Always . . . ethical rather than aesthetic," Mencken had "begotten a family of hammer and tongs men—insensitive, suspicious of glamor, preoccupied exclusively with the external, the contemptible, the 'national' and the drab" (*AA*, 119). The other was Sherwood Anderson, who had been imitated as a man of ideas instead of a writer with a brilliant style. American letters were looking up now, however, since Ernest Hemingway had just published *In Our Time*, containing "no food served up by the railroad restaurants of California and Wisconsin" (*AA*, 121).

Fitzgerald's own work exhibits "shaping" or "a molding of the confusion of life into form" and "pruning" or economy (*Price*, 263). These are well illustrated by the painstaking way he cut and revised material. In *This Side of Paradise* he "wrote and revised and compiled and boiled down" (*AA*, 85). From *The Great Gatsby* he deleted enough to make another novel, yet remained dissatisfied. Fitzgerald complained to Bishop that he had not reached the stage of "ruthless artistry which would let me cut out an exquisite bit that had no place in the context" (*CU*, 271). *Tender Is the Night*, composed between 1925 and 1934, went through three versions and numerous titles. Its author admitted composing more than 400,000 words for the book and throwing away three-fourths of them. Even after publication he struggled, finally deciding the plot should be chronological. But though Fitzgerald revised such manuscripts with considerable care, often making several drafts before arriving at the one he wanted, he tried not to overwrite. His type of style suffered through excessive reworking, he apprized Joseph Mankiewicz, and about *The Last Tycoon* he reminded himself: "Rewrite from mood. Has become stilted with rewriting. Don't look. Rewrite from mood."

Fitzgerald had a healthy respect for the single word and the single line. He believed that a single word could change the emphasis and the value in a scene or a setting. The "best . . . instance of artistic power," he wrote of Grace Flandrau's *Being Respectable*, was "the remarkable portrait of Valeria": "We have scarcely a glimpse of her, and she says only one line throughout. Yet the portrait is vivid and complete" (*Miscellaney*, 142). Despite the drastic revisions in his novels, he did not throw away anything he considered good. He went through the stories he did not intend to republish in a book, took out the best phrases and passages, had his secretary enter these in his notebooks, and then marked the stories "stripped" and not to be published again. Later, these same phrases and passages turned up in his novels. He felt similarly about the significance of scenes. He commented to Bishop, "I could tell you plenty [of] books in which the main episode, around which swings the entire drama, is over and accomplished in four or five sentences" (*Letters*, 366).

Fitzgerald's goal was "to develop a hard, colorful prose style" (*Daughter*, 25). This he achieved, but how? For one thing, he used verbs whenever possible instead of adjectives:

> About *adjectives*: all fine prose is based on the verbs carrying the sentences. They make the sentences move. Probably the finest technical poem in English is Keats' *Eve of Saint Agnes*. A line like:
>
> The hare limped trembling through the frozen grass,
>
> is so alive that you race through it, scarcely noticing it, yet it has colored the whole poem with its movement—the limping, trembling, and freezing is going on before your own eyes. (*CU*, 303)

He wrote natural sentences. In the Mankiewicz communication previously cited, he remarked: "People don't begin all sentences with *and, but, for* and *if*, do they? They simply break a thought in mid-paragraph, and in both *Gatsby* and *Farewell to Arms* the dialogue tends that way. Sticking in conjunctions makes a *monotonous* smoothness" (*Letters*, 562).

He avoided stilted language. Instead of such phrases as "pitched forward," which Edmund Wilson used in one of his short stories, Fitzgerald advised colloquialisms like "fell down," or "sorta sank down" (*CU*, 263). Because Wilson and Bishop were overcareful, they did not achieve "the queer slanting effect of the substantive, the future imperfect, a matter of intuition or ear to O'Hara" (*Notebooks*, 162). Fitzgerald's style appealed to the senses. He observed the Conrad definition of writing—to make the reader hear, feel, and above all else, see. In *McTeague*, by appealing "to the sense of smell or of hearing rather than by the commoner form of word painting," Frank Norris had created an air of authenticity (*Miscellany*, 127).

A critic of others, Fitzgerald desired, even encouraged sincere and detailed criticism from people whom he respected. With reference to a review Bishop was going to write on *The Beautiful and Damned*, he said: "Tell specifically what you like about the book and don't. . . . I'm so afraid of all the reviews being general" (*CU*, 258). If he felt criticism justified, he accepted it graciously. For example, he told Bishop that he had learned something from his comments on *The Great Gatsby* in spite of the fact that they had caused him pain. Often Fitzgerald was his own severest critic. He admitted that *Gatsby* had a serious fault, namely that he had not known or accounted for the feelings between the hero and Daisy from the time of their reunion to the end. By 1938 no one was harsher about *This Side of Paradise* than the author himself.

II

Along with craftsmanship—shaping and pruning—poetry and originality were essential for the development of a great style. Scott Fitzgerald had heard poems from his father's lips at an early age. This and his conviction that "the talent that matures early is usually of the poetic [type], which mine was in large part" (*Daughter,* 138), explains why much of his early writing was verse. But despite his success in having "The Way of Purgation" accepted by *Poet Lore* in 1917, Fitzgerald, through Amory of *This Side of Paradise,* confessed that he would "never write anything but mediocre poetry" because he was "not enough of a sensualist" and noticed only "obvious things."[1] Fitzgerald was quite right about his poetry. Only occasionally is the magic we often find in his prose revealed in his verse, which for the most part is undistinguished and dull. Nevertheless, his feeling for poetry was in large measure responsible for the beauty of his prose style. "Poetry," he wrote to his daughter on 3 August 1940, "is either something that lives like fire inside you—like music to the musician or Marxism to the Communist—or else it is nothing" (*Daughter,* 142–43). Once he informed her that he did not believe a person could write "succinct prose" without first attempting an "iambic pentameter sonnet" and reading "Browning's short dramatic poems" (*CU,* 304). On another occasion he warned her that her own style lacked distinction and that the way to achieve it was "to cultivate *your own garden,*" which could be done only through "poetry . . . the most concentrated form of style" (*Letters,* 86).

Originality was of the utmost importance, Fitzgerald believed. The inventor, he declared, was "infinitely superior" to those who simply did things well; for instance, Giotto or Leonardo was greater than Tintoretto and D. H. Lawrence than John Steinbeck (*CU,* 294). "The prose talent" depended on "having something to say and an interesting, highly developed way of saying it" (*Daughter,* 138). Once he advised Bishop to eliminate "all traces of other people." In Bishop's *Act of Darkness*, Fitzgerald thought there were "patterns . . . which derived background and drama from Faulkner, or cadence from Hemingway." Bishop should delete these passages "no matter how satisfactory" they were and acquire something that was more himself. Fitzgerald admitted in the same letter that he had had to fight this battle too, no doubt referring to the year and a half during which he deliberately stopped reading Hemingway because he feared the latter's rhythms were replacing his own (*Letters*, 365).

The young writer should ignore "the known, the admired and the currently accepted" as well as that false voice within that tells him that his feelings and actions are "not . . . universal nor generally interesting nor even right." Instead he should listen to that true voice within that "makes him write down those apparently exceptional and unimportant things" because they are "his style, his personality—eventually his whole self as an artist" (*Letters*, 591–92). Yet the young writer can do certain things that the older writer cannot afford to do. It was natural for Thomas Wolfe in *Look Homeward, Angel* to make one chapter practically a parody of a chapter in *Ulysses* and for Fitzgerald "to have done an equivalent thing half a dozen times in *This Side of Paradise*." If this becomes a habit, however, the writer will lose all chance of developing a personality (*Letters*, 365). Then, too, the early novel may be formless because "the lack of a pattern gives the young novelist more of a chance to assert his or her individuality, which is the principal thing" (*Miscellany*, 137).

Besides studying poetry, "the most concentrated form of style," in order to develop originality, the young artist should read other writers. Fitzgerald recommended that he "absorb half a dozen top-flight authors every year." If he does, his style will become "a subconscious amalgam" of what he has admired; if not, it will be "simply a reflection of the last writer" he has read, "a watered-down journalese" (*Daughter*, 139). This attitude is not a contradiction of his insistence upon eliminating "all traces of other people." Rather, he is saying that an effective style comes from soaking up many elements, the new concoction being an original, whereas an inferior style results from being influenced by one person only.

Fitzgerald described the kind of author the young artist should study: "If you were learning tennis you would form yourself not upon an eccentric like Tilden, for example, but upon players with classic styles like Cochet or La Coste (my references are of the dim past). You cannot imitate a mannerism with profit; a man might labor over Tilden's tennis style for six years, finding at the end that it simply couldn't be done without Tilden's 6'6" in height" (*Letters*, 593). He went on to enumerate some of the "great English classics": *A Farewell to Arms, Dubliners*, "The Eve of St. Agnes," "Ode on a Grecian Urn," *Huckleberry Finn, Daisy Miller*, and "The Drums of the Fore and Aft." But since these English classics tend to be more eccentric than the French, which are "the most *classical* classics," the young writer might profit more by reading something like Maupassant's "Maison Tellier." In any event, he should spend his time studying good things. On 29 July 1940 Fitzgerald reminded his daughter that after she had read Gertrude Stein's "Melanctha" she sold a *New Yorker* story, but when she was reading the average novel, she sank "back to a Kitty-Foyle-diary level of average performance" (*Daughter*, 140).

But achieving originality would not have been possible had Fitzgerald not had something to say. Having something to say is essential to finding a way of saying it. Indeed, in the creative artist, Fitzgerald insisted, style and subject matter become one:

> Nobody ever became a writer just by wanting to be one. If you have anything to say, anything you feel nobody has ever said before, you have got to feel it so desperately that you will find some way to say it that nobody has ever found before, so that the thing you have to say and the way of saying it blend as one matter—as indissolubly as if they were conceived together. . . .
>
> Let me preach again for a moment: I mean that what you have felt and thought will by itself invent a new style, so that when people talk about style they are always a little astonished at the newness of it, because they think that it is only *style* that they are talking about, when what they are talking about is the attempt to express a new idea with such force that it will have the originality of the thought. (*CU*, 303–4)

Although novels are not written with the idea of creating a philosophical system, the novelist must have "a sharp and concise attitude about life" (*Miscellany*, 156). Fitzgerald did not, however, write merely because he wanted to say something; on the contrary, he wrote because he had something to say. Fitzgerald felt that the writers in his time did not have sharply defined attitudes toward life, or diversified material. Joseph Conrad had avoided this "by being brought up in a métier utterly unrelated to literature" (*CU*, 301). Thomas Wolfe, on the other hand, had not escaped. Fitzgerald said of him, "His awful secret transpires at every crevice—he did not have anything particular to say! The stuff about the GREAT VITAL HEART OF AMERICA is just simply corny." Wolfe had recapitulated what Whitman, Dostoevsky, Nietzsche, and Milton had said before him, but "unlike Joyce and T. S. Eliot and Ernest Hemingway, has nothing really new to add." This was because he had failed to find "a solid gold bar like Ernest's courage, or Joseph Conrad's art, or D. H. Lawrence's intense cohabitations"; instead, he had told us what we already knew, that everything was a "mess" and that it was "too bad about the individual" (*Daughter*, 158).

But even better authors, perhaps because they have found "a solid gold bar," do not have a limitless stock of themes, Fitzgerald contended in "One Hundred False Starts":

> Mostly, we authors must repeat ourselves—that's the truth. We have two or three great and moving experiences in our lives—experiences so great and moving that it doesn't seem at the time that anyone else has been so caught up and pounded and dazzled and astonished and beaten and broken and rescued and illuminated and rewarded and humbled in just that way ever before.
>
> Then we learn our trade, well or less well, and we tell our two or three stories—each time in a new disguise—maybe ten times, maybe a hundred, as long as people will listen.
>
> If this were otherwise, one would have to confess to having no individuality at all. (*AA*, 132)

Those experiences or stories cannot be merely reported; rather, the author must express "the *profound* essence of what happened" so that "even a forlorn Laplander" may "*feel* the importance of a trip to Cartier's!" (*CU*, 304). Nor is it permissible to depart from reality. The author must illustrate that same "desire to imitate life which is in all the big shots" (*Notebooks*, 161). He has another responsibility as well. He must help the reader all he can with most of his observations, clothing only his "more radical" ideas in "sheep's wool" (*Correspondence*, 460).

III

Besides his convictions about the elements that compose a great style, there are at least two other important aspects of Fitzgerald's views on writing: the place of morality and the role of "subjectivity" and "objectivity."

Part 2

It must have come as a surprise to Fitzgerald's early contemporary readers who thought of him chiefly in connection with *This Side of Paradise*, which shocked with its apparently frank exposé of youthful manners and morals, to discover later that Fitzgerald was a highly moral author. Indeed, he has been considered "a spoiled priest," the term he used to describe Dick Diver in his *Tender Is the Night* notes, the same term, incidentally, with which James Joyce once referred to Stephen in *Ulysses*. Fitzgerald thought himself a moralist, as certainly he was. He tells us that he had "a New England conscience—developed in Minnesota" (*AA*, 134) and that in spite of his opposition to schoolteachers, there was "just the ghost of one in me" (*Letters*, 440). Most revealing is a comment from a letter of 1939: "I guess I am too much a moralist at heart, and really want to preach at people in some acceptable form, rather than to entertain them" (*CU*, 305). Let us briefly examine two or three typical attitudes showing Fitzgerald to be a moralist.

He said that his "stamp" was "taking things hard" (*Notebooks*, 163) and that "despite a tendency to self indulgence" he had "some essential seriousness" (*Daughter*, 23–24). It comes as no surprise, then, to find him observing of the postwar period that "living wasn't the reckless, careless business these people thought." America might be headed for "the greatest, gaudiest spree in history," but Fitzgerald, for one, could not share its naive optimism. All the plots he thought of "had a touch of disaster in them." He anticipated that lovely girls would go to ruin, that wealth would disintegrate, that millionaires would be "beautiful and damned" (*CU*, 87). In his college story "The Spire and the Gargoyle" he had stated that although Epicureanism had been "romantic" in his early days at Princeton, it was "rather disgusting in the city" because "it was much too easy; it lacked the penance of the five o'clock morning train back to college."

Lionel Trilling observed that the author's work is "innocent of mere 'sex.'"[2] As a romanticist Fitzgerald based relations between men and women on mental and spiritual rather than physical needs, while some of his contemporaries, particularly the naturalists, stressed only physical attraction. He felt that "'sex books,' . . . arouse pruriency and sometimes . . . kill the essence of romance" (*Miscellany*, 182). He did not approve of vulgarity. On 13 August 1936 he wrote to Bennett Cerf that he would like to eliminate the line in *Tender Is the Night* "I never did go in for making love to dry loins" because it was "definitely offensive" (*Letters*, 540). This does not mean that Fitzgerald was a prude.

He was simply opposed to vulgarity for vulgarity's sake. He was also opposed to hypocrisy in these matters. For instance, he considered the novel *Simon Called Peter* a "piece of trash" because "the characters move in a continual labyrinth of mild sexual stimulation" over which "the colored lights of romantic Christianity" played. But Sherwood Anderson's *Many Marriages* was not immoral. It was "the reaction of a sensitive, highly civilized man to the phenomenon of lust" (*Miscellany*, 139–40). Fitzgerald was against Puritanism in any form. As an anti-Philistine, he took an intense dislike to any group of "professional uplifters." He said that the Philadelphia Society, for example, possessed a "depressing conviction of sin" and that it appealed "to the intellect of farmers' wives and pious drug-clerks."[3]

Fitzgerald also disliked censorship. When William Woods, editor of *The Literary Digest*, asked for his opinion, he replied:

> The clean-book bill will be one of the most immoral measures ever adopted. It will throw American art back into the junk heap where it rested comfortably between the Civil War and the World War. The really immoral books like *Simon Called Peter* and *Mumbo Jumbo* won't be touched—they'll attack Hergesheimer, Dreiser, Anderson and Cabell whom they detest because they can't understand. George Moore, Hardy and Anatole France who are unintelligible to children and idiots will be suppressed at once for debauching the morals of village clergymen. (*Letters*, 476)

Later he expressed a similar opinion of the "halfwitting halfwit Hayes and his legion of decency." Although he had urged his daughter not to see the moving pictures of 1932–33 "because they were suggestive and salacious," now that the Hayes group wanted to interfere with "*all* strong themes" so that the only safe films were either "feeble and false" or dealt "with children," he went to the other extreme (*CU*, 303).

His notes to *The Last Tycoon* effectively illustrate Fitzgerald's concern about instilling a moral into his fiction. He says that Monroe Stahr's plane will crash and as had actually happened in an incident of 1933 the bodies of the dead will be rifled, but this time by three children. One boy, Jim, is to steal Stahr's possessions; Dan is to rifle the body of a ruined producer, Bradogue; and a girl, Frances, will rifle the body of an actress. The belongings they find, which reflect the character of the dead passengers, will determine the attitude of the children toward the theft. Frances, like the actress, will become selfish; Dan, like the unsuccessful producer, will become irresolute; but Jim, who has identified himself with Stahr, will redeem them by confessing the crime. Jim, therefore, will turn out "all right," while Frances, who has been corrupted, may become "anything from a gold digger to a prostitute," and Dan, whose morals have been completely demolished, will from this time forward always try "to get something for nothing." Since Fitzgerald is an artist as well as a moralist, he insists that his lesson be presented unobtrusively. Of Dan's new resemblance to Bradogue, he says: "This must be subtly done and not look too much like a parable or moral lesson, still the impression must be conveyed, but be careful to convey it once and not rub it in. If the reader misses it, let it go—don't repeat." At the end of the episode, he says:

> I cannot be too careful not to rub this in or give it the substance or feeling of a moral tale. I should [show] very pointedly that Jim is all right and end perhaps with Frances and let the readers hope that Frances is going to be all right and then take that hope away by showing the last glimpse of Frances with that lingering conviction that luxury is over the next valley, therefore giving a bitter and acrid finish to the incident to take away any possible sentimental and moral stuff that may have crept into it. (*LT*, Notes, 155ff.)

Like Keats, Scott Fitzgerald struggled between "objectivity" and "subjectivity," and, again like Keats, he was primarily a "subjective" writer. After his death, several American critics began to take this dualism into account. John Dos Passos called his work "a combination of intimacy and detachment" (*CU*, 342); Malcolm Cowley, "a sort of double vision."[4] But however they phrased it, the critics agreed that it was the author's ability to participate in his fiction and at the same time to stand aside and analyze that participation that gave his work maturity and power. This is best illustrated by *The Great Gatsby*, where, to a large extent, the author acts as Gatsby and observes as Nick.

Fitzgerald echoed Keats's statement that "Men of Genius" do not have "any individuality, and determined Character" (CU, 95), which agrees with another remark, namely that there has never been "a good biography of a good novelist" (*Notebooks*, 159). But perhaps the most telling comment Fitzgerald made on "objectivity" is the following: "Books are like brothers. I am an only child. Gatsby my imaginary eldest brother, Amory my younger, Anthony my worry. Dick my comparatively good brother but all of them far from home. When I have the courage to put the old white light on the home of my heart, then—" (*Notebooks*, 158). Since on 14 September 1940 he told Gerald Murphy that *The Last Tycoon* was "as detached from me as *Gatsby* was, in intent anyhow" (*Letters*, 430), he might well have added Monroe Stahr to his list.

But though Fitzgerald valued the aspect of detachment in his work and came to use it with considerable skill, he was more concerned about the "subjective" approach to writing: "Whether it's something that happened twenty years ago or only yesterday, I must start out with an emotion—one that's close to me and that I can understand" (AA, 132). Thus, he felt self-revelation to be one of the most vital components of creativity: "I used to think that my sensory impression of the world came from outside. I used to actually believe that it was as objective as blue skies or a piece of music. Now I know it was within, and emphatically cherish what little is left" (*Letters*, 427). Fitzgerald opposed the tendency toward psychoanalysis that was growing in his period on the grounds that it caused the disintegration of personality, and "the extinction of that light is much more to be dreaded than any material loss" (*Letters*, 538). Since everything he had written was himself, so much so in fact that he was not able to remember when he wrote anything because he had "lived in [the] story" (*Notebooks*, 159), any technique that would tend to destroy self would also destroy the springs of art. Nevertheless, in the psychoanalytically oriented "Author's House," Fitzgerald enters "a dark damp unmodernized cellar," where "all the complicated dark mixture of my youth and infancy that made me a fiction writer instead of a fireman or a soldier" exist. The "intangibles" of "why I chose this God awful metier of sedentary days and sleepless nights and endless dissatisfaction" reside here. Eyeing a "dark corner," he explains: "Well, three months before I was born my mother lost her other two children and I think that came first of all though I don't know how it worked exactly. I think I started then to be a writer." Nearby there lies "buried my first childish love of myself, my belief that I would never die like other people, and that I wasn't the son of my parents but a son of a king, a king who ruled the whole world." Upstairs again, the author looks outside at "some children playing football." This causes him to remember the time he was considered "yellow" during a game: "The point is it inspired me to write a poem for the school paper which made me as big a hit with my father as if I had become a football hero. So when I went home that Christmas

153

vacation it was in my mind that if you weren't able to function in action you might at least be able to tell about it, because you felt the same intensity—it was a back door way out of facing reality" (*AA*, 183–86).

As has been mentioned, Fitzgerald felt that the young writer must listen to that voice within that encourages him to record his feelings and actions because those feelings and actions are actually "his style, his personality—eventually his whole self as an artist." Developing individuality is so crucial that it is natural for the young writer to begin with a formless novel; the lack of pattern will give him a chance to exploit his selfness. If he starts with emotions that are close to him and that he can understand, eventually he will evolve two or three major themes. These become his "stamp." If he experiences them strongly enough, he will automatically present them in a new way. Thus it is that the artist creates a vision of life, a vision of utmost value to others: "The genius conceives a cosmos with such transcendental force that it supersedes, in certain sensitive minds, the cosmos of which they have been previously aware. The new cosmos instantly approximates ultimate reality as closely as did the last" (*Miscellany*, 138–39). Later, Fitzgerald elaborated: "Someone once said—and I am quoting most inexactly—'A writer who manages to look a little more deeply into his own soul or the soul of others, finding there, through his gift, things that no other man has ever seen or dared to say, has increased the range of human life'" (*Letters*, 591).

To a greater extent than he may have been aware, Scott Fitzgerald solved the conflict between "objectivity" and "subjectivity." In a letter of 9 November 1938 to Frances Turnbull, he tells her that he read her story but that "the price for doing professional work is a good deal higher" than she is willing to pay. The writer must sell his "heart," his "strongest reactions," and not just minor things that he "might tell at dinner." This pertains especially to beginning writers who "have not yet developed the tricks of interesting people on paper," who, because they lack technique, "have only . . . emotions to sell." He gives examples: "It was necessary for Dickens to put into *Oliver Twist* the child's passionate resentment at being abused and starved that had haunted his whole childhood. Ernest Hemingway's first stories, *In Our Time*, went right down to the bottom of all that he had ever felt and known. In *This Side of Paradise* I wrote about a love affair that was still bleeding as fresh as the skin wound on a haemophile." When the amateur sees the professional take "a trivial thing such as the most superficial reactions of three uncharacterized girls and make it witty and charming," he believes that he can do likewise. But, at that stage, he does not possess the professional's ability "to transfer his emotions to another person" in a skillful and subtle way; the amateur can effect this transfer only "by some such desperate and radical expedient as tearing your first tragic love story out of your heart and putting it on pages for people to see." Since, therefore, the admission price to a writing career is high, and often conflicts with one's "attitude on what is 'nice,'" the neophyte will have to decide whether he is willing to make the necessary sacrifices. Talent is only "the equivalent of a soldier having the right physical qualifications for entering West Point"; self-revelation is the other essential ingredient (*Letters*, 577–78).

This letter is interesting on two counts: first, it demonstrates Fitzgerald's conviction that all writers, beginners and veterans, inevitably exploit their own emotions and experiences; second, it shows the development that came about in both his fiction and his criticism. Whereas the beginning writer, because he lacks technique, may simply describe everything in a more or less direct way, the professional, because he has gained knowledge in living and technique in writing, is able to transfer to something or someone outside himself his deepest or most trivial feelings. In other words, subject matter is always highly personal, but while it remains merely personal to the young writer, the mature artist finds ways of projecting it objectively. This, of course, implies T. S. Eliot's "objective correlative."

Fitzgerald's career as an artist followed very closely his observations to Frances Turnbull. All his work is subjective, reflecting his own experiences and emotions, but the early work presents these in quite a direct way, while the subsequent work employs two devices discussed during part 1—"composite" character and observer-narrator—to transfer them to something or someone outside the author.

In *This Side of Paradise* the love affair between Amory and Isabelle is a fairly faithful rendition of Fitzgerald's own love affair with Ginevra King, which was "still bleeding as fresh as the skin wound on a haemophile." Monsignor Darcy is almost an exact replica of Monsignor Fay, a good friend of Fitzgerald in his college days, whose letters, Fitzgerald tells us, were transcribed with practically no changes. The autobiographical material throughout *The Beautiful and Damned* was also presented, by and large, directly. A comment the author made to his daughter on 14 June 1940, however, indicates that when he was writing this novel he was also groping for greater "objectivity": "Gloria [Patch] was a much more trivial and vulgar person than your mother. I can't really say there was any resemblance except in the beauty and certain terms of expression she used, and also I naturally used many circumstantial events of our early married life. However the emphases were entirely different. We had a much better time than Anthony and Gloria had" (*Correspondence*, 600). This "objectivity" reaches its apotheosis in *The Great Gatsby*, where composite characterization and first-person observer help build an American masterpiece.

We may well believe his daughter when she tells us that "sweat," "heart-breaking effort," and "painful hours of work under the most adverse circumstances" made Scott Fitzgerald's finest prose possible.[5]

IV

Clearly, then, the author held consistent and comprehensive views on the craft of fiction, which he presented in novelistic terms. That should not surprise us, for we know how much he esteemed the long form as artwork and scorned the short form as hackwork. Producing stories contributed to his "crack-up," he claimed: "I have asked a lot of my emotions—one hundred and twenty stories. The price was high, right up with Kipling, because there was one little drop of something—not blood, not a tear, not my seed, but me more intimately than these, in every story, it was the extra I had. Now it has gone and I am just like you now" (*CU*, 165).

Unlike most commercial writers, the creator of "The Diamond as Big as the Ritz," "The Rich Boy," and "Babylon Revisited" was never comfortable with formulaic fiction, despite his O. Henry orientation and his *Post* success; thus "even in years like '24, '28, '29, '30 all devoted to short stories I could not turn out more than 8–9 top price stories a year." Why? Because "all my stories are concieved [*sic*] like novels, require a special emotion, a special experience—so that my readers, if such there be, know that each time it'll be something new, not in form but in substance." Fitzgerald realized he could profit from "pattern stories," yet, when he tried writing them, "the pencil" went "dead" (*As Ever*, 221).

His memorandum about *The Last Tycoon*—"Rewrite from mood. Has become stilted with rewriting. Don't look. Rewrite from mood"—applied equally well to the short form, daughter Scottie learned in 1940:

> I read the story in *College Bazaar* and was very pleased with it.
> You've put in some excellent new touches and its only fault is the

jerkiness that goes with a story that has often been revised. Stories
are best written in either one jump or three, according to the length.
The three-jump story should be done on three successive days, then
a day or so for revise and off she goes. This of course is the ideal—
in many stories one strikes a snag that must be hacked at but, on
the whole stories that drag along or are terribly difficult (I mean a
difficulty that comes from a poor conception and consequent faulty
construction) never flow quite as well in the reading. (*Daughter*, 151)

Fitzgerald's "novelettes" naturally required more than "three successive days." For example, the seventeen-thousand-word "Rich Boy"
spanned April to August 1925.

The critical opinions regarding shaping and pruning, poetry and originality, subjectivity and objectivity, and so on, pertain to both novels
and stories; yet Fitzgerald almost always illustrated these with references taken from the former. Only twice did he write at length about
the short form: in "How to Waste Material" (1926), where *In Our Time*
was reviewed, he discussed the new Chekhovian art (see the Introduction to part 1), and in "One Hundred False Starts" (1933) he discussed
the compositional process. This process is also treated by a letter to
The Editor in June 1920. Here Fitzgerald explained the genesis of his
initial major story, "The Ice Palace" (see "Early Triumphs" in part 1).
It reveals more intricately and more vividly than any other document
how he wrote fiction.

Parallel conversations, the first involving an unidentified Northern
girl and the second an unnamed but recognizable Southern girl, inspired "The Ice Palace." "Riding . . . one November night" in St.
Paul, Minnesota, the Northern girl, noticing the snow, remarked,
"Here comes winter." Her escort wondered "if the Swedes aren't melancholy on account of the cold"; then he stopped, "for I had scented
a story." There followed two weeks during which Fitzgerald pondered
the idea without writing. With a single atmospheric detail—"the first
wisps of snow weaving like advance-guard ghosts up the street"—he
believed he could fictionalize some Anglo-Saxons enduring frigid
weather over several generations.

The second conversation transpired later in Montgomery, Alabama,
where, wandering through the local cemetery, Zelda contended Scott
did not "understand how she felt about the Confederate graves," but
he disagreed. It suddenly occurred to him on his return trip that these

two conversations constituted one story, "the contrast between Alabama and Minnesota." Reaching home, he possessed five points:

(1)   The idea of this contrast.

(2)   The natural sequence of the girl visiting in the north.

(3)   The idea that some phase of the cold should prey on her mind.

(4)   That this phase should be an ice palace—I had had the idea of using an ice palace in a story since several months before when my mother told me about one they had in St. Paul in the eighties.

(5)   A detail about snow in the vestibule of a railway train.

Fitzgerald proceeded to research the ice palace, asking relatives what they recalled and finding a sketch in the public library. Subsequently "I went through my notebook for any incident or character that might do," as was his wont, yet discovered nothing "except a conversation I had once with a girl as to whether people were feline or canine." Now he could start:

> I did an atmospheric sketch of the girl's life in Alabama. This was part one. I did the graveyard scene and also used it to begin the love interest and hint at her dislike of cold. This was part two. Then I began part three which was to be her arrival in the northern city, but in the middle I grew bored with it and skipped to the beginning of the ice palace scene, a part I was wild to do. I did the scene where the couple were approaching the palace in a sleigh, and of a sudden I began to get the picture of an ice labyrinth so I left the description of the palace and turned at once to the girl lost in the labyrinth. Parts one and two had taken two days. The ice palace and labyrinth (part five) and the last scene (part six) which brought back the Alabama motif were finished the third day. So there I had my beginning and end which are the easiest and most enjoyable for me to write, and the climax, which is the most exciting and stimulating to work out. It took me three days to do parts three and four, the least satisfactory parts of the story, and while doing them I was bored and uncertain, constantly re-writing, adding and cutting and revising— and in the end didn't care particularly for them.

Thus Fitzgerald "unintentionally" exemplified his "theory" that "what you enjoy writing is liable to be much better reading than what you labor over" (*Correspondence*, 61–62).

Notes

1. *This Side of Paradise* (1920; reprint, New York: Scribner, 1986), 84.

2. Lionel Trilling, "F. Scott Fitzgerald," in *F. Scott Fitzgerald: The Man and His Work*, ed. Alfred Kazin (Cleveland: World, 1951), 197.

3. "The Claims of the Lit.," *Princeton Alumni Weekly* (10 March 1920): 514.

4. Malcolm Cowley, "Third Act and Epilogue," in *F. Scott Fitzgerald: The Man and His Work*, 148.

5. Frances Scott Fitzgerald (Lanahan), "Princeton and F. Scott Fitzgerald," *Nassau Literary Magazine* 100, no. 3 (Hundredth Year Issue, 1942): 45.

Part 3

The Critics

Introduction

Although Scott Fitzgerald's short fiction had already provided the focus for several dissertations and one book—John A. Higgins's *F. Scott Fitzgerald: A Study of the Stories* (1971)—not until the late 1970s did the rising number of critical essays on the stories begin to reflect increasing interest in this part of his work. The essays that appear here—most of them from 1975 or later—concern seven of the eight major stories. (Because "The Ice Palace" receives such extensive treatment in parts 1 and 2, it did not warrant further attention.) Anthony J. Mazella discusses "The Tension of Opposites in Fitzgerald's 'May Day,'" and Marius Bewley explores "Scott Fitzgerald and the Collapse of the American Dream" in "The Diamond as Big as the Ritz." Gerald Pike treats "Four Voices in 'Winter Dreams,'" Robert Emmet Long analyzes "Absolution" in "Toward *The Great Gatsby:* The Apprenticeship Period," James L. W. West III and J. Barclay Inge examine "F. Scott Fitzgerald's Revision of 'The Rich Boy,'" Roy R. Male contributes " 'Babylon Revisited': A Story of the Exile's Return" and Stanley Grebstein offers "The Sane Method of 'Crazy Sunday.'" These essays on the short masterworks conclude with William Troy's brilliant review of *Taps at Reveille,* in which he calls Fitzgerald "a rather old-fashioned sort of storyteller." I have deleted the critics' notes and parenthetical citations throughout this part.

Anthony J. Mazzella

Considering that its themes belong to Fitzgerald's late period as well, it should also be noted that "May Day" was first published twenty years before his death. It, thus, turns out to be an early work of surprising complexity, structured on the careful modulation of opposites, of integration and disintegration. It is also a moving expression of order struggling against approaching chaos. In its carefully revised version for *Tales of the Jazz Age* (1922), the lives of several central characters—young, wealthy Philip Dean; penniless and dissipated Gordon Sterett, his former Yale roommate; and shallow, pretty narcissistic Edith Bradin—intersect in the story's eleven sections with the lives of returning soldiers, mob forces, social dilettantes. . . . The story, when examined closely, reveals in the young Fitzgerald a sophisticated and highly controlled writer, one quite unlike the novice usually depicted as antedating *The Great Gatsby.*

The content of "May Day" is chaos and destruction, but the story's form reverses the direction of the content, giving the reader attuned to form a sense of order and stability. It is this disparity between form and content that produces the story's tension. . . . And Fitzgerald has created a sense of triumph-in-despair through the "assertiveness" of the form running counter to the defeatism of its content.

The title, for example, is a paradox, specifying numerous opposites when related to the story. First, it denotes the day (May 1, 1919) when most of the random incidents occur—largely incidents involving violence and death. Next, besides denoting the date of occurrence, the title has several suggestive connotations which, because they are apt and capable of wide application, create a sense of life where the events in the story create an opposite effect: a sense of defeat, despair, the abyss. May Day, of course, commemorates the working class, but in the story we have confusion in the working class. . . . Thus, elements of the same class are working against each other; supposed allies be-

Excerpted from "The Tension of Opposites in Fitzgerald's 'May Day,'" *Studies in Short Fiction* 14 (Fall 1977): 380–81, 382–83, 384. Reprinted by permission.

come enemies, similarities become opposites, and the day of commemoration becomes the night of death and destruction. But May Day
connotes more than a commemoration—in the story, a commemoration
gone awry. It connotes the celebration of a spring festival, crowning a
May Queen, dancing around a May pole, the advent of new life; but
in the story we encounter the reverse. . . . Finally, "May Day," from
the French *m'aidez*, means "help me"; it is the familiar distress
call. . . . The title's amplitude, thus, in not only referring to the time
of the story but also in giving connotations of commemoration, celebration, and help, offers a richness that counterbalances the defeatism
of the plot and produces a tension of opposites which, as we shall see,
is sustained throughout the work.

If we examine the prologue to the story, for instance, we discover
another paradox, this time largely in a tone that is opposed to that of
the rest of the work, and in a form that appears nowhere else in the
story. The form is that of the fairy tale; the tone, that of pained as well
as mocking exaggeration. . . . The thematic oppositions that the rest
of the work presents to the fairy-tale form and exaggerated tone are
realistic form and serious tone. . . . The very structure of the work,
then, has a pulsating movement, a step in one direction followed by a
step in an opposite direction.

If this principle of structure—the pulsation of opposites—is examined against the story's eleven sections, the tight organic nature of the
work as a whole is evident. . . .

The second section ends with a pair of men (Sterrett and Dean), one
of whom is to die violently; the third section opens with a pair of men
(Carroll Key and Gus Rose), one of whom is also to die violently.
(Their names, in addition, are also paradoxes: the feminine sounds of
Carroll and Rose, but belonging to men rather than women.) Section
III ends with Rose and Key using metaphorical language to describe
the heat in a storeroom at Delmonico's ("'It's hot in here, ain't it?' . . .
'Hot as hell.'"); and section IV opens with a variation on that metaphor
and with a different character. Instead of heat as infernal we have heat
as choler ("She [Edith Bradin] was still quite angry"). Section IV ends
with the defeat of Sterrett as he mistakenly believes Edith Bradin is
sincere in loving him; section V begins with the defeat of Peter Himmel who is snubbed by the same Edith Bradin. Moreover, Himmel,
another of the world's rejected, is linked with Rose and Key here, and
with Dean in section X; thus, while we have a series of formal links,
these links in content do not in fact link as in harmony but end as in

dissolution. These structural links paradoxically do not link but disengage. . . .

By now, half-way through the story, a rhythm of simultaneous gain and loss is clearly evident; i.e., the structure metaphorically moves in a forward direction (with its various formal links), but that forward direction is checked by plot reversals that move in an opposite direction. Stated in different terms, the form's complexity may be seen as a positive factor while the story's plot may be seen as a negative one, the resultant antiphony contributing to the story's tension.

The stress in the next five sections (before the eleventh section or coda) is on imagistic as well as structural opposites and links. . . . Mr. In and Mr. Out not only refer to Himmel and Dean but also suggest the pulsation aspect of the structure, for on several occasions in the story we have seen that as things move in, they suddenly move out. . . .

The pulsating rhythm that we have seen throughout the story's form paradoxically gives the story's deadly content a sense of life. It is almost as if the pulsating structure were an analog for the human heartbeat in the story of death, where seemingly disparate but actually related incidents and brutal events culminate in paired climaxes of death—those of Key and Sterrett. These two characters die violently; and, in a similar way, the story's structure with its pulsing rhythm appears to end violently as well because the pulsation of Sterrett's heart and the pulsation of the story's structure both cease simultaneously. One feels a sense of futility in the story's content but at the same time one has to marvel at Fitzgerald's technique: a story about death told in a method that bespeaks life.

Marius Bewley

"The Diamond as Big as the Ritz" is a story of very genuine originality, and I can think of no classic American writer with whose work to associate it with the possible exception of Hawthorne in some of his short stories. There are aspects of it that make one think of "My Kinsman, Major Molineux." . . . The hero of Scott Fitzgerald's story, John T. Unger, enacts the parable of the young American who awakes from the American Dream. . . . As the title of "The Diamond as Big as the Ritz" suggests, it is in the tradition of the Western tall tale, and its Montana setting underlines this; but this is important only as supplying a traditional mould for a meaning and a seriousness that far exceed anything the genre had ever held before. . . .

I said that Scott Fitzgerald was the first of the great American writers to have found that a "treatable" class, with its accompanying manners, really did exist in America—to have found it sufficiently, at any rate, to have been able to create characters who are representative of a socially solid and defined group rather than symbolic embodiments of the ultimate American solitude, or two-dimensional figures in the American morality play. . . . If Scott Fitzgerald loved wealth he was not taken in by it, and some of his gaudiest celebrations of it are simultaneously the most annihilating criticisms. . . .

But to return to "The Diamond as Big as the Ritz," this story is one in which Fitzgerald's attitude to wealth as a constituent part of the American dream is most clearly revealed. . . . At school John forms a friendship with an aloof and uncommunicative boy who asks John to spend the summer vacation with him at his home "in the West." John accepts, and during the long train trip into a remote part of Montana the dream quality that has been present from the first is intensified. The form of the story just a little resembles *Through the Looking-Glass*.

Excerpted from "Scott Fitzgerald and the Collapse of the American Dream," in *The Eccentric Design: Form in the Classic American Novel* by Marius Bewley, (New York: Columbia University Press, 1963), 259–60, 261, 262–63, 264, 265, 267, 268–69. © 1959, 1963 Columbia University Press. Used by permission.

We don't quite know when the dream begins, but we are there for the awakening on the last page. . . .

But certainly the dream has begun by the opening of Part II when the Transcontinental Express stops at the forlorn village of Fish. . . . The Christian implications of the fish symbol are certainly intended by Fitzgerald, and these are enforced by the twelve solitary men who are apostles "beyond all religion." These grotesque and distorted Christian connotations are strengthened by their dream-like relation to Hades on the Mississippi where John was born. What we are given in these paragraphs is a queerly restless and troubled sense of a religion that is sick and expressing itself in disjointed images and associations, as if it were delirious. . . .

What we have to bear in mind is that this story is an attack on that American dream which critics have so often imagined Fitzgerald was engaged in celebrating throughout his writings. The fevered religious imagery of the passage I have quoted presents it, in the very beginning, as a kind of gaudy substitute for a sterile orthodoxy whose promises cannot compete with the infinite material possibilities that the dream seems to hold out to the faithful Americans. . . . Historically, the American dream is anti-Calvinistic—in rejecting man's tainted nature it is even anti-Christian. It believes in the goodness of nature and man. It is accordingly a product of the frontier and the West rather than of the New England and Puritan traditions. Youth of the spirit—youth of the body as well—is a requirement of its existence; limit and deprivation are its blackest devils. . . . *The Great Gatsby* is Scott Fitzgerald's great exploration of this theme, but first of all he explored its more degraded aspects as they had come to exist in the 'twenties in "The Diamond as Big as the Ritz.". . . The sick and portentous undertones that were struck by the twelve men of Fish, waiting under the poisoned sunset, give way to a riotous fantasy in a style that can only be called Babylonian-Hollywood. The implicit presence throughout of Hollywood criteria of values and taste (and Hollywood in its most barbaric age) is the technical means by which Fitzgerald makes his final point, and presses his condemnation. . . .

The major part of the story is concerned with giving us a series of glimpses of life in this American dream—a fantasy on the theme of material possibilities run wild. Fitzgerald's treatment of the theme is completely successful. The sense of a colossal Hollywood movie set, and a "plot" that unwinds along the lines of an old-time movie scenario, keeps the question of reality implicitly to the fore of the reader's mind. In fact, the total effect of the story duplicates the odd ambivalence of response that one brings to the moving pictures of the period—disbelief neatly balanced by exhilarated acceptance. . . .

It is indeed the American dream's idea of Heaven, and Hades is where all this is not. . . . The Washingtons maintain their Hollywood existence on the diamond mountain only at the price of the freedom of others. . . .

The scene in which Braddock Washington attempts to bribe God on the mountainside to withhold the impending destruction with a gigantic diamond held by two negro slaves, brings the dream sequence to its conclusion. . . . This morning scene, during which the giant diamond catches the first yellow light of the sun, balances the sunset scene in the first two paragraphs of Part II. Whether it was explicitly intended or not—perhaps not—it is appropriate that the American dream (the particular dream of John T. Unger) which began under a poisoned sky, should dissolve in the clear light of day, and that the ominous note in the religious imagery of the opening should reach its climax in the blasphemous prayer of Braddock Washington.

Gerald Pike

In "Winter Dreams," Fitzgerald experiments with distinct shifts in authorial voice, occasionally with less than felicitous effect, but always with a sense that the voice should match the texture of the thing described. I count four authorial voices in the story, but two dominate. The first of these uses the richly romantic prose style which many readers associate with Fitzgerald, the style for which he is either applauded or condemned: a selection of ornate terms so mutually dependent that to alter one is to alter all. . . .

This poetic voice primarily depicts Dexter Green's character and point-of-view. . . .

This voice works through the first four sections of the story to de-

Excerpted from "Four Voices in 'Winter Dreams,'" *Studies in Short Fiction* 23 (Summer 1986): 315, 316, 318, 319, 320. Reprinted by permission.

scribe the exteriors of characters and situations; it *shows* things. In counterpoint, a second voice, generally more sober and stylistically conventional gives editorial comment on action. This voice, from the American naturalistic tradition, *tells* us things about Dexter. . . .

So far, Fitzgerald is in control. When he wants to show youthful infatuation reaching for that fine sparkling jewel just beyond the out-stretched fingers, he uses a style at once excessive and selective, like the condition he wants to capture. But when he needs naturalistic ob-jectivity—in a sense, the adult's view of life—the voice becomes neu-tral and rational. When Dexter looks at things, the first voice dominates; when we look at Dexter, we hear the second. . . . the gap between the two creates certain obvious problems with point-of-view that he attempts to patch up with a third voice which imposes itself on the story like an uninvited pedant.

The second instance of this editorial voice, like the first, involves Dexter's motivation, his internal self. . . .

This behavioral analysis again verges on the naturalistic, and Fitz-gerald delivers it, as Dreiser or Anderson might, in a neutral style, universal in fit and scope. But it also reveals a distinctly inappropriate authorial insecurity: Fitzgerald fears his protagonist's development is insufficient to carry the weight of the author's tendency toward social analysis; thus, we are told what we might better be shown. . . . Fitz-gerald uses the imperative voice, then, by way of apology for shoving Dexter through the War, an awkwardness necessitated by the need for a fully mature Dexter. . . .

This last section employs a fourth voice, more stylistically reserved than the first, to show a mature protagonist's observations; and it suits a more deadened, reserved character—one compromised by age. . . .

Observing Fitzgerald struggling with these four voices early on in his career invites a view of "Winter Dreams" as a stylistic turning point, a smaller world in which the writer's difficulties with novels reveal them-selves, sometimes with the overt and vital confusion of the youth he describes. The first voice stylistically mirrors the protagonist's inflated point-of-view, an effect traditionally limited to first-person narration. The second voice offers naturalistic objectivity. The imperative third voice is an apologist for structural inadequacies. And the fourth voice, over which he labored extensively, repeats the function of the first but in a style appropriate to a mature protagonist. Because the four voices are discreet and their union is not seamless, readers may fault Fitzgerald.

Robert Emmet Long

But a much superior story is "Absolution" (1924), in which romantic illusion is focused forward in time, rather than backward into the past, as it is in "Winter Dreams" and "The Sensible Thing.". . .

In narrating the story, in fact, Fitzgerald uses Joyce's technique in *Dubliners*, working naturalistic detail and symbol tightly into the fabric of the tale. . . . The priest's watery eyes call attention to his failing vision and to vision itself as a theme to be explored in the story. . . .

The first paragraphs introduce the controlling images of the story—the sun and the wheat, light and darkness, the moon. . . . The story concludes with a Joycean epiphany, as the controlling images suddenly expand into completed revelation. . . . At the very end, reinforcing the sense of the boy's liberation, there is an evocation of release from constriction into intense life.

Father Schwartz (whose name in German means "black" or "dark," the color also of his clerical garments) is always presented in images of enclosure, contrasted with the "open world of wheat and sky." The two places where he is seen are his "haunted room" and the confessional booth. . . . In particular, Rudolph's eyes are a contrast with the priest's cold, watery eyes suggesting two kinds of vision, one almost unnaturally bright, the other almost unnaturally faded. . . .

The father's oddness is that he could have confused two such different entities as God and James J. Hill, the spiritual calling and the worldly life. Like Father Schwartz, divided between inward and outward life, the father searches ineffectually for transcendence, which he finds nowhere, not in the freight office, where he is merely a servant of Hill's greater, more powerful, and realized dream, or in his home, which seems as constricted and haunted as the priest's study. More-

Excerpted from "Toward *The Great Gatsby:* The Apprenticeship Period," in *The Achieving of "The Great Gatsby": F. Scott Fitzgerald, 1920–1925* by Robert Emmet Long (Lewisburg, Pa.: Bucknell University Press, 1979), 71, 72, 73, 74, 75, 76, 77. © 1979 by Associated University Presses, Inc. Reprinted by permission of Associated University Presses.

over, like the priest, he seems about to break down. He is depicted in his isolation even at home, and significantly sleeps in a separate bedroom from his wife, from whom he has apparently become estranged. . . .

The inwardly divided figures of the priest and the father are used by Fitzgerald to accentuate the inner conflict of the boy. . . . The story has moved suspensefully toward this moment, when the inner lives of the boy and the priest are revealed at once.

The unusually rich texture of the story is achieved in part through Fitzgerald's use of time, which has been handled impressionistically, the story beginning in the middle of a central action, then moving back in time through a flashback, and then forward to the present. This movement back and forth in time complements the important role of time—future, present, and past—in the story. . . . By the end the priest's dream-past flows into the boy's dream-future, and it is toward the future that the story looks at the end. But there is an irony involved in this future in which things go "glimmering," since the priest warns Rudolph not to "get up close because if you do you'll only feel the heat and the sweat and the life." The gorgeousness of the world, which has nothing to do with God, is more ominous than the boy yet understands.

James L. W. West III and J. Barclay Inge

"The Rich Boy," composed in 1925 and published early in 1926, is one of F. Scott Fitzgerald's finest short stories. An examination of the composition and revision of the story—as revealed by three separate versions of its text—has uncovered some interesting information about Fitzgerald's working methods. Collation of these three versions with one another helps to clear up some puzzling matters about Fitzgerald's anonymous narrator in the story, and also reveals how readers should view and judge Anson Hunter, the main character. . . .

Excerpted from "F. Scott Fitzgerald's Revision of 'The Rich Boy,'" *Proof* 5 (1975): 127, 129, 135, 136–37, 137–38, 144. Reprinted by permission.

The resulting textual situation is intriguing. Three versions of "The Rich Boy" survive: the ribbon typescript that Ober saved; *The Red Book* text; and the *All the Sad Young Men* text. . . . Fitzgerald's late revisions are revealing, because many of them are aimed at modifying the attitude of the narrator toward Anson Hunter.

Here one must recall some details about "The Rich Boy." The story is told by an unnamed first-person narrator who claims to be Anson Hunter's friend. This narrator, in the famous prologue to the story, promises to view Anson objectively, as an individual and not as a representative of his class. . . . In the prologue, this narrator claims that he will be objective, but his comments about Anson have a noticeably ironic edge throughout. Anson is frequently undercut by the narrator: the disapproval is subtle but unmistakable. And, too, this unnamed narrator recounts information that he has no way of knowing, and reports conversations—in quoted dialogue—at which he was not present. How far is this narrator to be trusted?

The narration here is similar to the narration by Nick Carraway in *The Great Gatsby*. Nick also professes objectivity—he claims that he will withhold judgment of the characters in his tale—but his contempt for Tom and Daisy Buchanan, for their wealth and amorality, and for the gaudy and corrupt East are clear to the reader in the end. The narrator in "The Rich Boy" is cut from Nick's pattern: he professes objectivity but does not truly practice it. Nick Carraway must have been much on Fitzgerald's mind while he was composing "The Rich Boy": *The Great Gatsby* was published on 10 April 1925, shortly after Fitzgerald began "The Rich Boy," and Fitzgerald was carefully watching his sales figures and reading his reviews all during the time he worked on the story. The similarity between Nick and the narrator of "The Rich Boy" is therefore not surprising.

But the unnamed narrator in "The Rich Boy" has been the subject of some critical controversy. The disagreement, it is fair to say, centers around the narrator's identity. Most critics have identified him as Fitzgerald's mouthpiece. . . .

This view—that the narrator is Fitzgerald himself—is, to say the least, critically unsophisticated. Fitzgerald, in 1925, was fresh from a careful study of Joseph Conrad's writings and had just recently created Nick Carraway. Surely, then, he must have been very much aware of the effect of a first-person observer/narrator on a work of fiction, and must have known that such a narrator has an identity distinct from the identity of the author. . . . The collations do show that [Joseph] Katz in probably right: Fitzgerald appears deliberately to have been creating a biased narrator, a character in his own right who deserves as much attention as Anson. The collations indicate that the reader must not allow his attention to be diverted from the narrator, because the real key to the meaning of "The Rich Boy" lies in the realization that this narrator is a biased, unsympathetic, middle-class observer who cannot properly understand Anson or Anson's class. . . . The narrator in the revised version portrays Anson as more isolated, less charming, and less popular than he had been in the version sent to Ober. And the narrator, after Fitzgerald's revision of the carbon, pictures Anson as less intelligent and less trustworthy in his profession. Finally, the narrator in the revised version implies more clearly that Anson is incapable of the emotion of love. . . . But if Fitzgerald was in control of his material and technique—and in a story so finely wrought as "The Rich Boy," it is difficult to believe otherwise—then he intentionally created a narrator whose subtle bias against Anson is the real point of the story.

Roy R. Male

From this point of view, "Babylon Revisited" belongs with a number of stories in which the protagonist returns after a prolonged absence, either to his home or to some substitute for it. This category we may call the story of the Exile's Return. . . .

The hero may ask about the men, his former friends, but the essential motivation for his return is always a reunion with some form of feminine principle. . . .

As anyone who has returned home after a long absence will testify, the experience often has a dreamlike quality, a curious mixture of pain and pleasure as one feels his identity dissolving into two selves, past and present, private and public. . . . And this theme of split identity recurs, as we shall see, in "Babylon Revisited," where the basic ques-

Excerpted from "'Babylon Revisited': A Story of the Exile's Return," *Studies in Short Fiction* 2 (Spring 1965): 271, 272, 273, 275, 277. Reprinted by permission.

tion about Charlie is whether he is indeed "the old Wales," as his former friends call him, or the new.

A final theme given in the situation of the returning exile is that of freedom and responsibility. . . . This double vision of actor and spectator, with the mature spectator no longer a gawky outsider but a judge, informs all of Fitzgerald's best work, and in this story it allows him to view Charlie Wales with both sympathy and ironic detachment.

[Stephen Vincent] Benét's remark about Fitzgerald's "almost magic" phrasing also provides a clue to the all-important relation between art, spending, and morality in this story. . . .

The basic conflict of the story, then, is not just between Charlie and Marion; it is between Charlie Wales (who presumably takes his last name from the prince who was the epitome of the good-time Charlies in the twenties) and "Mr. Charles J. Wales of Prague," sound businessman and moralist, between the regally imaginative but destructive past and the dull, bourgeois but solid present. . . . For the trouble with Charlie is that he *still* wants both worlds. The harsh fact is that if he had not stopped in the Ritz bar in the first place, had not tried to get in touch with Duncan Schaeffer, he would have won back his daughter. . . .

The acrobats, the imagery of the vaudeville, remind us, finally, that this is a story of suspension between two worlds. Charlie's dream of his wife concludes with this vision: "she was in a swing in a white dress, and swinging faster all the time, so that at the end he could not hear clearly all that she said." Fitzgerald continues this image in the climactic scene when the drunken Lorraine and Dunc invade the Peters' apartment. After they leave, Lincoln is "still swinging Honoria back and forth like a pendulum from side to side." Up to this point Charlie has virtually convinced even Marion that his feet are "planted on the earth now," but actually, as we have seen, he is caught between two worlds. Fitzgerald has arranged their representatives with a symmetry reminiscent of James. On the one hand is the pale blonde, Lorraine, with her escort Duncan Schaeffer; on the other, Marion, clothed in a "black dress that just faintly suggested mourning," with her husband, Lincoln, who appropriately works in a bank. . . . The prodigal has returned, but his effort to "conciliate something," to redress the balance, has failed, and he remains an exile.

Sheldon Grebstein

As its most obvious theme or subject, "Crazy Sunday" contrasts the physical beauty, charisma, or talent of its major characters—Joel, Stella, Miles—with the element of instability, weakness, or tendency toward self-destruction which seems to coincide, even be necessary to their beauty and talent. Joel drinks to excess. Miles is exhausted, marked for death. The alluring Stella is emotionally fragile, subject to hysteria. . . .

The story's atmosphere and action are thus intensely psychological, not only in the specifically psychiatric sense conveyed in Miles's talk of his psychoanalysis and personal troubles, but more important in that the narrative emphasizes states of feeling and the impressions people make upon one another from moment to moment. . . . Relationships that would take months, even years, to develop in "real" or "normal" life are accelerated, foreshortened, developed in one or two brief encounters. In this concentration and distillation of experience, Fitzgerald both exercises the economy of the short story form and evokes the method of a film scenario.

The story's title alerts us to its psychological focus, although it is also deliberately ambiguous. "Crazy" applies less obviously to the day than to the characters. . . .

Appropriately, the emphasis on the psychological dimension is reinforced by the story's dramatic structure. This structure basically depends not upon the five formal sections into which Fitzgerald has overtly divided it, although these are important as phases in the action, but upon three crazy Sundays. In turn, each of these Sundays serves as the occasion for the exposure and humiliation of each of the main characters. . . .

Excerpted from "The Sane Method of 'Crazy Sunday,'" in *The Short Stories of F. Scott Fitzgerald: New Approaches in Criticism*, ed. Jackson R. Bryer (Madison: University of Wisconsin Press, 1982), 280–81, 282, 283, 284, 285, 286. © 1982 by the Board of Regents of the University of Wisconsin System. Reprinted by permission of the publisher.

176

Inextricably intertwined with the "crazy" motif, and equally important as a thematic and structural element, is the story's emphasis upon
the artificiality and theatricality of this microcosm and the conduct of
its inhabitants. This motif of frenetic make-believe is rendered both
metaphorically and as direct exposition. It begins at once in the simile
of the characters as enchanted puppets infused temporarily with life.
It is soon reinforced by the description of the producer's home as a vast
theater or auditorium. . . . Even nature seems sensitive to the histrionic conduct of these Hollywood people, for in each of the major
scenes the condition of sea or sky collaborates with the Calman house
or some other extreme feature of the California setting to supply a
fittingly cinematic backdrop for the plot. . . . The pseudo-romantic
moon and the sexy streetlights combine to anticipate the action and,
in retrospect, to offer an ironic commentary upon it.

Within this prevailing context of theatricality, each of the main characters appears both genuine and artificial. Stella seems especially at
home in the melodramatic mode and glows as the story's most vivid
incarnation of the enchanted puppet motif. . . . In accordance both
with the norms of her Hollywood status and to enhance further our
sense of the theatrical, Fitzgerald usually presents Stella to us in vi-
brant color and exquisite clothing or, said otherwise, in the suitable
makeup and costume for her role.

As actor in his own life story, Miles Calman creates almost as much
fantasy and melodrama in his career and marriage as in the films he
produces. . . . In the first scene, Joel plays the lead, Stella a highly
visible but nevertheless supporting role, and Miles the smallest part.
His presence is important; we know he stands in the background as
one of the crowd, but we do not observe him directly or hear him
speak. He really serves as audience or witness. In the second scene,
however, Miles and Stella are co-featured, with Joel relegated to the
role of audience or witness. The final scene casts Joel and Stella together again, this time as co-stars but with Stella's lines and action
paramount. As in the first scene, Miles again functions as distant on-
looker; indeed, even though he is physically absent, he exists more
than ever as a dominant presence in the minds of the others. Note also
that the varying interplay of the three characters, staged primarily in
the Calman house in each of the three "Crazy Sunday" scenes, occurs
at equivalent intervals in the story's formal divisions, Section I, III,
and V, and provides an unobtusive but pleasing structural symmetry.
Moreover, the placement of the Joel-Stella scenes at the beginning and

end of the story works as a form of closure. . . . This evolution in Joel's character from weakness toward strength is clearly evident by a simple comparison of his conduct and speech in Section I with that of Section V. . . . Joel's self-control in this final scene is emphasized all the more by Stella's hysteria. . . . What occurs, then, as intrinsic to the selective-omniscient mode when properly rendered, is a merging of the writer's voice and vision with those of his central character. The story is told in the third person, but it assumes the impact and the immediacy of a first-person narrative. . . .

Concomitant with the story's portrayal of film people and its dramatic structure, much of its aesthetic method depends upon the *visual*, both as the reader's attention is focused upon the characters' eyes and in the visual exchange among the characters. With the exception of a few bright splashes of color—especially the red-gold and ice-blue associated with Stella—the story's most vivid imagery is reserved for eyes. I count about forty direct references in the story either to eyes or to actions of sight: seeing, looking, watching, staring, etc. Whatever the clothing, manners, physical structure, or presence of the characters, their *eyes* betray the deepest truth about them.

William Troy

Although it is one of the most obvious statements that can be made of any novelist, it has never exactly been pointed out about Scott Fitzgerald that what he is principally concerned with in all his novels and tales is character. "She was a fine girl—one of the best," remarks the hero of one of the stories in this collection [*Taps at Reveille*], of the wife who has abandoned him to follow her own career. "She had character." All the important personages in the book have character or are trying to have character, or have irretrievably lost their character. Whether the emphasis is on achievement or struggle or failure the theme is one and the same. Whatever may be their age or sex or background all of them

Excerpted from "The Perfect Life," *Nation*, 17 April 1935. Copyright 1935 *The Nation Magazine*/ The Nation Co., Inc. Reprinted by permission of the publisher.

are sooner or later confronted, like the adolescent Basil Lee, with the vision of "the perfect life.". . .

Now the problem of character, which is first and last the moral problem, is not popular with many of the writers and readers of contemporary fiction; it has been relegated to that class of quaint antiquities which includes Malthusianism and the Boston rocker. . . . What used to be called character has dissolved in the confused welter of uncoordinated actions, sensations, impressions, and physico-chemical reactions which currently passes for the art of fiction.

Mr. Fitzgerald, in his persistent concentration on "those fine moral decisions that people make in books," is fundamentally, therefore, a rather old-fashioned sort of storyteller. He has more in common, let us say, with George Eliot, Henry James, and Joseph Conrad than with any of the more prominent members of his own generation. One should not be misled by the strong sense of the Zeitgeist reflected in his choice of subjects and characters. Although the experience is as contemporary as that of Faulkner or of Hemingway, the focus on the experience is very different, and the technique that is the result of this focus is different. It is not experience *qua* experience that is important but the ordering of experience, the arrangement of experience according to some scheme of developing moral action. This is the reason why Mr. Fitzgerald in even his worst lapses, such as the story called "Majesty," is always able to sustain a certain interest, to provide the kind of interest that we are accustomed to receive from prose narrative.

Chronology

1853   Edward Fitzgerald born near Rockville, Maryland.

1860   Mary ("Mollie") McQuillan born in St. Paul, Minnesota.

1890   Edward Fitzgerald and Mollie McQuillan marry.

1896   Francis Scott Key Fitzgerald born 24 September at 481 Laurel Avenue, St. Paul.

1898   Between 1898 and 1908 the Fitzgerald family lives in Buffalo and Syracuse, New York, before returning to St. Paul.

1900   Zelda Sayre born in Montgomery, Alabama.

1901   Fitzgerald's sister, Annabel, born.

1908   Enters St. Paul Academy.

1909   First appears in print with the publication of "The Mystery of the Raymond Mortgage" by the *St. Paul Academy Now & Then*.

1911   Writes his first play, *The Girl from Lazy J.*, for the Elizabethan Dramatic Society. By 1914 three others will be produced. Enters the Newman School, Hackensack, New Jersey.

1913   Enters Princeton University, where he will meet Edmund Wilson and John Peale Bishop.

1914   Contributes to *The Princeton Tiger*. *Fie! Fie! Fi-Fi!*, Fitzgerald's first Triangle Club show, is produced in December. *The Evil Eye* (1915) and *Safety First* (1916) will follow. At Christmas, meets Ginevra King in St. Paul.

1915   *The Nassau Literary Magazine* publishes "Shadow Laurels," the first of several Fitzgerald contributions, in April.

1917   Is commissioned as an infantry second lieutenant after failing to graduate from Princeton. At Fort Leavenworth, Kansas, begins his first novel, "The Romantic Egotist," which will eventually become *This Side of Paradise*.

1918   Meets Zelda Sayre at a country club dance in Montgomery.

1919   Discharged from the army, works for the Barron Collier advertising agency in New York City. *The Smart Set* accepts "Babes in the Woods," Fitzgerald's first commercial story sale. In June Zelda breaks their engagement. Quits his job and returns to St. Paul, where he rewrites *This Side of Paradise*, which Scribner editor Maxwell Perkins accepts for publication on 16 September. Harold Ober becomes Fitzgerald's agent. The *Saturday Evening Post* buys "Head and Shoulders," initiating a long professional relationship between this magazine and Fitzgerald. Between November 1919 and February 1920 *The Smart Set* publishes "The Debutante," "Porcelain and Pink," "Benediction," and "Dalyrimple Goes Wrong."

1920   Resumes engagement to Zelda. Between March and May, the *Post* publishes "Myra Meets His Family," "The Camel's Back," "Bernice Bobs Her Hair," "The Ice Palace," and "The Offshore Pirate." *This Side of Paradise* appears 26 March. On 3 April marries Zelda in New York. In July *The Smart Set* publishes "May Day." Publication of *Flappers and Philosophers*, Fitzgerald's first short story collection, 10 September.

1921   The Fitzgeralds make their first trip to Europe. Others will follow. Their daughter Scottie is born 26 October.

1922   *The Beautiful and Damned* appears 4 March. *The Smart Set* publishes "The Diamond as Big as the Ritz" in June. *Tales of the Jazz Age* appears 22 September. *Metropolitan Magazine* publishes "Winter Dreams" in December.

1923   Fitzgerald's only full-length play, *The Vegetable*, is published on 27 April, but soon fails in Atlantic City.

1924   *The American Mercury* publishes "Absolution" in June. During the summer and fall writes *The Great Gatsby*. *Liberty* publishes "The Sensible Thing" in July. The Fitzgeralds meet Gerald and Sara Murphy at Cap d'Antibes.

1925   *The Great Gatsby* appears 10 April. The Fitzgeralds meet Hemingway in Paris.

1926   Zelda Fitzgerald takes the "cure" at Salies-de-Béarn. *Red Book* magazine publishes "The Rich Boy" during January and February. Owen Davis's play version of *The Great Gatsby* is produced on Broadway. *All the Sad Young Men* appears 26 February.

1927 Makes the first of several trips to Hollywood, one of which will inspire "Crazy Sunday." Meets actress Lois Moran.

1928 In April the *Post* publishes "The Scandal Detectives," the first of eight Basil Duke Lee stories.

1929 In March the *Post* publishes "The Last of the Belles."

1930 Zelda Fitzgerald experiences her first breakdown in Paris. She enters the Malmaison clinic, then the Valmont clinic (Switzerland). She will be hospitalized from time to time throughout the 1930s. The *Post* publishes "First Blood," launching the five-story Josephine Perry series.

1931 Edward Fitzgerald dies. In February the *Post* publishes "Babylon Revisited."

1934 *Tender Is the Night* appears 12 April.

1935 *Taps at Reveille* appears 20 March.

1936 Mollie Fitzgerald dies.

1937 Meets Sheila Graham in Hollywood. Between September 1937 and January 1938 works on *Three Comrades*, which will be Fitzgerald's only screen credit.

1939 In February the Dartmouth College drinking spree fictionally recorded in Budd Schulberg's *The Disenchanted* occurs. Break with Harold Ober.

1940 In January *Esquire* publishes "Pat Hobby's Christmas Wish," the first of a seventeen-story sequence. In May moves to 1403 North Laurel Avenue, Hollywood. From May to August, works on "Cosmopolitan." Dies of a heart attack 21 December at Sheila Graham's apartment. Is buried 27 December in the Rockville Union Cemetery, Rockville, Maryland.

1941 *The Last Tycoon* (unfinished) appears 27 October.

1948 Zelda Fitzgerald dies in a fire at Asheville, North Carolina.

Selected Bibliography

Primary Sources

Story Collections

Afternoon of an Author. Edited by Arthur Mizener. 1957. Reprint. New York: Macmillan Scribner Classic, 1987. This selection of uncollected stories and essays includes "How to Waste Material," "One Hundred False Starts," "Outside the Cabinet-Maker's" and "One Trip Abroad" among its twenty pieces.

All the Sad Young Men. New York: Scribner, 1926. Contains "The Rich Boy," "Winter Dreams," "The Baby Party," "Absolution," "Rags Martin-Jones and the Pr-nce of W-les," "The Adjuster," "Hot and Cold Blood," "The Sensible Thing," and "Gretchen's Forty Winks."

The Apprentice Fiction of F. Scott Fitzgerald, 1909–1917. Edited by John Kuehl. New Brunswick, N.J.: Rutgers University Press, 1965. Contains twelve prep-school and college stories, as well as the previously unpublished document "The Death of My Father."

Babylon Revisited and Other Stories. 1960. Reprint. New York: Macmillan Scribner Classic, 1988. Contains "The Ice Palace," "May Day," "The Diamond as Big as the Ritz," "Winter Dreams," "Absolution," "The Rich Boy," "The Freshest Boy," "Babylon Revisited," "Crazy Sunday," and "The Long Way Out."

The Basil and Josephine Stories. Edited by Jackson R. Bryer and John Kuehl. 1973. Reprint. New York: Macmillan Scribner Classic, 1987. Contains all nine Basil and all five Josephine stories, as well as a lengthy introduction.

Bits of Paradise: 21 Uncollected Stories by F. Scott and Zelda Fitzgerald. Selected by Matthew J. Bruccoli with the assistance of Scottie Fitzgerald Smith. 1973. Reprint. New York: Pocket Books, 1976. Among the pieces in this volume are Fitzgerald's "Jacob's Ladder" and "The Swimmers."

Flappers and Philosophers. 1920. Reprint. New York: Macmillan Scribner Classic, 1988. Contains "The Offshore Pirate," "The Ice Palace," "Head and Shoulders," "The Cut-Glass Bowl," "Bernice Bobs Her Hair," "Benediction," "Dalyrimple Goes Wrong," and "The Four Fists."

The Pat Hobby Stories. 1962. Reprint. New York: Scribner, 1968. Contains all seventeen Pat Hobby stories, as well as the unused revision of "A Patriotic Short."

184

The Price Was High: The Last Uncollected Stories of F. Scott Fitzgerald. Edited by Matthew J. Bruccoli. New York: Harcourt Brace Jovanovich/Bruccoli Clark, 1979. Contains fifty selections.

The Short Stories of F. Scott Fitzgerald: A New Collection. Edited by Matthew J. Bruccoli. New York: Scribner's, 1989.

Six Tales of the Jazz Age and Other Stories. 1960. Reprint. New York: Scribner, 1968. Contains "The Jelly-Bean," "The Camel's Back," "The Curious Case of Benjamin Button," "Tarquin of Cheapside," "'O Russet Witch!,'" "The Lees of Happiness," "The Adjuster," "Hot and Cold Blood," and "Gretchen's Forty Winks," as well as an introduction by Fitzgerald's daughter, Frances Fitzgerald Lanahan.

The Stories of F. Scott Fitzgerald. Edited by Malcolm Cowley. 1951. Reprint. New York: Macmillan Scribner Classic, 1986. This collection of twenty-eight stories is a good supplement to the ten selections in *Babylon Revisited and Other Stories.* The editor has provided a lengthy introduction and sectional notes.

Tales of the Jazz Age. New York: Scribner, 1922. Contains "The Jelly-Bean," "The Camel's Back," "May Day," "The Diamond as Big as the Ritz," "The Curious Case of Benjamin Button," "Tarquin of Cheapside," "'O Russet Witch!,'" "The Lees of Happiness," "Mr. Icky," and "Jemina."

Taps at Reveille. 1935. Reprint. New York: Scribner, 1960. Contains "The Scandal Detectives," "The Freshest Boy," "He Thinks He's Wonderful," "The Captured Shadow," "The Perfect Life," "First Blood," "A Nice Quiet Place," "A Woman with a Past," "Crazy Sunday," "Two Wrongs," "The Night of Chancellorsville," "The Last of the Belles," "Majesty," "Family in the Wind," "A Short Trip Home," "One Interne," "The Fiend," and "Babylon Revisited."

Novels

The Beautiful and Damned. 1922. Reprint. New York: Macmillan Scribner Classic, 1988.

The Great Gatsby. 1925. Reprint. New York: Macmillan Scribner Classic, 1986.

The Last Tycoon. 1941. Reprint. New York: Macmillan Scribner Classic, 1986.

Tender Is the Night. 1934. Reprint. New York: Macmillan Scribner Classic, 1986.

This Side of Paradise. 1920. Reprint. New York: Macmillan Scribner Classic, 1986.

Plays

F. Scott Fitzgerald's St. Paul Plays, 1911–1914. Edited by Alan Margolies. Princeton, N.J.: Princeton University Library, 1978. Contains the four previously unpublished plays Fitzgerald wrote for the Elizabethan Dramatic Club of St. Paul, Minnesota.

The Vegetable; Or, from President to Postman. 1923. Reprint. New York: Macmillan Scribner Classic, 1987.

Nonfiction

As Ever, Scott Fitz–: Letters Between F. Scott Fitzgerald and His Literary Agent, Harold Ober, 1919–1940. Edited by Matthew J. Bruccoli. New York: Lippincott, 1972.

Correspondence of F. Scott Fitzgerald. Edited by Matthew J. Bruccoli and Margaret M. Duggan. New York: Random House, 1980.

Dear Scott/Dear Max: The Fitzgerald-Perkins Correspondence. Edited by John Kuehl and Jackson R. Bryer. New York: Scribner, 1971.

F. Scott Fitzgerald's "Ledger." Edited by Matthew J. Bruccoli. Washington, D.C.: NCR Microcard Editions, 1973.

The Letters of F. Scott Fitzgerald. edited by Andrew Turnbull. New York: Scribner, 1963.

Letters to His Daughter. Edited by Andrew Turnbull. New York: Scribner, 1963.

The Notebooks of F. Scott Fitzgerald. Edited by Matthew J. Bruccoli. New York: Harcourt Brace Jovanovich, 1978.

Thoughtbook of Francis Scott Key Fitzgerald. Introduction by John Kuehl. Princeton, N.J.: Princeton University Library, 1965. This was also printed in the *Princeton University Library Chronicle* 26, no. 2 (Winter 1965): 102–8. The dated entries of Fitzgerald's childhood diary run from August 1910 to 24 February 1911.

Miscellaneous

The Crack-Up. Edited by Edmund Wilson. 1945. Reprint. New York: New Directions, 1956. This contains a variety of primary and secondary material, including Fitzgerald's three "crack-up" articles and an abbreviated version of his "note-books."

F. Scott Fitzgerald in His Own Time: A Miscellany. Edited by Matthew J. Bruccoli and Jackson R. Bryer. Kent, Ohio: Kent State University Press, 1971. Contains "Miscellany by Fitzgerald" ("Poems," "*The Princeton Tiger* Humor," "*The Nassau Literary Magazine* Humor," "Introductions and Blurbs," "Public Letters and Statements," "Love, Marriage, and Sex," "Autobiographical," "Unclassified") and "Miscellany about Fitzgerald" ("Interviews," "Reviews," "Essays and Editorials," "Parodies," "Obituary Editorials and Essays").

Secondary Sources

Books and Parts of Books

Allen, Joan M. *Candles and Carnival Lights: The Catholic Sensibility of F. Scott Fitzgerald.* New York: New York University Press, 1978.

Bewley, Marius. *The Eccentric Design: Form in Classic American Literature.* New York: Columbia University Press, 1963. See chapter 11, "Scott Fitzgerald and the Collapse of the American Dream," 259–87.

Bruccoli, Matthew J. *Some Sort of Epic Grandeur: The Life of F. Scott Fitzgerald.* New York: Harcourt Brace Jovanovich, 1979.

Bryer, Jackson R., ed. *The Short Stories of F. Scott Fitzgerald: New Approaches in Criticism.* Madison: University of Wisconsin Press, 1982. Contains overviews by Richard Lehan, Lawrence Buell, Kenneth E. Eble, C. Hugh Holman, Alan Margolies, Scott Donaldson, Joseph Mancini, Jr., Ruth Prigozy, Robert A. Martin, James L. W. West III, and essays on individual stories by John Kuehl ("The Ice Palace"), James W. Tuttleton ("May Day"), Neil D. Isaacs ("Winter Dreams"), Irving Malin ("Absolution"), Victor Doyno ("Rags Martin-Jones and the Pr—nce of W—les"), Christiane Johnson ("The Adjuster,") Peter Wolfe ("The Rich Boy"), Melvin J. Friedman ("The Swimmers"), James J. Martine ("The Bridal Party"), Carlos Baker ("Babylon Revisited"), Sheldon Grebstein ("Crazy Sunday"), and George Monteiro ("Financing Finnegan"). Also included is useful bibliographic information in the appendix, "The Short Stories of F. Scott Fitzgerald: A Checklist of Criticism."

Donaldson, Scott. *Fool for Love.* New York: Congdon & Weed, 1983.

Eble, Kenneth. *F. Scott Fitzgerald.* 1963. 2d. ed. Boston: Twayne, 1977.

Gullason, Thomas A. "The American Short Story in the 1920s." In *The American Short Story: 1900–1945,* edited by Philip Stevick. Boston: Twayne, 1984.

Higgins, John A. *F. Scott Fitzgerald: A Study of the Stories.* Jamaica, N.Y.: St. John's University Press, 1971.

Hindus, Milton. *F. Scott Fitzgerald: An Introduction and Interpretation.* New York: Holt, 1968.

Kazin, Alfred, ed. *F. Scott Fitzgerald: The Man and His Work.* Cleveland: World, 1951. Contains thirty selections by writers and critics.

Kimbel, Ellen. "The American Short Story: 1900–1920." In *The American Short Story: 1900–1945, edited by Philip Stevick. Boston: Twayne, 1984.*

Latham, Aaron. *Crazy Sundays: F. Scott Fitzgerald in Hollywood.* New York: Viking, 1971.

Lehan, Richard D. *F. Scott Fitzgerald and the Craft of Fiction.* Carbondale: Southern Illinois University Press, 1966.

LeVot, André, *F. Scott Fitzgerald: A Biography.* Trans. William Byron. Garden City, N.Y.: Doubleday, 1983.

Long, Robert Emmet. *The Achieving of "The Great Gatsby": F. Scott Fitzgerald, 1920–1925.* Lewisburg, Pa.: Bucknell University Press, 1979.

Mellow, James R. *Invented Lives: F. Scott & Zelda Fitzgerald.* New York: Ballantine Books, 1984.

Milford, Nancy. *Zelda.* New York: Avon, 1970.

Miller, James E., Jr. *F. Scott Fitzgerald: His Art and His Technique.* New York: New York University Press, 1967.

Mizener, Arthur. *The Far Side of Paradise: A Biography of F. Scott Fitzgerald.* 1951. 2d. ed. Boston: Houghton Mifflin, 1965.

———, ed. *F. Scott Fitzgerald: A Collection of Critical Essays.* Englewood Cliffs, N.J.: Prentice-Hall, 1963. Contains nineteen essays on Fitzgerald's career, his early work, *The Great Gatsby,* and his late work.

Perosa, Sergio. *The Art of F. Scott Fitzgerald.* Translated by Charles Matz and Sergio Perosa. Ann Arbor: University of Michigan Press, 1965.

Petry, Alice Hall. *Fitzgerald's Craft of Short Fiction: The Collected Stories 1920–1935.* Ann Arbor: UMI Research Press, 1989.

Phillips, Larry W. *F. Scott Fitzgerald on Writing.* New York: Scribner, 1985.

Piper, Henry Dan. *F. Scott Fitzgerald: A Critical Portrait.* New York: Holt, 1965.

Shain, Charles E. *F. Scott Fitzgerald.* Minneapolis: University of Minnesota Press, 1961.

Sklar, Robert. *F. Scott Fitzgerald: The Last Laocoön.* New York: Oxford University Press, 1967.

Stavola, Thomas J. *Scott Fitzgerald: Crisis in an American Identity.* New York: Barnes & Noble, 1979.

Stern, Milton. *The Golden Moment: The Novels of F. Scott Fitzgerald.* Urbana: University of Illinois Press, 1970.

Trilling, Lionel. "F. Scott Fitzgerald." In *The Liberal Imagination: Essays on Literature and Society.* New York: Scribner, 1950.

Voss, Arthur. *The American Short Story: A Critical Survey.* Norman: University of Oklahoma Press, 1973.

Way, Brian. *F. Scott Fitzgerald and the Art of Social Fiction.* London: Arnold, 1980.

Wright, Austin McGiffert. *The American Short Story in the Twenties.* Chicago: University of Chicago Press, 1961.

Articles

Arnold, Edwin T. "The Motion Picture as Metaphor in the Works of F. Scott Fitzgerald." *Fitzgerald/Hemingway Annual* 9 (1977): 43–60.

Atkinson, Jennifer McCabe. "Lost and Unpublished Stories by F. Scott Fitzgerald." *Fitzgerald/Hemingway Annual* 3 (1971): 32–63.

Bodeen, DeWitt. "F. Scott Fitzgerald and Films." *Films in Review* 28 (May 1977): 285–94.

Brondell, William J. "Structural Metaphors in Fitzgerald's Short Fiction." *Kansas Quarterly* 14 (Spring 1982): 95–112.

Burhans, Clinton S., Jr. "'Magnificently Attune to Life': The Value of 'Winter Dreams.'" *Studies in Short Fiction* 6 (Summer 1969): 401–12.

Cardwell, Guy A. "The Lyric World of Scott Fitzgerald." *Virginia Quarterly Review* 38 (Spring 1962): 299–323.

Cass, Colin S. "Fitzgerald's Second Thoughts about 'May Day': A Collation and Study." *Fitzgerald/Hemingway Annual* 2 (1970): 69–95.

Casty, Alan. "'I and It' in the Stories of F. Scott Fitzgerald." *Studies in Short Fiction* 9 (Winter 1972): 47–58.

Cushman, Keith. "Scott Fitzgerald's Scrupulous Meanness: 'Absolution' and 'The Sisters.'" *Fitzgerald/Hemingway Annual* 11 (1979): 115–21.

Daniels, Thomas E. "Pat Hobby: Anti-Hero." *Fitzgerald/Hemingway Annual* 5 (1973): 131–39.

———. "The Texts of 'Winter Dreams.'" *Fitzgerald/Hemingway Annual* 9 (1977): 77–100.

———. "Toward a Definitive Edition of F. Scott Fitzgerald's Short Stories." *Papers of the Bibliographical Society of America* 71 (Third Quarter 1977): 295–310.

Donaldson, Scott. "Scott Fitzgerald's Romance with the South." *Southern Literary Journal* 5 (Spring 1973): 3–17.

Drake, Constance. "Josephine and Emotional Bankruptcy." *Fitzgerald/Hemingway Annual* 1 (1969): 5–13.

Edenbaum, Robert I. "'Babylon Revisited': A Psychological Note on F. Scott Fitzgerald." *Literature and Psychology* 18 (1968): 27–29.

Elstein, Rochelle S. "Fitzgerald's Josephine Stories: The End of the Romantic Illusion." *American Literature* 51 (March 1979): 69–83.

Fulkerson, Tahita N. "Ibsen in 'The Ice Palace.'" *Fitzgerald/Hemingway Annual* 11 (1979): 169–71.

Gervais, Ronald J. "The Snow of Twenty-Nine: 'Babylon Revisited' as *Ubi Sunt* Lament." *College Literature* 7 (Winter 1980): 47–52.

Griffith, Richard R. "A Note on Fitzgerald's 'Babylon Revisited.'" *American Literature* 35 (May 1963): 236–39.

Gross, Seymour L. "Fitzgerald's 'Babylon Revisited.'" *College English* 25 (November 1963): 128–35.

Gruber, Michael Paul. "Fitzgerald's 'May Day': A Prelude to Triumph." *Essays in Literature* (University of Denver) 2 (1973): 20–35.

Hagemann, E. R. "Should Scott Fitzgerald be Absolved for the Sins of 'Absolution'?" *Journal of Modern Literature* 12 (March 1985): 169–74.

Holmes, Charles S. "Fitzgerald: The American Theme." *Pacific Spectator* 6 (Spring 1952): 243–52.

Houston, Penelope. "Visits to Babylon: F. Scott Fitzgerald and Hollywood." *Sight and Sound* 21 (April–June 1952): 153–56.

Ishikawa, Akiko. "From 'Winter Dreams' to *The Great Gatsby.*" *Persica (Journal of the English Society of Okayama)* no. 5 (January 1978): 79–92.

Johnston, Kenneth G. "Fitzgerald's 'Crazy Sunday': Cinderella in Hollywood." *Literature/Film Quarterly* 6 (Summer 1978): 214–21.

Kane, Patricia. "F. Scott Fitzgerald's St. Paul: A Writer's Use of Material." *Minnesota History* 45 (Winter 1976): 141–48.

Katz, Joseph. "The Narrator and 'The Rich Boy.'" *Fitzgerald Newsletter* no. 32 (Winter 1966): 2–3.

Kolbenschlag, Madonna C. "Madness and Sexual Mythology in Scott Fitzgerald." *International Journal of Women's Studies* 1 (May/June 1978): 263–71.

Kreuter, Kent, and Gretchen Kreuter. "The Moralism of the Later Fitzgerald." *Modern Fiction Studies* 7 (Spring 1961): 71–78.

Kuehl, John. "A la Joyce: The Sisters Fitzgerald's Absolution." *James Joyce Quarterly* 2 (Fall 1964): 2–6.

———. "A Note on the Begetting of *Gatsby.*" *University* 21 (Summer 1964): 26–32.

———. "Scott Fitzgerald's Critical Opinions." *Modern Fiction Studies* 7 (Spring 1961): 3–18.

———. "Scott Fitzgerald's Reading." *Princeton University Library Chronicle* 22 (Winter 1961): 58–89.

———. "Scott Fitzgerald: Romantic and Realist." *Texas Studies in Literature and Language* 1 (Autumn 1959): 412–26.

LaHurd, Ryan. "'Absolution': *Gatsby's* Forgotten Front Door." *College Literature* 3 (Spring 1976): 113–23.

Larsen, Erling. "The Geography of Fitzgerald's St. Paul." *Carleton Miscellany* 13 (Spring/Summer 1973): 3–30.

LeGates, Charlotte. "Dual-Perspective Irony and the Fitzgerald Short Story." *Iowa English Yearbook* 26 (1977): 18–20.

Lehan, Richard D. "F. Scott Fitzgerald and Romantic Destiny." *Twentieth Century Literature* 26 (Summer 1980): 137–56.

Lueders, Edward. "Revisiting Babylon: Fitzgerald and the 1920s." *Western Humanities Review* 29 (Summer 1975): 285–91.

Male, Roy R. "'Babylon Revisited': A Story of the Exile's Return." *Studies in Short Fiction* 2 (Spring 1965): 270–77.

Margolies, Alan. "A Note on Fitzgerald's Lost and Unpublished Stories." *Fitzgerald/Hemingway Annual* 4 (1972): 335–36.

Martin, Robert A. "The Hot Madness of Four O'Clock in Fitzgerald's 'Absolution' and *Gatsby.*" *Studies in American Fiction* 2 (Autumn 1974): 230–38.

Martin, Robert K. "Sexual and Group Relationships in 'May Day': Fear and Longing." *Studies in Short Fiction* 15 (Winter 1978): 99–101.

Mazella, Anthony J. "The Tension of Opposites in Fitzgerald's 'May Day.'" *Studies in Short Fiction* 14 (Fall 1977): 379–85.

Mizener, Arthur. "The Voice of Scott Fitzgerald's Prose." *Essays and Studies* (English Association), n.s. 16 (1963): 56–67.

Morrison, Gail Moore. "Faulkner's Priests and Fitzgerald's 'Absolution.'" *Mississippi Quarterly* 32 (Summer 1979): 461–65.*

Moses, Edwin. "F. Scott Fitzgerald and the Quest to the Ice Palace." *CEA Critic* 36 (January 1974): 11–14.

Murphy, Garry N., and William C. Slattery. "The Flawed Text of 'Babylon Revisited': A Challenge to Editors, a Warning to Readers." *Studies in Short Fiction* 18 (Summer 1981): 315–18.

Murphy, Patrick D. "Illumination and Affection in the Parallel Plots of 'The Rich Boy' and 'The Beast in the Jungle.'" *Papers on Language and Literature* 22 (1986): 406–16.

Nettels, Elsa. "Howell's 'A Circle in the Water' and Fitzgerald's 'Babylon Revisited.'" *Studies in Short Fiction* 19 (Summer 1982): 261–67.

Nilsen, Helge Normann. "A Failure to Love: A Note on F. Scott Fitzgerald's 'The Rich Boy.'" *The International Fiction Review* 14, no. 1 (1987): 40–43.

Osborne, William R. "The Wounds of Charlie Wales in Fitzgerald's 'Babylon Revisited.'" *Studies in Short Fiction* 2 (Fall 1964): 86–87.

Perlis, Alan. "The Narrative Is All: A Study of F. Scott Fitzgerald's 'May Day.'" *Western Humanities Review* 33 (Winter 1979): 65–72.

Petry, Alice Hall. "Love Story: Mock Courtship in F. Scott Fitzgerald's 'The Jelly-Bean.'" *Arizona Quarterly* 39 (Fall 1983): 251–60.

———. "The Picture(s) of Paula Legendre: Fitzgerald's 'The Rich Boy.'" *Studies in Short Fiction* 22 (Spring 1985): 232–34.

Pike, Gerald. "Four Voices in 'Winter Dreams.'" *Studies in Short Fiction* 23 (Summer 1986): 315–20.

Piper, Henry Dan. "Scott Fitzgerald's Prep-School Writings: Several Newly-Discovered Additions to the Canon of His Published Works." *Princeton University Library Chronicle* 17 (Autumn 1955): 1–10.

Podis, Leonard A. "Fitzgerald's 'The Diamond as Big as the Ritz' and Hawthorne's 'Rappaccini's Daughter.'" *Studies in Short Fiction* 21 (Summer 1984): 243–50.

Powers, J. F. "Dealer in Diamonds and Rhinestones." *Commonweal* 42 (10 August 1945): 408–10.

Prigozy, Ruth. "The Unpublished Stories: Fitzgerald in His Final Stage." *Twentieth Century Literature* 20 (April 1974): 69–90.

Rees, John O. "Fitzgerald's Pat Hobby Stories." *Colorado Quarterly* 23 (Spring 1975): 553–62.

Staley, Thomas F. "Time and Structure in Fitzgerald's 'Babylon Revisited.'" *Modern Fiction Studies* 10 (Winter 1964–65): 386–88.

Stewart, Lawrence D. "'Absolution' and *The Great Gatsby*." *Fitzgerald/Hemingway Annual* 5 (1973): 181–87.

Taylor, Dwight. "Scott Fitzgerald in Hollywood." *Harper's* 218 (March 1959): 67–71.

Toor, David. "Guilt and Retribution in 'Babylon Revisited.'" *Fitzgerald/Hemingway* Annual 5 (1973): 155–64.

Twitchell, James B. "'Babylon Revisited': Chronology and Characters." *Fitzgerald/Hemingway* Annual 10 (1978): 155–60.

Wells, Elizabeth. "A Comparative Statistical Analysis of the Prose Styles of F. Scott Fitzgerald and Ernest Hemingway. *Fitzgerald/Hemingway Annual* 1 (1969): 47–67.

West, James L. W. III. "Fitzgerald Explodes His Heroine." *Princeton University Library Chronicle* 49, no. 4 (Winter 1988): 159–65. Fitzgerald's previously unpublished story "The Vanished Girl" (retitled "A Full Life") follows this introduction.

West, James L. W. III, and J. Barclay Inge. "F. Scott Fitzgerald's Revision of 'The Rich Boy.'" *Proof* 5 (1977): 127–46.

White, William. "The Text of 'Babylon Revisited.'" *Fitzgerald Newsletter* 28 (Winter 1965): 4–7.

———. "The Versions of F. Scott Fitzgerald's 'Babylon Revisited': A Textual and Bibliographical Study." *Papers of the Bibliographical Society of America* 60 (Fourth Quarter 1966): 439–52.

Yates, Donald A. "The Road to 'Paradise': Fitzgerald's Literary Apprenticeship." *Modern Fiction Studies* 7 (Spring 1961): 19–31.

Index

Index

Index

Subjectivity, objectivity, and double
vision, *45–46*, 53, 58, 73, 88,
89, 115–16, 124, *152–56*
Subjects, 16, 17, 26
Symbolism, 28, 37, 39, 42, 51, 61,
68, 125, 128

Tarkington, Booth, 94; "Gentle
Julia," 94; *Penrod and Sam*, 94,
98
Taylor, Dwight, *87–88*, 123–24
Thalberg, Irving, 87, 88, 91
Tilden, William Tatem, Jr. ("Bill"),
147–48
Tintoretto, [Jacopo Robusti], 146
Toor, David, 80
Triangle Club, 17
Trilling, Lionel, 12, 150
Troy, William, 62, *178–79*
Turnbull, Frances, 45, 154
Tuttleton, James W., 40, 43–44

Twain, Mark (Samuel Langhorne
Clemens), 29, 47, 51, 133n36,
142

Velez, Lupe, 87

West, James L. W., III, 70, 136n69,
172–74
West, Nathanael: *The Day of the
Locust*, 91
Wharton, Edith, 9; *Glimpses of the
Moon*, 88
Whitman, Walt, 143, 149
Williams, Kiddy, 15, 16
Wilson, Edmund, 102, 142, 145
Wolfe, Peter, 73
Wolfe, Thomas, 143, 149; *Look
Homeward, Angel*, 147; *Of Time
and the River*, 142
Woman's Home Companion, 128–29
Woods, William, 151

The Author

John Kuehl is professor of English at New York University, where he specializes in contemporary American literature and modern drama. A graduate of the University of Iowa, Professor Kuehl received his M.A. in English from U.C.L.A. and his Ph.D. in English from Columbia University. He is the author or editor of ten previous books, including *The Apprentice Fiction of F. Scott Fitzgerald, 1909–1917; Write and Rewrite: A Study of the Creative Process;* (with Jackson R. Bryer) *Dear Scott/Dear Max: The Fitzgerald-Perkins Correspondence;* (with Jackson R. Bryer) *The Basil and Josephine Stories; John Hawkes and the Craft of Conflict;* (with Steven Moore) *In Recognition of William Gaddis;* and *Alternate Worlds: A Study of Postmodern Antirealistic American Fiction.*

The Editor

Gordon Weaver earned his Ph.D. in English and creative writing at the University of Denver, and is currently professor of English at Oklahoma State University. He is the author of several novels, including *Count a Lonely Cadence, Give Him a Stone, Circling Byzantium,* and most recently *The Eight Corners of the World.* His short stories are collected in *The Entombed Man of Thule, Such Waltzing Was Not Easy, Getting Serious, Morality Play,* and *A World Quite Round.* Recognition of his fiction includes the St. Lawrence Award for Fiction (1973), two National Endowment for the Arts fellowships (1974 and 1989), and the O. Henry First Prize (1979). He edited *The American Short Story, 1945–1980: A Critical History* and is currently editor of the *Cimarron Review.* Married and the father of three daughters, he lives in Stillwater, Oklahoma.